Land of Exile

CONTEMPORARY KOREAN FICTION

Land of Exile

CONTEMPORARY KOREAN FICTION

Translated and edited by

Marshall R. Pihl
Bruce & Ju-Chan Fulton

Foreword by Kwon Youngmin

An East Gate Book

M. E. Sharpe / UNESCO Publishing

An East Gate Book

UNESCO COLLECTION OF REPRESENTATIVE WORKS
Korean Series
The publication of this work was assisted by a contribution of the Government of the Republic of Korea under UNESCO's Funds-in-Trust Programme.

"Kapitan Ri" and "Seoul: 1964, Winter" previously appeared in *Listening to Korea*, ed. Marshall R. Pihl (New York: Praeger, 1973).

"The Bronze Mirror" previously appeared in *Modern Korean Literature*, ed. Peter H. Lee (Honolulu, HI: University of Hawaii Press, 1990).

"The Man Who Was Left as Nine Pairs of Shoes" was previously published in *The House of Twilight,* ed. Martin Holman (London: Readers International, 1989). Used with permission of Readers International.

Library of Congress Cataloging-in-Publication Data

Land of exile : contemporary Korean fiction / translated and edited by Marshall R. Pihl and Bruce & Ju-Chan Fulton ; foreword by Kwon Youngmin.
p.   cm. — (UNESCO collection of representative works)
"An east gate book"—T.p.
ISBN 1-56324-194-3 (cloth).—ISBN 1-56324-195-1 (pbk.)
1. Korean fiction—20th century—Translation into English.
I. Pihl, Marshall R. II. Fulton, Bruce, 1942–
III. Fulton, Ju-Chan. IV. Series.
PL984.E8L36   1993
895.7′3408—dc20
93-25238   CIP

Cover design by Ted Palmer.
Cover painting by Shin Pong-ja.

Printed in the United States of America

∞

The paper used in this publication meets the minimum requirements of American National Standard for Information Sciences— Permanence of Paper for Printed Library Materials, ANSI Z 39.48-1984.

MV   10 9 8 7 6 5 4 3 2 1
MV   10 9 8 7 6 5 4 3 2 1

Contents

Foreword

Currents in
Contemporary
Korean Fiction

In general, we can consider that contemporary Korean fiction developed in three stages.

First, we can identify the short course of growth that began immediately after the end of World War II and lasted until the outbreak of the Korean War in 1950. During this period, Korean fiction ceased to be a scarce item. However, it is difficult to single out works of fiction from this first stage, one reason being that the very conceptions of literature divided into "pure" and "class" orientations and, in a context where criticism and exculpation had collided, served to summon up the emotions of the history of recent decades or to depict dismal realities of the present. The fiction of this period is thus noted for re-creating the tragedy of the colonial experience or for criticizing the humiliations and frustrations of this period.

The second stage ran from the end of the Korean War through the early 1960s. In this period the literary establishment was reorganized with the emergence of the so-called postwar writers' group. Within the grim existence defined by the civil war, which hardened the national division, and the subsequent refugee experience and recovery of Seoul from the northern side, literature sought some sort of response to Korea's tragic realities. The postwar writers' group, depicting the ruins in which they stood, evinced a rootless and frustrated struggle and saw the world with critical and rejecting eyes. One might say that Korean postwar fiction is best characterized by the intensity of its concern with issues, an intensity that appears in its resistance to and criticism of the current scene and that is revealed in its self-referential satire and its search for the meaning of existence. But despite the intensity of its orientation toward issues, we can identify in postwar fiction a general atmosphere of unrest and despair, of frustration and sorrow.

We can think of the third stage as extending from the middle 1960s to the present day. In this period fiction began to overcome what some describe as its postwar mentality. Emerging from the depressing nature of postwar realities, it began to evince a petty-bourgeois consciousness and a sense of lifestyle. As this kind of consciousness of oneself as an individual expanded to a broad and growing interest in social realities after the mid-1960s, the central task of fiction was to somehow comprehend both the individual in particular and the society in general. But at around this time, Korean society encountered the sudden changes that are by-products of industrialization. Waves of industrialization intensified differences between urban and rural life and widened the gap between social classes. With the addition of political unrest to these social conditions, tension became endemic in the reality that was Korea. In this context, it was fiction that took the lead in laying bare the illogical conditions of life. Fiction turned more acrimonious as it exposed the reality of rural life, contradictions in the social structure, and anguish in the lives of urban laborers. Around the same time, critical disputes over literary nationalism and the use of realism as a method were directly reflected in the creative process of fiction. Consequently, fiction sought to give concrete form to the new critical understanding of Korea's territorial division. This area of writing, which is directed toward overcoming "division consciousness," has garnered such breadth and diversity that it has been separately identified as Division Literature.

Moreover, among these fictional developments, internal changes in fiction itself are leading to even more important literary innovations. Whereas fiction from Liberation through the postwar period was dominated by a short-story form that stuck closely to the slice-of-life approach, the 1970s witnessed an increase in novellas and linked-story novels. Rather than treating this growing diversity of literary genres simply as a change in literary convention, we can also see it as bespeaking a change in world view of writers who are closely watching life around them. Furthermore, we should recognize that such change will ultimately lead to the maturation of the full-length novel.

Kwon Youngmin
Seoul National University

Preface

This book owes its existence to a landmark four-volume anthology of post-1945 Korean literature compiled by Kwŏn Youngmin of Seoul National University—*Haebanghu sashimnyŏn ŭi munhak* (Scoul: Minŭm sa, 1985). Indeed, the two volumes of fiction therein may be considered in large part the canon of post-1945 Korean stories and novellas. We are grateful to Professor Kwŏn not only for producing this and other indispensable anthologies and reference works, but for supplying a foreword to the present volume.

Eight of the twelve stories in *Land of Exile* are appearing for the first time in English translation in book form. Of the remaining four, previously published elsewhere, two, "Kapitan Ri" and "Seoul: 1964, Winter," have long been out of print; the remaining two, "The Bronze Mirror" and "The Man Who Was Left as Nine Pairs of Shoes," were published after first being scheduled for inclusion in the present volume. Readers may with justification point to the paucity of modern Korean fiction in quality translations and protest this recycling. Properly chastened in advance, we would nonetheless hope that the importance of these four works justifies a second anthologizing.

We are honored that UNESCO has included this volume in its series of representative translations. Our thanks to Secretary-General Chung Hee-chae of the Korean National Commission for UNESCO and to Mr. Huh Kwon, Chief of the Culture Section of that organization, and to Mr. Fernando Ainsa, Chief, Collection of Representative Works, UNESCO Publishing, in Paris.

We also wish to thank Douglas Merwin of M. E. Sharpe for his patience. Finally, we are grateful to the editors of *Hanguk munhak* (Korean Literature), *Korea Journal*, and the *Asian & Pacific Quarterly* for publishing earlier versions of several of the translations.

M.R.P.
B.&J.C.F.

Introduction

Baptized by fire, sundered by civil war, tempered by autocracy and galloping modernization, Korea has undergone a series of dizzying transformations in its recent history. Literature, often a useful means of painting a portrait of the times, is crucial to understanding modern Korea, especially in the period dating from 1945, when the nation was released from colonial rule. There are several reasons for this. First, modern Korean literature was initially modeled to a large extent on Western forms. In the case of fiction, French and Russian realism were dominant influences, and realism has strongly colored much of Korean fiction to the present day. This is not to deny the presence of extra-realistic currents in Korean fiction; one has only to consider the sur-realistic stories of Yi Sang, produced as early as the 1930s. Rather, the great majority of Korean writers of fiction have found realism conge-nial to their chosen themes, and those themes—often involving the isolation, alienation, and frustration of individuals caught in a rigid, stifling social and political structure—frequently mirror the realities of modern Korea.

Second, Korean writers of fiction have, consciously or not, helped socialize generations of Korean readers into the harsh realities of the nation's modern history—the oppressiveness of colonial rule, the political chaos of the postwar period, the increasing divisions on the peninsula culminating in civil strife, the tragedy of territorial divi-sion, the imposition of military rule, and the strains of headlong industrialization. In short, twentieth-century Korean literature can be read as a chronicle of a history rife with conflict.

This is a volume of contemporary Korean fiction. In using the term *contemporary* we follow colleagues in Korea who distinguish between pre-1945 (*modern*) and post-1945 (*contemporary*) literature. Though some might argue that the period labeled *contemporary* stretches a bit far back, the distinction is a useful one. For one thing, post-1945 fiction could be composed and published in Korean, which had been banned as a public language during the latter years of the occupation period. Equally important, the writers who began their education after 1945 had the Korean language, rather than Japanese, as their medium of instruction. Indeed, they even have their own name, the Liberation Generation. Post-1945 Korean fiction is in this sense a more self-conscious literature. Many Korean authors who have debuted since 1945 write of a society and a people now autonomous, if still subject to great-power rivalries, and now responsible in greater part for their own future. This acknowledgment of voluntarism, societal and individual, is epitomized by Sŏnu Hwi's novella "Flowers of Fire" (Pulkkot, 1957).

But if the individual shows increasing signs of empowerment in post-1945 fiction, the risks attendant upon personal choice are also evident. One of those risks, isolation—or, in the context of this anthology, exile—has long been a central theme in Korean literature. Korean writers who have dealt with this theme often speak from personal experience. Great poets of the Chosŏn period like Chŏng Ch'ŏl (1536–1593) and Yun Sŏndo (1587–1671)—masters of the *kasa* and *shijo* forms, respectively—sang frequently of their several banishments, earned when they ran afoul of the throne. And in our age, Hwang Sŏgyŏng, one of the authors represented in this volume, underwent self-exile abroad rather than face a certain jail term for his unauthorized visit to North Korea in the late 1980s.

Isolation and exile hold a special significance for Koreans, who often describe themselves as one of the most homogeneous peoples on earth. Because of Korea's rigid social structure, the person who does not fit in is at a greater disadvantage than he or she would be in the more individualistic societies of the West. For in Korea, one's identity is determined almost exclusively by relationships with others, whether family, clan, classmates, or colleagues. In extreme cases, misfits are virtually nonpersons—people without a society, internal exiles. It is the status of such individuals that lends tension to a great deal of contemporary Korean fiction, and to many of the stories in this volume.

In Ch'ae Manshik's "The Wife and Children," for example, a husband and father twice leaves home. We are never told why, but we suspect he has found himself on the wrong side of the political fence in the post-occupation period. While we read of the effect of the man's absence on his family, we wonder, as he himself does, about the "terrible crime" he must have committed; we wonder what would await him were he to remain at home instead of moving to a "distant land."

In "The Post Horse Curse" Kim Tongni is searching dimensions of human existence that have been shunned by our scientific century and asking whether we, like young Sŏnggi in his story, live fated lives. Is it possible that Sŏnggi is cursed by destiny with wanderlust and, thus, is denied his heart's desire by that same force? Must he forever be a wanderer in his land, finding love one night at a time?

"Mountains" by Hwang Sunwŏn presents two kinds of exiles. A band of soldiers detached from the main army during the civil war are lost in a rugged, virtually uninhabited wilderness of rock and wood. Increasing privations strip away layers of decorum one by one until the men turn on each other in a naked struggle to survive. In contrast with this forced isolation is the reclusive existence chosen by the family of the story's central figure, Pau. Though their decision to seclude themselves from society is voluntary, it is motivated by an especially harsh tradition in the social system, as we learn late in the story.

Chŏn Kwangyong presents another kind of exile, one who is a tragic by-product of Korea's twentieth-century experience. Yi Inguk, M.D., of "Kapitan Ri" is a chameleon, a parasitic Korean who forsakes his ethnic identity to buy the favor of a succession of foreigners—Japanese, Russian, and American. Not surprisingly, his children have left to take up lives in other countries.

Kim Sŭngok was the first literary spokesman of the alienated Liberation Generation. By education, outlook, politics, and culture, the members of this generation distinguished themselves from the generation of their parents, who had grown up in the Japanese colony before they were born and had endured the horrific violence of the Korean War when their children were still toddlers. Kim's "Seoul: 1964, Winter" reflects their alienation in its brash arrogance and slangy confidence, but by the end of the story two young men, Kim and An, are given second thoughts about their lives by an unforeseen event.

"The Boozer" is an impressionistic tour de force that erupts with language unseen in Korean fiction before. Author Ch'oe Inho conjures up memorable characters who are the wreckage of war and the refuse of an industrializing society that has moved beyond them. They live their lives in a dark and bizarre other world that is no longer in contact with modern Korea.

Hwang Sŏgyŏng's "A Dream of Good Fortune" and Yun Heung-gil's "The Man Who Was Left as Nine Pairs of Shoes" deal with a marginal social group especially visible in the 1970s—urban squatters. Refugees from the countryside, these people often band together in communities united by a common home in the provinces. Much of the tension of these two stories springs from the tenuous existence of the squatter communities. Lacking legal claim to the land they occupy on the outskirts of the capital, they find themselves at the mercy of the government. In "A Dream of Good Fortune," a squatter neighborhood is leveled in a day. In the Yun story, squatters in the satellite city of Sŏngnam are uprooted by draconian and sometimes contradictory pronouncements by city and provincial authorities. Paralleling the group struggle to maintain community is the individual struggle to maintain dignity in degrading circumstances, illustrated by Yun's Kwŏn and his nine pairs of shoes.

In an informal survey conducted by *Sosŏl munhak* magazine in the early 1980s, ten writers and critics were asked to identify the most memorable women writers of the 1970s. Nine of the respondents mentioned Pak Wansŏ, eight O Chŏnghŭi. Each in her own way, these two women have spoken for the isolation and frustration of Koreans today. O's "The Bronze Mirror" examines a rarity in modern Korean society —a childless couple. Their only child having died a generation earlier, the husband enduring forced retirement, the man and woman are reduced to contemplating physical debilitation and emotional starvation. The horror of their lonely existence is ultimately revealed when the husband becomes obsessed with a kindergarten girl, who then turns on the wife with a demonic intensity. When it comes to portraying gaps in the family fabric, gaps that mirror rents in a society fast evolving from rural and traditional to urban and modern, O has few equals among contemporary authors.

Pak Wansŏ, on the other hand, is often referred to by readers and critics as the *yŏp chip ajuma*—the "auntie next door." In contrast with the dark, austere world of O Chŏnghŭi's fiction, Pak's stories radiate warmth, even when dealing with such tragic situations as that of Grandmother No-no in "Winter Outing." While the outcome of the story suggests a heartening revelation, the story begins with the narrator's sudden feeling of estrangement from her husband and step-daughter, which deepens into a frigid isolation as events unfold.

The title work of this collection, Cho Chŏngnae's "Land of Exile," tells of a man who, as a tragic victim of history, is condemned to the life of a wandering exile in his own land. The man, Mansŏk, is unable to return to his hometown because of things he did there during the Korean War. His life's story reveals not the superpower conflict of the Western imagination but another war that racked Korea, one that was played out in the villages and was not confronted in literature until the last twenty years.

Another familiar exile figure in contemporary Korean fiction is the student dissident. Student protesters apprehended during the three decades of military rule beginning in 1961 often had no future in their homeland. Though some went underground, like the fugitive depicted in Im Ch'ŏru's "A Shared Journey," they were only postponing the inevitable. What is interesting about this story is not simply the isolation of the fugitive but also the narrator's guilt-ridden estrangement from him, the knowledge that this friend's decision to become an exile will forever undercut the close relationship the two once enjoyed as college classmates.

The most ironic yet formative experience of the twentieth century for Korean literature began with Liberation on August 15, 1945. On that day, Koreans regained a country that had been lost to Japanese rule only to lose it again to Russian and American influence. What has remained since then are two distortions of Korea—a "north" and a "south"—which have been further altered by war and industrialization. In Korean, the 1945 Liberation is called Kwangbok, "Glorious Recovery." But it ended up neither glorious nor a recovery. Worse, it was capped by an internecine war that spared no corner of the country. Of the Koreans who survived, 10 million today remain separated from members of their families by the impassable truce-line. These events have so informed contemporary Korean literature in one way or another that some critics define literature since 1945 as the Literature of an Age of Division.

We find, as a recurrent underlying theme in Korean literature of the twentieth century, an expression by the Koreans of their awareness of themselves as a people. Although enlightenment literature early in the century had never been more than transitional, its intellectual momentum stimulated an awareness of Korean cultural identity that emerged in colonial literature and could champion a sense of moral victory over unrelenting Japanese rule. Contemporary literature, initiated by Liberation in 1945, promised the opening of a new literary age, one dedicated fundamentally to the establishment of a national literature in the truest sense—an ironic concept for a divided nation.

Land
of
Exile

CONTEMPORARY KOREAN FICTION

The Wife and Children

Ch'ae Manshik

Ch'ae Manshik—fiction writer, playwright, essayist, critic—was born in Ŭmnae, a coastal village in North Chŏlla Province, in 1902. Like many of the intellectuals of his generation, he studied for a time in Japan, then returned to Korea to work at a succession of writing and editorial jobs. He died of tuberculosis in 1950.

Ch'ae is one of the great talents of modern Korean literature. His penetrating mind, command of idiom, utterly realistic dialogue, and keen wit produced a fictional style all his own. The immediacy of some of his narratives, the sense of the storyteller speaking directly to the reader, is reminiscent of the traditional oral narrative *p'ansori*.

Often pigeonholed as a satirist, Ch'ae was much more. Long before satirical sketches such as "My Idiot Uncle" (Ch'isuk, 1938), about a political misfit during the Japanese occupation, and "Mister Pang" (Misŭt'ŏ Pang, 1946), set during the American military occupation, Ch'ae had written "Age of Transition" (Kwadogi, 1923), an autobiographical novella about Korean students in Japan testing the currents of modernization that swept urban East Asia early in this century. In other early works, such as "In Three Directions" (Segillo, 1924) and "Sandungi" (Sandungi, 1930), he dealt with the class differences that are so distinct in Korean society past and present. In these earlier stories Ch'ae is concerned as well with the plight of the unemployed young intellectuals turned out by the modernization movement. The impecunious young intellectual making the rounds of publishing houses and

3

pawnshops is portrayed with devastating accuracy in "A Ready-Made Life" (Redimeidŭ insaeng, 1934). Ch'ae was also at home depicting the rural underclass, so long suppressed as to be almost incapable of autonomous action, in stories such as "On a Train" (Ch'ajung esŏ, 1941). *Peace Under Heaven* (T'aep'yŏng ch'ŏnha, 1938), on the other hand, is a pointed treatment of traditional Korean etiquette in the person of one who thrived materially but wasted spiritually during the Japanese occupation; it has been acclaimed one of the great Korean novels.

Ch'ae's later works are somewhat more bitter and introspective. "Public Offender" (Minjok ŭi choein, 1948–49), for example, is a semi-autobiographical apologia for those branded as collaborators for their failure to actively oppose Japanese colonial rule. In these stories, the author's wit is tempered by the spiritual turmoil of having to come to grips with the role of the artist in a colonized society.

"The Wife and Children" (Ch'ŏja; not to be confused with a posthumously published work of the same name) first appeared in 1948 in the weekly *Chugan sŏul*. One of the author's more somber stories, it echoes premodern Korean political history, in which victims of factional infighting were frequently banished to the countryside, as well as prefiguring contemporary history with its record of house arrests of dissidents.

Pak the teacher calmly set out from home again. He wore an old Japanese army uniform that was dull and faded, patched here and there with a different material. But the jacket and trousers both looked neat, for his wife had washed them clean and starched and ironed them. His black, rubber-soled shoes were likewise patched, stitched, and well worn. A fowling cap rested gently on his closely cropped head, and around his shoulders was a small cloth bundle containing fresh underwear, a towel, and a few other necessities. One hand held a walking stick of long-jointed bamboo, and in the other arm he carried a puppy. Thus accoutered, Pak looked for all the world like a typical destitute rural provincial on his way to visit relatives.

It was July 10, 1948—the day after the stranger had come to his house.

In mid-June, about a month earlier, Pak had returned home after an absence of one whole year.

He had left home around the same time the previous year. And then on August 15, the anniversary of Liberation, he was apprehended in Seoul and sentenced to a year in jail, which he began serving in September. He was released in June after nine months. In prison he had done as he was told and hadn't caused trouble, earning himself recognition as a model prisoner as well as a three-month commutation. The suddenness of his early release prevented him from notifying anyone, so no family members or close friends had welcomed him out of prison, and he had made his way home by himself.

From the train station to his village—a walk of two or three miles with a small hill to cross midway. . . .

The early-summer afternoon was hot, and Pak was quite weakened. But being free after so long, he drank in the refreshing breeze and feasted his eyes on the fields and hills, which he was just in time to see at their greenest. Under such conditions, what could be more exhilarating than a leisurely walk?

The first weeding was under way in the paddies where the rice shoots had already been planted. In other paddies the farmers had taken advantage of rain a day or two earlier to do their planting. By the traditional reckoning, this was a *muja* year. Previous *muja* years were said to have been marked by droughts and lean harvests, and this year seemed true to form. The farmers felt threatened, and so the weeding and planting were an attempt, more than anything else, to set their minds at ease.

The cry of a cuckoo.

The call circled the green hills and trailed off in the distance. There was nothing quite like the feeling it gave Pak.

Across the hill and a bit farther on were the willows that bordered the source of the village stream.

It wasn't Pak's hometown, but it might as well have been. For he had lived there fifteen years before departing late the previous spring, fifteen years teaching at a grammar school.

Now all things gave him fresh pleasure. How many times had he strolled those familiar streamside hills that delighted him so? How many times had he sat in the shade of the willows soaking his feet while pondering, contemplating, lamenting something or other?

A flock of boys were playing in the stream. Most were naked, but a few little fellows were splashing about in the loose shorts that farmers wore. All were about the same age—not quite old enough for school.

Pak searched the group for his son Ch'ŏl, who must be among them. Surely he was. Several boys frolicked boisterously in the water—but not Ch'ŏl. Instead there he sat all by himself on the bank, wearing a dispirited, listless expression, gazing at the others.

The boy was rather timid, like Pak himself, and didn't relish throwing himself into the other boys' games. But that didn't mean he had always had this touch of the hangdog. Now, though, the boy wore that look.

Added to this impression was his slight neck, which appeared barely able to support his head, and the sallow color of malnourishment—this seemed to show Pak the sum total of what his wife and children had gone through emotionally, physically, and materially in the year he had been away. He was suddenly overcome with a choking sensation.

Pak remained for a time looking at his son, who was gazing in the opposite direction, then approached and called the boy's name.

Ch'ŏl turned and studied his father with a doubtful expression. Finally recognizing him, he rushed over, eyes brimming, and grabbed hold of his father's legs. Burying his face there, he burst into tears.

The other children, when they realized it was Pak, looked up and gazed in wonder at this reunion between father and son.

Pak patted the boy's head, then led him off, Ch'ŏl wiping away the tears with his fist.

"Is Mommy home?" Pak asked.

Ch'ŏl shook his head. "She went over to Yongman's house to mill some barley. Their mortar works real well."

Pak said nothing.

"All we eat is barley. And when we're out of barley we eat gruel."

"Did you have to buy the barley?"

"No, Grandfather brought us a sack."

Pak had heard that his in-laws had made big money on the black market following Liberation. But thank god for the barley, whatever its source.

As a so-called public employee, Pak had been receiving a more generous monthly ration of foodstuffs than other nonfarming households. Even so, there was barely enough food for half a month, and they had to buy rice to make up. With Pak gone it seemed the family had survived on the ration alone, eating gruel to stretch it out from one month to the next, before good fortune had arrived in the form of the barley.

Father and son walked on in silence. And then,

"Father?"

"Yes?"

"Why didn't you come home? Hmm?"

"I had a lot of business to look after, and it held me up."

Pak had left home promising to return in ten days.

"But Father, the boys made fun of me. 'Your father did something bad and went to jail'—that's what they said."

Pak could say nothing.

"And they called Mommy names and they hit her. That bad boy Pyŏngshik's big brother and some other people came to our house."

Pak remained silent. What could he say in response to this youngster who was barely seven? If only the boy were fifteen or so, Pak could have made himself understood, but. . . .

"Ch'ŏl?"

"Yes?"

"What would you like to eat?"

Pak gave his son a smile and looked down at his face. That face told him there were many things Ch'ŏl wanted.

Ch'ŏl was happy enough already and lacked a ready answer. He looked up at his father as he groped for words. And finally,

"Cucumbers."

"Mmm-hmm. And?"

"Uh . . . meat."

"Hmm, meat. And?"

"Uh . . . uh . . . cookies—and candy."

"Cookies and candy—is that all?"

"Uh . . . gum."

"Gum?"

"Yeah, gum."

"All right. Well, Father brought cookies and candy—you can have them when we get home. He'll buy you the gum and cucumbers later."

"Won't Mommy scold me for eating between meals?"

"If Mommy was scolding you when Father was away, it was probably because she didn't have money to give you for snacks. So if you kept crying and pestering her to buy you something, why sure she'd scold you."

The house looked terrible. Holes had appeared in the roof, and the fence had collapsed in a heap. It was a small cottage, really not much to begin with, but each fall they had rethatched the roof and the fence, replacing the rotted parts of the fence with millet stalks and putting in new posts. And so the house had never looked as bad as it did now.

At home, Pak handed over the entire bag of cookies and candy to Ch'ŏl, to the boy's delight. Then he washed up in the yard and sat down to wait for his wife. He waited and he waited, and finally she arrived. Cloth bundle of barley carried on her head, sleeping baby Sŏk slipping far down from his perch high on her back, hemp summer jacket with threadbare shoulders, hemp skirt wrapped about her, sun-burned, sweat-drenched face with jet-black discolorations, tangled hair, heelless straw sandals dragging along—this was the sight that greeted him as his wife entered the brushwood gate.

Just twenty-six years old—a young age, a time of full bloom. There was nothing about her that struck Pak as pretty, but her roundish, expressive face had a certain charm. She was a cheerful sort—couldn't have been gloomy if she'd tried.

But who could have known she had once been like that, so merci-lessly had she aged, so emaciated had she become after a single year's worth of troubles.

Gaunt cheekbones, hollows scooped beneath them. Black discolor-ations, so many Pak could hardly tell her nose from her eyes.

Dark despair clouded her eyes, lined her face. The tired way she carried herself, as if she were about to collapse, the unbecoming clothes hanging from her body, her hair untouched for days, and what's worse, the baby dangling low on her back. . . .

The unexpected sight of her husband sitting on the veranda instantly brought a smile of surprise to her lips. She probably wondered if it weren't an illusion.

Pak's head bobbed in amazement as he observed his wife's face. Only a year, and look at her! Pak couldn't keep from sighing.

Pak was thirty and his wife eighteen when they first met. Pak had been married earlier as a child, but hadn't so much as held his spouse's hand before they were separated. Even so, that woman still appeared as his wife on the Pak family register. His present wife, Suni, was the daughter of the family who lived next door to where Pak used to lodge. In grammar school she had twice been in Pak's class.

After finishing her schooling, Suni had stayed with her family, then married at seventeen. But only three months later she was back home, turned out by her husband. Six months later she was a widow. With the new year came a rumor that Suni would soon go south to become a rich old man's concubine.

Suni's family had never been well off, and they were not the sort to blush at the monstrous notion of sending a daughter—and especially one who was not in mint condition—down such a road.

Suni's father was quite the prodigal, but not a vulgar person. Her stepmother, on the other hand, a former tavern hostess and occasional bedmate for the customers, had become the father's concubine and ended up replacing his wife when she died. Well, what do you expect from someone like that? It was this woman who exercised the power in the family. She had brought with her a son (Suni's stepbrother), and together the two of them farmed and occasionally worked as merchants, at the same time handling all household matters. The old gentleman spent all his time fiddling around and became just another mouth to feed. And so the wife held sway in all family matters; the old gentleman's opinions had no force.

One evening late in the fall, Suni stole out to Pak's room. The purpose of her expedition? Her mother had been pressuring her to become the concubine of a rich old man. Her stepbrother insisted that as long as she was leaving, she ought to work in a tavern. And her father, who'd been siding with Suni but was outnumbered by the other two, couldn't speak out and had to retreat to the back room. What was she to do?

"Well, Suni, do you have a preference?"

"Either way, I don't want it," she said, emphatically shaking her head.

"You don't? Then what do you think you'll do?"

"That's why I came to see you, since you're a teacher. I thought you could give me some good advice."

"Good grief—what am I supposed to do, contradict your parents?"

"Whatever you have to do, Teacher. Won't you help me—please? I hate it! Who'd want to go live with some old. . . . I'd rather drink lye. And working at a bar? That's even worse. . . ."

Pak fell deep into thought, then changed to a softer tone: "Suni?"

"Yes?"

"If you don't want to marry an old man or go work in a bar, then you're probably thinking somewhere down the line of meeting a decent man—you don't intend to live by yourself, do you?"

"No, but right now my family's pushing me so. . . ."

"Well, then, what about me? Better than the old gentleman or the bar, isn't it? Why not? Like they say, fainting's better than dying."

Suni buried her head in her chest, unable to respond, and fingered the ties of her jacket, blushing furiously.

But the moment Suni lowered her head, Pak had plainly seen a spark of delight in her eyes.

It was not that Pak had been interested in Suni as a woman. Nor had he been dearly fond of her as a student. And his was not a heroic decision to sacrifice himself as a result of some deep, sentimental feeling experienced then and there. It was just that the time was right. For several years now Pak's bachelor existence had been dreary and lacking in domestic conveniences, and Pak had been thinking he might like a taste of what people called settling down. He wasn't picky—any old skirt would do.

Pak did some thinking:

Hell, if she can do any better with me than she can with an old man or at a bar, then why would she object?

As long as she's a used wife and I'm a used husband . . . so what if a couple of secondhand people happen to meet and start living together? I mean, it's not a capital offense—we're not traitors or anything.

And I'm not going to worry myself blue about the family register.

You can't be choosy, not in my situation, not at my age. And you can't expect to marry a virgin two times over. Hell, I ought to be thankful.

Pak's mind was exceedingly lucid and detached as he considered these matters.

In general, Pak felt that reading and the truth realized through reading offered the best life; marriage and family-related things were secondary at best.

The next day, Pak set aside three hundred of the thousand or so wŏn he had saved—he would need at least that much to set up housekeeping with Suni. Then he visited Suni's family. After presenting them with seven hundred wŏn, he brought Suni home. They would have received three hundred from the old gentleman, five hundred from the drinking house, and so it would appear that they had netted an extra two hundred wŏn.

Suni, true to the meaning of her name, was a docile sort, and she venerated Pak to the heavens—indeed, if he had asked her to die she would have rolled over and played dead. Apart from this, though, Pak came to realize after living with her awhile that she was not a woman to lose your head over.

She didn't have an ounce of initiative. She wasn't capable of coming up with an idea, devising a plan, and then putting the plan into action.

All she could do was cook the rice he would buy for her. She would prepare only the side dishes he bought, then set the table. Even if he gave her money, she didn't know how to buy the proper ingredients for side dishes.

She was utterly incapable of selecting colors or patterns for her own clothing. Pak would purchase fabric after his own taste, and all Suni would do was make the garments, believing the fabric to be the best quality. In the end, she was a kind of automaton. Without an operator she would never move by herself, but just sit idle.

But his wife's helplessness was not something to disillusion Pak or cause him to complain; nor was it a burden. For he had always been a considerate, attentive person. Except for cooking the rice, mending the clothes, doing the wash, and bearing and nursing children, Pak did all the things that should be done in a proper household: He would check the rice chest and stock it with grain; he would lay in fuel. When it was time to make kimchi for the winter, he would purchase appropriate quantities of radishes, cabbages, salt, and all the other seasonings. When it was time to make soy sauce and soybean paste, he bought soybeans and salt. In spring he bought pickled fish, in fall he purchased fabric for cold-weather clothing.

The little woman was helpless and unadaptable, but thanks to the husband's prudence, his attention to detail, the couple got on well, with no rips in the family fabric—but only as long as Pak had his teaching position, only as long as he was tied to the family and oversaw its workings.

Pak was well aware that his wife lacked the ability and resourcefulness to carry on a life of her own, without her husband at the wheel. For this reason, he had found it especially difficult to set aside his worries about the family while he was away the previous year.

When Pak had departed then, he had left behind close to twenty thousand wŏn he had scraped up through saving and lending. But even if this amount were to be spent on grain and fuel alone, Pak had wondered, would it last more than half a year?

And even if his wife were to somehow make do for that long, then what next? She didn't have the perseverance, the resourcefulness, the nerve to eke out a living by striking out with a bundle of something to sell on the black market. Instead, she and the children would probably starve. Or at best she just might sell this shack they lived in and that way at least be able to fill their bellies.

What he saw now was not so different from what he had imagined. My god, he muttered to himself. This is the family I left behind—look at them . . . it must have been a terrible crime I committed. Again he sighed deeply.

His wife stepped up onto the veranda and began breast-feeding the baby, who had just awakened. He was thinner than their big one, Ch'ŏl, and his complexion was not good. The baby hadn't reached its one hundredth day when Pak had left, but it had grown after a fashion in his absence.

"Well, how did you manage?"

This wasn't so much an inquiry about the past year as it was an attempt to comfort his wife.

She looked down and remained silent for a time.

"Well, we're still alive—if you call this living." And, after another silence, "I thought for sure we'd starve. But then Father visited, and when he saw Ch'ŏl bothering me for something to eat, he went away crying. And then a sack of barley and half a bushel of rice arrived. . . ." She became choked up and couldn't finish.

A month or so passed uneventfully, and then on the morning of July 9 a stranger visited Pak.

Master and visitor had a long, quiet discussion. After lunch Pak saw the visitor off, then informed his wife he would be leaving early the next morning for a distant land.

Wrapped in silence, his wife wept the whole night through.

Early the next morning: Pak had finished his preparations and was about to depart. Suddenly an idea occurred to him.

"Would any of the neighbors have a puppy I could buy?"

"What are you going to do with a puppy? Give it to someone?"

"I have my reasons."

"Well . . ."

His wife thought for a moment, eyes blinking.

"Yongman's family, where we hull our barley, I heard they have a lot of puppies, already weaned.... They're supposed to be a good breed, too."

"I'm not concerned about the breed," said Pak as he took a wad of hundred-wŏn notes from inside his shirt. He peeled off ten and handed them to his wife. "Hurry on over and buy one, would you?"

His wife didn't know what to say. There must have been more than ten thousand wŏn in that wad. He was going to take all that money with him and not leave her any—not even enough for a tiny little bag of rice. How heartless her husband was!

Where had this money come from? The day he'd returned home the previous month he had emptied his pockets—eight hundred and some wŏn. He'd earned it in prison, he said. "Go buy a chicken or something, and have it with Ch'ŏl." And that was it as far as money was concerned. So it was clear to her that the wad of bills inside his shirt was someone else's money, entrusted to him by the stranger.

But no matter whose money it was, he must have seen, plain as day, that there was no way to keep the family in food now. To think he wouldn't even leave them a measly hundred wŏn . . .

After a time, Pak's wife returned with a puppy in her arms. She gave back the thousand wŏn—how could they accept money from a neighbor, Yongman's family had said. Just take the puppy.

"Well, what can you do?" Pak put the money away, then took the puppy from his wife. "I know you'll have a hard time, but I can't help it. Like I said last night, try to forget I'm alive." He turned away.

His wife plopped down on the spot. She felt an urge to cry. This was the last straw—her husband really was heartless. The least he could do was let her keep the money for the puppy. What difference would it make?

Pak set out, then stopped after a few steps. He deliberated a moment, then called his wife over.

"I'm going to drop by a friend's house over in Kunsan and send him here with a bookseller—I want you to sell all my books. I never thought this would happen—I swore I'd never get rid of those books! . . . They're hard to come by these days. Anyway, there must be about seven hundred of them—at a hundred a volume, they'll bring you seventy thousand wŏn. You ought to be able to get by on that for a while. . . ."

Shortly thereafter, Pak the teacher abruptly set out from home again. He wore an old Japanese army uniform that was dull and faded, and patched here and there in a different color. But the jacket and trousers both looked neat, for his wife had washed them clean and starched and ironed them. His black, rubber-soled shoes were likewise patched, stitched, and well worn. A fowling cap rested gently on his closely cropped head, and around his shoulders was a small cloth bundle containing fresh underwear, a towel, and a few other necessities. One hand held a walking stick of long-jointed bamboo, and in the other arm he carried the puppy. Thus accoutered, Pak looked for all the world like a typical destitute rural provincial on his way to visit relatives. The last thing he did was soothe Ch'ŏl, stroking the boy's hair and promising to return in ten days.

Translated by Bruce and Ju-Chan Fulton

The Post Horse Curse

Kim Tongni

For nearly sixty years, Kim Tongni (b. 1913) has written more—and has had more written about him—than any other living Korean author. He so embodies the history of modern Korean literature that one critic has asserted, "For all the credit we give Europe as our model, modern Korean fiction did not take root for sure until we were given the writing of Kim Tongni. What we did before him can be dismissed as practice."

Some regard him as a voice of the Korean ethos, as a writer who seeks understanding of what it means to be Korean. Accommodating ethnic materials in a perfectly modern aesthetic, he is anything but a "folk" writer. Two early, still acclaimed works, "Portrait of a Shaman" (Munyŏdo, 1936) and "Loess Village Story" (Hwangt'ogi, 1939), demonstrate his ability to be Korean and worldly at the same time. While set in the Korean countryside, these works are invested with a universality that links the national with the shared human experience.

Even in his early works, Kim was giving voice to a "humanistic nationalism," which he believed could "overcome cultural barriers and seek identity with universal trends in world literature." It is the universal language of symbols that lets his work reach out to readers beyond Korea's borders, even while heavily laden with local color.

Kim Tongni is the recipient of the Freedom Literary Prize (1955), the National Academy of Arts Award (1958), the Samil Literary Award (1967), the Order of the Camellia (1968), the Order of the

15

Peony (1970), the Seoul City Cultural Prize (1970), and the May 16
National Award (1983).

"The Post Horse Curse" (Yŏngma) first appeared in *Paengmin* magazine in 1948.

Three rivers meet at Hwagae Market, flowing alongside the roads. One
comes from the direction of Kurye in Chŏlla Province and another
flows down through Hwagae Valley in Kyŏngsang Province. Here they
form the mainstream of the Sŏmjin River, which, reflecting green
mountains and dark old trees, moves quietly as a lake while meander-
ing farther and farther south to mark the boundary between Kyŏngsang
and Chŏlla.

Lying at an intersection of the roads to Hadong, Kurye, and Ssanggye Temple, Hwagae bustled even when the market itself was closed.
Of all the many roads into the Chiri Mountains, the best known went
by way of Hwagae and up five-mile Hwagae Valley, which held both
Ssanggye Temple and its Sei Rock. There were several other such
spots along the Kyŏngsang–Chŏlla border, but it was Hwagae of which
people spoke. On market days, the wild carrots, bellflower roots, aralia
shoots, and bracken fern of slash-and-burn farmers in the Chiri Mountains were brought down through Hwagae Valley; thread, needles,
hand mirrors, scissors, belts, purse strings, tweezers, and face powder
of the Chŏlla sundries peddlers came over the road from Kurye; and
fishmongers of the lower Sŏmjin brought laver, dried green and red
seaweed, pollack, salted yellow corvina, and salted mackerel up along
the Hadong road. Though quite prosperous for an isolated mountain
market, Hwagae was known for more than just its market days.

Even when the market was not open, the place was popular with the
people of neighboring villages for the unusually clear and cool *makkŏlli* and the spanking-fresh sliced raw fish they could find at any of
the taverns that lined the Hwagae Valley stretching up beyond the
marketplace. This could have been the reason for its fame. Or perhaps
it was the sad and moving melodies that filtered through the drooping
fronds of the willows fronting the taverns. Or maybe the popular song-
and-dance troupes, country opera companies, and troubadors from the
Chŏlla region that would often come here to rehearse and perform as a

final test of their skills and enthusiasm before crossing over into Kyŏngsang Province.

Best known among the taverns at Hwagae was Okhwa's place, where the drink was good, the prices reasonable, and the owner—Okhwa herself—hospitable. Okhwa's mother had died not long before, leaving her with an unmarried son to raise alone while she awaited the return of a husband who had long since disappeared. Perhaps this was why her customers were all the more loyal and sympathetic. What is more, they would inevitably seek out Okhwa's tavern when low on cash or short of supplies.

"I'll settle with you when I get back from my trip to Kyŏngsang," was the sort of thing a customer might say.

It was toward sunset one summer day, when the drooping willow fronds washed themselves in the river's water and you could see the silvery shine of the sweetfish jumping in the evening breeze.

An old sieve peddler, who must have been well over sixty, sought out Okhwa's tavern. He carried sieve frames and linings on his back, a walking stick in one hand, and a fan in the other. Just behind him stood a slender girl of about fifteen who had a small bundle tucked under one arm. They both looked very tired.

"Just two, including that big girl?" asked Okhwa, looking directly at the "big girl" instead of the old man. The old man nodded quietly.

That evening, after the dinner table had been cleared away, the old man introduced himself to Okhwa. He lived in Kurye but was now on his way toward Kyŏngsang in hopes of making a little money. A native of Yŏsu, as a youth he had joined some friends to live awhile in Kurye, and later took to wandering around Mokp'o and Kwangju. Then he crossed over to Chin Island and, after staying there some seventeen or eighteen years—during which time his hair turned gray—he went back to live in Kurye once again. That was several years before. When Okhwa asked how he managed traveling with the girl, he explained he once had vowed not to move again for life but had no choice. The alternative was to stay put and simply starve.

"Is that big girl your daughter, then?" asked Okhwa, gazing at the soft shoulders of the girl, who sat in a corner against the wall—half illuminated by the light of a kerosene lamp—and glanced with bright eyes in their direction from time to time.

The old man nodded again. Having spent his life in alien places, he had now returned to the only place he knew as home to find it, too, unfamiliar. He complained of their lonely lot: a father and daughter in need of some source of strength but with nowhere to turn for support.

"I really did enjoy myself when I was young. My friends and I formed a touring song-and-dance troupe. Once you begin playing around as a youth, you can't settle down for the rest of your life, I guess. That was early in the year I turned twenty-four, just thirty-six years ago. In fact, I even had a one-night fling back then, right here at this marketplace."

The old man looked quietly around, searching the interior of the room, as if for some clue to the past he recollected.

"Oh, my! Such a long time ago!" exclaimed Okhwa, showing surprise.

It rained the next day.

Sŏnggi, who operated his bookstall only when the market was open, came down to the village from Ssanggye Temple a day early to get ready for the next day's market.

The road from the temple to Hwagae Market was a good five miles, but its magnificent scenery—water, rocks, and steep valleys revealed at every turn—always kept him from feeling bored. He had first visited the temple when his grandmother had practically dragged him there by the hand to learn Chinese writing. And he had gone again later, urged by older friends. But of late he had grown weary of the incessant daily sound of drums and wooden clappers, and even of the surprisingly white gingko trees and the lindens.

He had long desired to flee this place. But his mother's eyes would redden with anger at the mere suggestion of going anywhere.

"Have I a husband? Any family? It's my fate to live alone with only you to help. Now even you talk day and night of leaving! Who am I to turn to?"

By now, he had become hardened to his mother's rantings, as if he had grown calluses in his ears.

Worse than his mother was his grandmother, who had placed him in the temple at the age of ten to study for the priesthood. But she had died suddenly, secretly content to have seen him settled and freed from the wanderlust caused by his "post horse" curse. His grandmother, enthralled by the Chinese fortune-telling book *Tangsaju,* had looked up Sŏnggi's fortune when he was three and was aghast to discover "post horse nature" entered under the year, month, day, and hour of his birth. Grandmother thought the tiny old lady in the silk clothing, who said she lived in Hadong, might have mistakenly reckoned the date and time of his birth. So she went to ask an old monk at Ssanggye Temple and even showed the papers to a tall old man who said he had studied the Way in the Chiri Mountains. The "post horse nature" was unquestionably correct.

"He's got his father's character," said the grandmother, pointedly but without any deep sense of rancor.

"As the parent, so the child, they say. The fault all begins with you, Mother!" Okhwa shot back in agitation, trying to trap her mother in her own words.

"Don't get bitchy with your mother! So I slept with a song-and-dance man. . . . Did I leave you and go running after the fellow? Did I make you go find him for me?"

Thirty-six years before, the grandmother had fallen for the plaintive melodies of a song-and-dance man who dallied with her just one night and left her pregnant with Okhwa. Later, Okhwa had realized her own karma with a monk who had floated through like a cloud, and so she had come to have Sŏnggi. Neither mother nor daughter—both born in Hwagae Market taverns—had cause to lay blame on anyone in particular. Sŏnggi was cursed with wanderlust because his mother had taken up with a monk, and the mother had taken up with the monk because the grandmother had fallen for a song-and-dance man. That being the case, then, Sŏnggi's curse to wander was basically the grandmother's doing.

The grandmother had hastened to make Sŏnggi a monk to break the curse, and when that had failed, Okhwa tried to undo the curse by setting him up as a bookseller. One could see that Sŏnggi was clearly more interested in novels than in Buddhist scriptures and preferred being a salesman to being a monk, but Okhwa let him have the bookstall only after he promised that he would confine himself to Hwagae Market.

When she saw Sŏnggi stepping up onto the embankment in front of the porch, Okhwa sat up in surprise.

"In all this heat. . . . Why come down from the temple now?" she asked, handing him the towel and fan that were beside her.

A girl Sŏnggi had never seen before, and who appeared to have been reading a novel to Okhwa, stopped her recitation and lifted her face to gaze at him. The whites and pupils of her eyes, set in an oval face, were as bright as flowers. Sŏnggi felt a momentary tingle in his heart and quickly turned his suddenly brightened eyes to stare into the willow fronds that drooped in front of the house.

The girl soon went inside, and then Okhwa came back out, carrying a small dining tray set with Sŏnggi's lunch.

"She's a sieve peddler's daughter," said his mother with a cheerful look.

"Sieve peddler?"

Sŏnggi accepted the lunch tray but was slow to begin eating. Instead, he studied his mother's face.

"He says they're from Kurye. They're on their way to Chinju, through Hadong, to do business, it seems. He headed up Hwagae Valley last night."

The girl was the sieve peddler's only child. Okhwa had agreed to take care of her until he returned from Hwagae Valley and fetched her for the trip to Hadong, she explained, glancing casually at Sŏnggi to catch the look in his eyes.

"How long did he say he would be in Hwagae Valley?"

"It seemed like he was going to go even farther into the Chiri Mountains if sales are good," she said, and then added, "She doesn't look like a peddler's daughter, does she?" Her name was Kyeyŏn.

Sŏnggi silently lifted his spoon. He pushed away from the table without eating even half of his rice.

The next day, when Sŏnggi was at his bookstall, the sieve peddler's daughter arrived with his lunch. Though the stall was so close to his house that you could raise a shout and be heard, the kitchenmaid would still bring his lunch out to him every day. Sŏnggi felt embarrassed to have the task given to a stranger's daughter, who was already showing maidenly signs. But to the girl, nothing was amiss. With eyes as bright as flowers and full of cheer, she demurely placed his lunch basket in front of him and quickly turned to look over the other stalls, where rice cakes, taffy, and melons were sold.

"Has the kitchenmaid gone off somewhere?"

Sŏnggi was stirred by the delight that brimmed in Kyeyŏn's lovely eyes, but he queried her in gruff tones, his head cocked at a surly angle.

"The porch was full of customers and she was all alone. She was so busy trying to take care of them that Mother told me to bring it, instead."

Kyeyŏn, who until that time had hardly spoken at all, responded to Sŏnggi's question in an unexpected and unpolished Chŏlla Province dialect. He had no idea how so strong and buoyant a voice could emerge from such a slender neck and delicate shoulders. For all he knew, it was because of her well-developed arms and legs, plump hands, and full lips, which contrasted with a slender torso and a waist he could circle with his hands.

"Kyeyŏn! Fetch some water for Brother to wash his hands and face!"

The next morning as well, Okhwa left the maid at work in the kitchen while she had Kyeyŏn take care of Sŏnggi. And it went beyond just fetching wash water. She had Kyeyŏn take care of all Sŏnggi's needs—bringing hot broth after his meals, carrying in the meal tray, getting towels.

"The girl seems to be kindhearted, not at all sly or resentful," commented Okhwa, as if taking pride in her.

"You know, her father said—almost forcefully, I thought—that I was the only one he trusted. He seemed to suggest he wanted to leave her with me as an adopted daughter. . . ." Okhwa broke off for a moment and studied Sŏnggi's expression.

"So, I allowed as how I should listen to what you had to say. But I did think it was worth hearing him out. . . . You ought to take her with you sometime to see the Seven Buddhas," she continued, with every appearance of seeking Sŏnggi's approval.

She went on, passing on what Kyeyŏn had told her. What served as their house in Kurye was little more than a grass hut, set at the foot of a mountain outside of town, apart from any neighbors.

"What do they do about their possessions when they travel?"

"Whatever little they have they just lock up inside, that's all. The real worry, though, is traveling around with Kyeyŏn."

From the way she spoke, it was clear that Okhwa was inclined to adopt Kyeyŏn as soon as the old sieve peddler returned from Hwagae Valley. Her primary concern, it appeared, was whether Sŏnggi would object. Before then, Okhwa had repeatedly urged Sŏnggi to get married, but he had never been receptive. She had hired girls on occasion to sell drinks in their tavern but, while their one-sided affections stirred gossip about Sŏnggi, he had never once returned their feelings. With these thoughts in mind, Okhwa now seemed to be stressing the girl's strong points lest Sŏnggi take a dislike to her.

When Sŏnggi returned with a pair of straw sandals he had bought at the fruit and sundries shop down the way, Okhwa, smiling brightly, offered him a bowl of *makkŏlli*.

"Too hot today, isn't it?" she remarked.

Okhwa liked to pass out samples whenever she filtered fresh *makkŏlli*. Kyeyŏn was in the next room changing.

"Kyeyŏn! Come on out! You must be thirsty, too. Have a sip before you go," called Okhwa in the direction of the room.

Kyeyŏn emerged wearing a ramie jacket and dress. The whites and pupils of her clear eyes put one in mind of fresh young lotus blooms afloat in the water.

"I wore that just twenty years ago," said Okhwa with apparent feeling as she surveyed the attractive girl.

"I got it out yesterday and took in the top a bit. It fits quite naturally. You're actually somewhat more developed than you look. Ah, child. . . . Well, drink up, now! No need feeling shy just because Brother's here."

Kyeyŏn took the bowl with a smile and went back to the other room—to drink her *makkŏlli*, it seemed.

Sŏnggi was already out by the willows, softening his new sandals in the water. Kyeyŏn followed soon after.

When Sŏnggi had mentioned the day before that he was going up to Seven Buddha Hermitage to collect a book payment, Okhwa asked if he wouldn't take Kyeyŏn with him. He was going up there anyway, and she had been planning for some days to go pick mountain greens. He ought to take her just once to see Seven Buddha Hermitage. Sŏnggi was a bit agitated. What did he know about wild greens? he asked. He didn't like the idea. Who was asking him to pick greens? she persisted. All he had to do was lead the way. In the end, Sŏnggi had given up protesting to his strong-willed mother.

From the start, Sŏnggi avoided the main roads, choosing instead untraveled and overgrown hilly paths. These were the untouched foothills of the Chiri Mountains, and not even the woodcutters' paths were clearly visible. Although this was country in which he had grown up, Sŏnggi several times found himself lost in the densely overgrown woods.

If they looked up, they saw mountain peaks high enough to pierce the sky; below, beyond their feet, there was only a blurry, sealike forest; above them white sunshine poured down like streams of water.

Wild grapes, silvervine, and akebi were just now barely sprouting green, but the bright red raspberries and mulberries, already late for their season, were deepening in color.

While Sŏnggi went ahead, pushing aside the viny jumble with a stick he had fashioned for himself from a green hawthorn branch, Kyeyŏn dropped farther and farther behind, as she gathered aralia leaves and picked raspberries.

"What are you doing, dawdling back there?"

When Sŏnggi would stop to scold her, Kyeyŏn would leave off her picking and gathering to run and catch up with him, her small, round lips closed in a tight pout. But before long she would fall behind again.

"Oh, no! What am I to do now?" shouted Kyeyŏn suddenly from behind.

Looking back, Sŏnggi saw Kyeyŏn up in an oak tree, her skirt caught on a branch. What in the world was she doing there? Sŏnggi moved close to have a look. Just within Kyeyŏn's reach, a raspberry branch from below had overlain the oak. Since she couldn't get at the raspberry because of its thorns and because it was rooted high on a slope, it appeared she had approached the raspberry by way of the oak tree, with whose branches it was entangled. To lean over and reach down to free the hem of her skirt, she would have to let go of the upper branch she had barely grasped. And if she released her grip, she would fall out of the tree. Sŏnggi looked up from the base of the tree. Inside the widely opened skirt were hemp pantalets, barely reaching her shins, that caught the bright sunlight and revealed a creamy whiteness within them.

Sŏnggi tried to free the hem of her dress with the wooden stick he was carrying. Perhaps because it was too short, but quite without Sŏnggi himself really knowing, the tip of the stick was only tickling Kyeyŏn's pink and wholesome calves.

"Oh, stop it! I'll fall!" she cried.

And then, as luck would have it, a squirrel appeared along the silvervine runners. It sat poised to skip across the very oak branch that Kyeyŏn was now holding.

"Oh, I'm going to fall! Get that squirrel with your stick! Oh, please!" screamed Kyeyŏn, with most of her lower half brightly revealed in the sunlight but apparently more troubled by the cocky squirrel that worked its jaw as it looked across at her from the silvervine runner.

"Damned squirrel!"

Only by climbing into the lower branches of the tree was Sŏnggi able to unhook the hem of her skirt and whack his stick at the spot on the silvervine runner where the squirrel had been sitting a moment before. Evidently startled by the sound of the impact, several wild pigeons fluttered down to a wild grapevine below them.

"It would be nice if we could find a spring," said Kyeyŏn as she caught up the hem of her skirt to wipe the sweat off her forehead.

With each mountain spur they rounded and each new run of foot-hills they climbed, the more steep were the peaks they encountered; and whenever they emerged from the dark woods and looked down at the vista afforded by the open sky, they could see the valley floor, wide and even as the sea, lush with wild grapes, silvervine tangles, raspber-ries, and the fresh growth of arrowroot vines. The deeper they climbed into the mountains, the more chaotic the chorus of cuckoo cries, the call of occasional pheasants flying across the ravines, and even the sounds of autumn insects—all adding to a sense of confusion.

As the sun neared the center of the sky, it poured down fire on their heads; and, in the shadows of the dark woods, there stretched black snails as big as sea slugs, stuck to the ground by their silvery ooze.

Increasingly hot, sweaty, and thirsty, they plunged like beasts deeper and deeper into the dense undergrowth. They picked raspber-ries, wild berries and peaches, hawthorn fruit, and mulberries as they came to hand and stuffed them into their mouths. The fruit melted like snow, and they swallowed it whole with saliva that flowed tartly sweet. The unripened pieces of wild peach and hawthorn berries that caught in their teeth—both the bitter and the tart—they chewed together with the juices of the squashed berries and gulped them down. At first, their lips were darkened by the juices of the fruit but, later, even their cheeks were stained. Kyeyŏn was giving Sŏnggi a mixture of the thirst-provoking berries and green mountain peaches, piled high on round arrowroot leaves. Sŏnggi took these in his cupped palms and, bending his head forward as if to drink water, put them into his mouth. After eating them, he tossed the arrowroot leaves helter-skelter onto the vines and lay back at an angle against a tangle of silvervine that was completely choked by arrowroot vines.

Kyeyŏn gave a second arrowroot concoction to Sŏnggi. As if irked, he took it where he lay and poured himself a mouthful, which he gulped down, and then tossed the remainder onto the vines. It wasn't long before he started to snore.

Kyeyŏn had gathered more berries and grapes and placed them on a third arrowroot leaf, only to find that Sŏnggi had fallen asleep in the meantime. This time she ate the fruit herself, in the manner that Sŏnggi had adopted.

"Well, he's sure having himself a nice nap!" Kyeyŏn mumbled to herself, as she also lay back against the silvervine and tried to get comfortable. But she began to sneeze. Her throat was parched and she was hungry.

All of a sudden, the cuckoo cries seemed scary to her.

"There ought to be a spring somewhere in all this undergrowth."

As Kyeyŏn pushed aside the vines and made her way into the undergrowth, she unexpectedly came across an akebi vine loaded with fruit and entangled in the branches of a quince tree.

"How nice it would be if these were ripe!" murmured Kyeyŏn as she picked three of the largest akebi fruit, which were still green and as hard and lumpy to the touch as cucumbers. She carelessly bit off a mouthful—just as they had done with all the other fruit that they had found that day—and started to chew. Her mouth was immediately filled with a harsh, tart grassiness.

"Urrgh, it tastes like grass!" she exclaimed and spit out the contents of her mouth.

Kyeyŏn went back to Sŏnggi's side. By the look of the sun, it seemed already after lunchtime. She was both hungry and thirsty.

"Get up so we can go find a spring," she said as she shook Sŏnggi's shoulder.

Sŏnggi opened his eyes. Kyeyŏn, flustered, shoved the two remaining akebi fruits under Sŏnggi's nose. Sŏnggi sat up and put his arms around her soft shoulders up to the nape of her neck. Their lips met each other. On her small, round lips, Sŏnggi found the grassy smell left by the raspberries, mulberries, peaches, and akebi they had eaten, together with a warm and fleshy scent that was as fragrant as the fertile yellow soil.

A lonely crow flew out of nowhere and soared, cawing, above their heads.

"Are the Seven Buddhas still far from here?" asked Kyeyŏn, taking down the lunch basket she had left hanging on a branch of silvervine.

More than a fortnight had passed, and still the old sieve peddler had not returned from Hwagae Valley. From what he had said when he left,

Okhwa and Kyeyŏn expected he had gone into the Chiri Mountains.

"He must be spending all summer in the mountains," said Okhwa from time to time.

And the two of them would sit together, sharing novels. As Kyeyŏn read aloud, her appealing Chŏlla dialect was taking on greater clarity and a more touching melodic quality with each passing day.

If there was anything new between Okhwa and Kyeyŏn during those days, it was Okhwa's discovery of a small mole high on the rim of Kyeyŏn's left ear.

While Okhwa was combing Kyeyŏn's hair one morning, the hand that held the comb began to tremble, as if she had lost control of herself.

"What's wrong, Mother?" Kyeyŏn asked, surprised.

Okhwa only stared vacantly into Kyeyŏn's eyes without saying anything.

"Please, Mother, what's wrong?"

When Kyeyŏn asked the question a second time, Okhwa released a long sigh, appearing to have just barely regained her senses.

"It's nothing, nothing at all," she said, and began combing again.

Kyeyŏn sensed something but could not very well press Okhwa when she claimed there was nothing wrong.

The next morning Okhwa, saying she had business in Agyang, combed her hair early and left the house. Sŏnggi was napping in his mother's room. It began to shower.

"What's Mother going to do? She'll get soaked!" said Kyeyŏn as she brought in an armload of folded laundry from outside.

The hem of her dress, dampened by the rainy wind, brushed against Sŏnggi's sleeping face. As he opened his eyes, Sŏnggi reached out his hand and grabbed the hem. Her arms still laden with laundry, Kyeyŏn swung her head round and calmly studied Sŏnggi. Just when two small dimples began to deepen in her cheeks, they heard the sound of people outside.

"Mother's clothes are going to get soaked!" said Kyeyŏn, repeating herself as she went out onto the porch. After a moment, Sŏnggi began to snore once more.

When Sŏnggi woke again, guests were drinking out on the porch.

"We have nothing but pollack and green peppers to go with the drinks," came the sound of Kyeyŏn's voice from the kitchen. Apparently Kyeyŏn was busy waiting on the customers.

"I told you not to accept customers when Mother's not here," Sŏng-gi said to her after the customers had all left. His tone was a little gruff.

"True, but *makkŏlli* sours overnight. If we left it unsold, Mother would be angry when she got home, wouldn't she?" reasoned Kyeyŏn.

A little later, she appeared at Sŏnggi's side, a smile on her face.

"Brother, would you buy me a hand mirror? Just one little mirror, the round kind."

The next day happened to be a market day. When Kyeyŏn brought his lunch to him, Sŏnggi presented her with a small mirror and some rice cake he had bought.

"Oh, look here!" Kyeyŏn exclaimed in happy surprise when she saw the mirror and cake.

Her flowery eyes filled with delight as she held up the mirror and glanced into it several times before tucking it away into her jacket. Then, as Sŏnggi began to eat his lunch, she seated herself with her back demurely turned and began to eat the rice cake. She was soon chewing with noisy gusto.

To prevent her from being seen eating in public, Sŏnggi shifted his body to screen her from view whenever the shadows of passersby appeared at the front of the stall. She seemed to have a natural fondness for food. Besides cake, she particularly liked melon, peaches, taffy, honey pastries, and all kinds of snacks. If she caught sight of a melon peddler or taffyman passing by the house, Kyeyŏn would drop her sewing—mending thimbles and pincushions—and leap to her feet. She would stand, gazing dreamily after the man, until he disappeared from view.

Once, when Sŏnggi came down from the temple, he found his mother out somewhere and only Kyeyŏn, perched on the edge of the porch, sharing melons with a loafer from the tavern next door. She rose quickly when she saw Sŏnggi and managed a pleased expression, but her face was slightly flushed, as if she were a bit embarrassed.

"Ah, Brother!"

But Sŏnggi took no notice of her and went directly to his room. Kyeyŏn's eyes widened with concern as she left the half-eaten melon on the porch and followed Sŏnggi.

"What's the matter, Brother? Tell me!"

But Sŏnggi did not answer. When she placed her arms on Sŏnggi's shoulders and tried to close them in a hug around his neck, Sŏnggi violently twisted his body and, shaking off her arms, flew at her madly and slapped her on the face.

"Brother! Brother!" she cried, staring at Sŏnggi through a grimace as she raised her hands to fend off the beating. But, as his hands made contact with her face a second time, then a third time and more, she went and buried her head in a corner of the room, letting her body accept the blows he gave.

When she brought lunch to him in the market the next day, Kyeyŏn kept her small, round lips tightly and wordlessly closed. But her lovely, flowerlike eyes did not seem to hold the least rancor for the night before.

That evening, seeing that Kyeyŏn had come out alone to the riverbank, Sŏnggi followed after her. The stars shone steely blue in the sky, but the shadows of the trees shrouded the riverbank in utter darkness.

"Brother," she murmured in a low voice.

Sŏnggi had gotten to her side, when Kyeyŏn rose and moved close up by his chin to speak.

"Brother, how come you stay at the temple all the time nowadays?" she whispered in her strongly inflected Chŏlla accent.

Lately, except for market days, Sŏnggi didn't come down from the temple at all. He sensed that Okhwa had somehow begun keeping a closer eye on his relationship with Kyeyŏn ever since she had visited the seer in Agyang and gotten soaked in a shower on the way back. Being basically faint of heart and particularly loath to face the displeasure of others, Sŏnggi ended up hiding in the temple rather than dealing with his feelings of anger toward his mother.

And now this evening, before Sŏnggi could say anything in response to Kyeyŏn's question, he heard Okhwa calling, "Kyeyŏn! Kyeyŏn!"

Frowning, Sŏnggi gave up what he was going to say and shut his mouth. Oh, Mother! How can you be so unfeeling? He felt a sudden tightening in his throat.

The light of a firefly flashed past. Kyeyŏn, straddling a boulder, grabbed at some smartweed and whispered something, as if talking to herself. But her voice, masked by the sound of the rushing water, was not audible.

Early the next morning, when Sŏnggi peeked into the rooms and the kitchen as if looking for someone and then gave up and left for the temple with a look of apparent disappointment, Kyeyŏn was down at the river again, near where the smartweed grew, washing the cleaning rags.

Four days later, when Sŏnggi came back down from the temple, he found the old sieve peddler on the porch drinking *makkŏlli* and Kyeyŏn sitting at the edge of the porch with her head down, a small bundle at her side. Her hair was washed and combed and she was dressed in new clothes—that is, the ramie jacket and dress that she had worn before, now freshly washed and ironed. Kyeyŏn seemed depressed, but as soon as she caught sight of Sŏnggi she straightened up, a sparkle of joy in her blossomy eyes. Then, in a moment, the hint of anger playing on her small, round lips signaled to Sŏnggi that imminent misfortune threatened them.

"Kyeyŏn's leaving," blurted Okhwa, who was offering a bowl of *makkŏlli* to the old man when she saw Sŏnggi.

According to Okhwa, the old man had returned on the evening of the day that Sŏnggi had gone back up to the temple. When he announced that he meant to depart with Kyeyŏn the next day, that is, yesterday, Okhwa talked him into staying over to rest one more night. And so, planning on an early start, they had gotten their things together and were now about to set out.

All these things he understood only after Okhwa had explained them to him, later on. But at first he was stunned, as if clubbed over the head. He felt as though his entire body, from the top of his head to the tips of his toes, was being swept by a combination of vertigo, rage, and anxiety; as though all his blood was suddenly pooling in one spot, both his ears being drawn straight up from his head, his tongue curling down into his throat, and steely stars flashing before his eyes. Until then, he had no idea how attached he had become to her, so much so that he couldn't bear to live apart. Had it been inevitable that only now, at this moment when they were to separate forever, that only now such feelings would flare up, suddenly igniting both heart and mind? It was like a dream. He was on the verge of letting loose a howl, bursting into sobbing tears with no care for dignity or shame, when he realized he couldn't show such a face to his mother, and so, biting his trembling lips, he sat down heavily at the end of the porch.

"Your son is certainly a handsome young man."

The old man was obviously talking about Sŏnggi. But Sŏnggi sat without turning his head in their direction, nursing his anger.

Okhwa, all the while, continued her narration to Sŏnggi of the old sieve peddler's story. While in the Chiri Mountains, he had happened to meet a young stranger who turned out to be the son of an old friend from his hometown of Yŏsu. By the time he had explained that he was an industrialist operating a large factory in Yŏsu and was now on holiday in the Chiri Mountains, the two of them found themselves on friendly terms. He urged the old man to go back home with him and settle there. With nostalgic thoughts of his old hometown and a belief that he might somehow improve his life with the young man's help, the old man decided to go back with him to Yŏsu. Okhwa went on in this vein for some time, but her story made no sense to Sŏnggi, who was distracted by his anxious, dizzy, and angry feelings. Her words were no more than a buzzing in his ears, like the sound of swarming bees.

"Why, the *makkŏlli* is so good, I'm already full!" said the old man, who had just finished off his bowl and was picking up his fan and walking stick.

"If you go to Yŏsu, we may never see you again," said Okhwa, also getting up.

"Who can understand our lives? We'll meet again if it's our destiny," said the old man, slipping his feet into huge cord sandals.

"Good-bye, child," said Okhwa to Kyeyŏn in parting, as she put a flowered purse containing money into the girl's small bundle as a present.

Kyeyŏn stared for a while into Okhwa's face with red eyes that seemed to plead for mercy.

"Come back again," said Okhwa simply, stroking Kyeyŏn's head. Whereupon, Kyeyŏn buried her face in Okhwa's bosom and began to sob loudly. Okhwa patted her shoulders, which were undulating like waves.

"No more crying, dear. Your father's waiting," said Okhwa in a voice that had quite lost its spirit.

"Be well, then," said the old man in parting to Okhwa.

"If you find that life in Yŏsu is not what you expected, please come back and live here with us, Grandfather," said Okhwa.

"I wish you well, Brother," said Kyeyŏn in parting, searching for Sŏnggi's last glance with reddened eyes.

Seemingly wakened by Kyeyŏn's words, Sŏnggi leapt down from the porch and began to stagger bewilderedly toward her only to stop, as if suddenly regaining his senses. He stood planted like a post, staring blankly for some time at her face.

"I wish you well, Brother."

Even with this second word of parting, Kyeyŏn's reddened eyes sought some miraculous deliverance in Sŏnggi's face. But Sŏnggi, himself close to collapsing on the spot, could barely manage to grab hold of a willow branch for support.

Oblivious to the stares of Okhwa and her father, Kyeyŏn had turned her brightly flushed face toward Sŏnggi's and fixed on him a penetrating gaze. But in his eyes, as he leaned against the willow, he revealed only blazing flames with no new message or miracle for her.

"I wish you well, Brother," she said, leaving behind a tearful voice as she turned away.

Sŏnggi stood amidst the streaming sunshine, drooping willows, and echoing cries of cuckoos, staring vacantly after the ramie jacket now disappearing into the distance.

Sŏnggi was finally able to get out of his sickbed only after the seasons of Rain Water and Waking of Insects had passed, at about the time of Pure Brightness, when the April drizzle had set in. The thready fronds of the willows lining the front of the tavern had turned green again; and, between the paths and in the foothills, apricots, peaches, and azaleas were colorfully blooming and falling.

Okhwa had brought her son's meal tray set with rice gruel and waited until she saw him finish the bowl before she asked, "Do you still want to take a trip up through Kangwŏn Province?"

Sŏnggi quietly shook his head.

"Are you going to get married and live here with me?"

Sŏnggi again shook his head.

That year, before spring had come, when everyone had nearly given up all hope of his recovery, Okhwa decided that if he was going to die, she should let him go with the knowledge of what was in her heart. So she revealed to him that the old sieve peddler was without doubt her own father, who had come to Hwagae Market thirty-six years before with his song-and-dance troupe and had himself a one-night fling. She also disclosed that Kyeyŏn was clearly her own younger sister, in view of the mole high on the rim of the girl's left ear. Okhwa even showed him that same black mole high on the rim of her own left ear.

"When the old man referred to 'thirty-six years ago' that first night, my heart skipped a beat. At first I tried to ignore the whole thing—how could it be? But I was still troubled and so I visited the seer in Agyang to ask her. It was almost as if she were looking right inside of me! I was devastated!"

Okhwa stopped for a moment. Sŏnggi stared into his mother's face, his eyes blazing with a fiery intensity.

"If I had never known, then things might well have been different, perhaps. But once I found out, what could I do? There are moral laws."

Okhwa's tears fell on her son's hand, now wasted and bony, as she asked him not to think her cold and heartless.

Sŏnggi unexpectedly seemed to draw strength from this confession, which Okhwa had given as her parting words to him. Sŏnggi stared with blazing eyes at the ceiling for a while and then set his teeth lightly into his lips as if making a new commitment.

Okhwa no longer insisted on her earlier plans for Sŏnggi, who wished neither to go search for his father in Kangwŏn Province nor to get married and settle at home.

"So, what do you think you'll do? Let it be what you think best."

Sŏnggi lay back down on his bed without saying anything.

It was more than a month after this, on a market morning in early summer, when the various wild greens that Sŏnggi liked so much were coming down Hwagae Valley, one kind after another. Sŏnggi gulped down the bowl of *makkŏlli* he was having with a dish of fresh, seasoned aralia leaves.

"Mother, would you have a taffyman's backrack made for me?" he asked.

Okhwa, struck dumb by Sŏnggi's request, could only stare vacantly into his face.

Another fortnight had passed since then. It was a morning when cuckoos were once again calling in their fluently echoing tones and sunlight was soaking into the fronds of the willows. A brief drizzle at dawn had yielded a day that was unusually bright and clear. In the intersection at Hwagae Market, Sŏnggi was saying good-bye to his mother. He was dressed in linen jacket and pants, his hair tightly bound with a silk scarf. A newly made, bright white wooden backrack was loosely strapped to his lower back. The top tray of the rack was more than half filled with long white sticks of taffy, and the lower tray held several volumes of his unsold books and a few knickknacks for ladies.

Before him were three roads, branching out along the rivers. But from the outset Sŏnggi kept Hwagae Valley to his back. To the southeast lay the road to Hadong. And to the southwest lay the road to Kurye, a hilly path over mountain spurs that she had crossed together with the old sieve peddler after the tearful parting about this time a year ago, a sunshine-flooded path, even now, that wound above the marketplace before it headed out toward Kurye. After a while, Sŏnggi turned away from it. He set his back to Kurye and started moving slowly toward Hadong.

With each step he took, his heart grew lighter; and by the time he had lost sight of his mother's tavern, from where she might have watched him disappearing through the willows, he had begun to hum the lively melody of a drinking song.

Translated by Marshall R. Pihl

Mountains

Hwang Sunwŏn

Hwang Sunwŏn was born in 1915 near Pyongyang. He was educated there and in Tokyo, where he received a degree in English literature from Waseda University in 1939. By that time he had already published two volumes of poetry. In 1940 his first volume of stories, *The Marsh* (Nŭp), was published, and since then Hwang has concentrated on fiction. In May 1946 Hwang and his family moved from the Soviet-occupied northern sector of Korea to the U.S.-occupied South. He began teaching at Seoul High School in September of that year. Like countless other Koreans, the Hwang family was displaced during the civil war of 1950–53. From 1957 to 1993 Hwang taught Korean literature at Kyung Hee University in Seoul.

Hwang is the author of some of the best-known stories of modern Korea: "Stars" (Pyŏl, 1941), "Old Man Hwang" (Hwang Noin, 1949), "The Old Potter" (Tokchinnŭn nŭlgŭni, 1950), "Pierrot" (Kogyesa, 1952), "Cranes" (Hak, 1953), "Shower" (Sonagi, 1959), and "Drizzle" (Karangbi, 1961), among others. In a burst of creativity in the mid-1950s, Hwang produced the story collection "Lost Souls" (Irŏbŏrin saram dŭl, 1958). This volume, a series of variations on the theme of the outcaste in a highly structured society, is unique among Hwang's eight collections of short fiction in its thematic unity.

Hwang began publishing novels in the 1950s. *The Descendants of Cain* (K'ain ŭi huye, 1954) is an autobiographical account of the uprooting of landowners in the Soviet-occupied zone in the immediate aftermath of Liberation. But it was during the next two decades that he produced his most important work in this genre. *Trees on the Cliff* (Namu tŭl pit'al e sŏda, 1960), perhaps his most successful novel, deals with the effects of the civil war on three young soldiers. *The Sun and the Moon* (Irwŏl, 1962–65) is a portrait of a *paekchŏng*, or untouchable, in urban Seoul. *The Moving Castle* (Umjiginŭn sŏng, 1968–72) is an ambitious attempt to synthesize Western influence and native tradition in modern Korea.

Also in the 1960s and 1970s, Hwang's short fiction became more experimental. Some of his most memorable and challenging stories date from this period: "Conversations in June About Mothers" (Omŏni ka innŭn yuwŏl ŭi taehwa, 1965), "The Curtain Fell, But Then. . . ," (Mak ŭn naeryŏnnŭnde, 1968), "A Numerical Enigma" (Sutcha p'uri, 1974). Hwang's creative powers were undiminished as late as 1984, as the highly original "A Shadow Solution" (Kŭrimja p'uri) demonstrates.

Indeed, the length of Hwang Sunwŏn's literary career, spanning six decades, is virtually unparalleled in modern Korean letters. But it is his craftsmanship that sets Hwang apart from his peers. Despite critics' quibbles about the social relevance of his fiction, it is safe to say that Hwang is *the* consummate short story writer of twentieth-century Korea. His command of dialect, his facility with both rural and urban settings, his variety of narrative techniques, his vivid artistic imagination, his spectacularly diverse constellation of characters, ranging from hermaphroditic shamans to effete intellectuals, and his insights into human personality make Hwang at once a complete writer and one who is almost impossible to categorize. If there is one thread that runs through Hwang's fiction, it is a lyrical humanism that is affirmative without being naive, compassionate without being lachrymose, spiritual without being otherworldly.

"Mountains" (San) first appeared in 1956 in *Hyŏndae munhak* magazine and was subsequently included in the story collection *Lost Souls*.

Again the traps were empty. In autumn you could always count on a rabbit or two and some pheasants, but not this year. Where had all the animals gone? Pau moved his snare and fowling net to a different game trail.

Pau was on his way to Acorn Hollow. There were oak trees nearer home, but the grove in Acorn Hollow had big, fat acorns just waiting to be gathered from the ground.

It was the season for foliage. Dark green firs and mixed pines grew halfway up the mountains. Higher up were groves of thorny ash, linden, and elm, and those birches that were so white, the maples blazing red among them. The vivid green, white, yellow, and crimson of the nearby mountains became muted in the distant mountains, then blurred and dissolved at the horizon. Wherever you looked it was the same—mountains and more mountains.

There was nothing resembling a road through these mountains. But Pau easily negotiated the roadless terrain and didn't find it a problem at all.

The concept of loneliness was unknown to Pau, for he had never had much social contact with others. Until he was seven he saw no one other than his mother and father. And then one day he followed his parents out to their fire-field patch, and there they heard a voice. Someone down below was shouting up to them, a man in a traditional white topcoat and black horsehair hat. He appeared to be asking directions. Pau's father stopped what he was doing and turned toward the man, but didn't immediately respond. It had been so long since he had talked with outsiders that he had lost the ability to speak freely. The passerby gave up trying to shout to them and walked away. He moved quite fast, and to Pau it seemed the man was somehow scared of them. He and his parents watched until the man's white topcoat had flickered out of sight around a bend in the path. Suddenly Pau's father shouted in that direction at the top of his lungs—"Hey!" Back came an echo—"Heyyy!" And then another echo and another, and finally the shout trailed off in the distance.

Some years later, after he had buried his father, Pau, young as he was, would sometimes feel stifled, and shout at the top of his lungs—"Hey! Heyyy!"

His father had died after being gored by a boar. Pau was in his early teens at the time. One morning his father had left the house and hadn't returned at the usual time. Pau would have tagged along but for a stomach-ache that had bothered him since the night before. He and his mother knew where his father had gone, for they had seen him taking a trap. And so they set out to look for him. They found him on the hillside that faced their house. A glancing blow from the boar had sent him tumbling halfway down an outcrop, and he had fetched up against a pine tree. Pau and his mother returned home for a linden-bark rope and barely managed to haul his father up. He had suffered a slight gash on his right side—nothing serious, it seemed. But in time it became infected. Pau and his mother ground up an elm root and applied it to the wound, but it didn't seem to help. His father took to bed and began repeating the same thing over and over:

"Just my luck—the one time mother boar decides to take her young ones on a different path, and this is what happens. As long as you live in the mountains, watch out for large animals—don't even think of going near them."

True to his words, using a pitfall or similar trap, his father had never hunted larger game. And in turn, the tiger whose tracks they sometimes saw on winter mornings in the snow outside their house was never to be seen slinking around, or leaving any other trace of itself.

"If you're going to live in the mountains," his father continued, "don't look at a large animal as an enemy—think of him as one of us." And a few days before he died, he said, "After I'm gone, I want you to move someplace where there aren't so many large animals." But not once did he tell Pau to leave the mountain country. Honoring his father's request, Pau had moved with his mother to Bush Clover Hollow, where they now lived.

Pau scared up a roe deer as he passed a clump of firs. The animal bounded off. And then a pheasant, flushed from a grassy thicket, took wing.

"That's more like it," said Pau. "I was wondering where all you pheasants were. You'll be walking into my trap any time now."

Pau crossed several ridges high and low and arrived at a pass wooded with flowering cherries. Below was the gravel stream of Trickle Hollow. If he continued on, skirting an alder grove, he would reach Acorn Hollow.

At the stream Pau cupped his hands and drank. As he wiped the moisture from his lips, his reflection in the water drew his gaze. He recalled what his mother had told him that morning. As a rule, there was little conversation between mother and son. It had been the same when his father was alive. If one of them picked up the farming tools, it was time to go out to the fields; when one of them stopped working, that meant it was time for a rest; and if one of them looked up at the sun and slung the tools over a shoulder, it was time to return home. With his father gone, Pau and his mother spoke even less. And then that morning, while his mother was cutting his hair, she had blurted out: "You look just like your father." Pau had said nothing. But now, as he observed his reflection in the water, he removed the towel he used as a headband. Father had a topknot, he thought, but my hair's been cut. And Father had black hair on his chin, but not me. What could his mother have meant?

Pau quickly filled his large basket with acorns. He was about to retrieve the backrack he had removed when something about ten yards in front of him caught his eye. An animal? But when he looked closer he saw it was a man. The man gestured behind his back, and several other men rose from the bushes. There were five of them in all.

Pau had never come face to face with so many people in the mountains. Even after moving to Bush Clover Hollow, he and his mother caught sight of only one or two people a year at best. And in most cases, they saw these others only at a distance as they rounded a hillside and disappeared. Pau encountered the most people during his annual spring visit to Flatland Village, some ten miles from home. There he would barter pine-root fungus, bracken fern, bellflower root, pine mushrooms, and agaric for salt and other necessities. It wasn't much of a village—only four households. In any case, Pau was happy to see so many people during these trading visits. He had grown up not knowing the meaning of loneliness, but as you might expect, he couldn't help enjoying these encounters with other people.

The five men quickly surrounded Pau. All of them wore dirty, olive-colored clothing. Dry grass and branches sprouted from their shoulders and from low on their backs.

The first man approached Pau and prodded him with a metal contraption that had a hole bored in it.

"Who are you?" he said bluntly.

The prodding reminded Pau of the time he had seen his father and a hunter carrying something called a rifle. The hunter had said he could down a bear or a tiger just like that with one shot.

Pau shuddered.

"Where are you from?"

The words still wouldn't come.

"Sucker must be deaf."

"Hey, look at those acorns!" One of the men ran to the basket. "Big as chestnuts!"

The others rushed over.

Freed from the touch of the muzzle, Pau breathed more easily.

The five men plopped down around the basket and began cracking the acorns.

Pau studied the men as they chomped away. The first man was the only one carrying that fearsome gun barrel. One of the others had something like a sack strapped to his shoulders. The rest of the men carried nothing. All were badly in need of a shave, except for one fellow with long hair who had no beard at all. He was the smallest of the five, and looked the youngest.

The men ate for some time.

"Hey, you—where's the nearest stream?"

This man had an extra tooth beside one of his canines.

Pau remained silent, wondering what this question meant.

"Sure enough, sucker's deaf."

The man with the rifle pantomimed someone drinking.

"Know what I mean?"

Pau finally understood that they wanted water.

"You have to go to Trickle Hollow. . . ."

"Well, what do you know, he's not deaf after all. . . . All right, then, where is it?"

"If you go around like this. . . ."

Pau, thinking he would guide the men to the stream on his way back home, put the basket on his backrack.

"Leave the backrack here," said the man with the extra tooth.

As soon as they heard the trickle of water on rocks, the men ran to the stream, stretched out on their stomachs, and slurped the water. Only the young, beardless man drank from cupped hands. After drinking their fill, the men washed their faces and feet.

Snaggle Tooth went behind an alder and relieved himself. As he returned, Pau noticed a palm-sized leather pouch hanging from his side.

Snaggle Tooth sat down, produced a piece of paper from his pocket, and spread it out on his lap.

The man with the rifle sat down in front of Snaggle Tooth. "Where do you think we are, sir?"

Instead of answering, Snaggle Tooth continued to study the piece of paper. Then he turned to Pau.

"You, what county are we in? And what township?"

Pau didn't understand these questions, either.

"We're just not connecting with you, are we?" said Rifleman in frustration. "What we want to know is the name of the village where you live."

"Bush Clover Hollow."

"And where's that?"

"Couple of miles from here."

"Really? How many families there?"

"Just us."

"You're the only family? Doesn't anybody else live around here?"

Pau shook his head.

This was sobering news to the five platoon members. Seeing Pau, they had assumed there was a hamlet nearby. Armed with a single rifle and revolver, they had clung to the hope that they could get what they wanted, emaciated though they were. But now even this hope evaporated. That this backwoods fellow's home was several miles away, that there was just the one family, that their living conditions compelled him to come all the way here just to gather acorns—the men despaired at this realization.

"How about if we take a rest around here, sir?" asked Rifleman. "The men look done in."

Snaggle Tooth folded the piece of paper.

"First we'd better get higher up. We have to keep out of sight of those damned jets."

"Fighter planes been overhead?" Rifleman asked Pau.

Pau didn't understand.

"Whoosh, whoosh." The other man spread his fingers wide and made a couple of swooping motions in front of his forehead. "See anything like that?"

Pau finally understood.

"Yeah."

The previous summer, when Pau was weeding their fire-field plot, he had heard a tremendous, roaring wind. Startled, he had looked up to see something like a huge bird flashing by overhead. On instinct he had buried his head in one of the furrows. Every time afterward when he heard that roaring wind, he would cover his head. And now, realizing that he too could boast of having seen this wondrous thing, he broke into a broad smile.

"Look at him grin—doesn't know shit. Wait till he gets a taste of those babies."

The platoon members rose silently. The beardless young man was the last to get up. For some time he had been sitting apart from the others, looking out at the pass that lay ahead of them.

They all drank once more.

"Don't forget to fill up."

The man with the sack on his back produced a metal container with a cap hanging from it. After filling it with water he gave it to the beardless young man to carry.

The men returned to Acorn Hollow but didn't release Pau. Instead, after he had retrieved his backrack and the basket, he was put at the head of the line. They then started up into the mountains. Pau would guide them, the platoon leader had decided.

They stopped where a stand of fir merged with a grove of whitish birch. One of the men produced a small shovel from the knapsack.

All sorts of interesting things in there, Pau thought.

The men ordered Pau to dig them a cave. Meanwhile, they ate more acorns. And then one man after another lay down. The beardless young man alone remained sitting against a tree, forehead resting on clasped hands against drawn-up knees.

The platoon leader sat up. He produced the map again, spread it out, and passed a fingertip along the main axis of the T'aebaek Mountains.

"I think we're on Odae Mountain," he muttered, producing a cigarette butt from his shirt pocket.

He lit up, took a drag, and exhaled. Instantly the other men jerked upright. The platoon leader realized he'd made a mistake.

"You've got a stash there, sir," said Rifleman, salivating at the thought of a cigarette. His adam's apple bobbed.

"It's the last one."

"All the more reason to share it."

The platoon leader reluctantly handed him the butt.

Rifleman took a puff, followed by a man with a lighter-colored beard than the rest, and finally the man with the knapsack. The young man with no beard was left out.

After Knapsack took his puff, Brownbeard snatched back the butt, which by now was little more than a crimson spark. He took one last drag, almost burning his lips. Suddenly dizzy, he closed his eyes and collapsed on his back. Then he turned to his side and opened his eyes to see Pau stop shoveling, remove his headband, and wipe his face. This amused him. Look at the sucker's hair, he felt like telling the man next to him—looks like a crow pecked at it. But, still giddy from the cigarette, he said nothing. Content with the tingling sensation, he closed his eyes again.

Before dark, Pau collected some dry grass and a load of dead twigs and branches. After making a fire, he spread out the grass and the men lay down again.

The platoon leader would occasionally look up and warn Pau to keep the flames low so they wouldn't be visible at a distance. Beardless remained hunched up beside the fire, knees drawn up and forehead resting on clasped hands, but before long he too had curled up on his side. In their sleep, the men instinctively inched toward the fire. Now no one cautioned Pau to keep the flames low.

The next morning Pau roasted some acorns and the men eased their hunger pangs. The acorns were more tart when cooked, but more tender as well, and the men could eat more of them that way.

Pau was happy to have come across so many people here in the mountains. And he was glad to be able to help them. Thoughts of his waiting mother faded from his mind. Taking up the shovel, he threw himself into digging the rest of the cave.

Brownbeard appeared, buckling his pants.

"Dammit, I'm all stopped up—just what I need!"

"Count your blessings. Would you rather be shitting on an empty stomach? I'd like to have some nice white rice and a thick soup full of meat, and then stuff my asshole with concrete. That way I'd never go hungry again. All I think about is food; can't even remember what the little woman and the kids look like. The only thing I can see is a big, steaming bowl of rice. Plain rice, rice with barley—anything's fine, so long as there's plenty of it."

The platoon leader took out his map again and peered at it.

"Shouldn't there be houses somewhere?" asked Rifleman.

"Looks like there's a village to the southwest."

"Well, what are we waiting for? We're so hungry, the lice are starving."

The platoon leader looked up. "You," he said to Brownbeard, "see if you can find a village." He pointed to the southwest. "Even if it's only a couple of houses."

Pau was taken along as a guide.

The woods were dank, even in the full light of day. Occasionally the men sank to their ankles in the damp, rotting leaves mixed with animal droppings. Underfoot it was peaceful and calm—almost lonely—but above, the restless wind whistled through the treetops. Often the trees would open up only to present a dropoff. So instead of taking a direct route, they would have to contour all the way around. In such terrain, Brownbeard constantly fell behind.

"Hey, slow down, will you," the man said as they rounded a hillside after walking about five miles. He decided to strike up a conversation to kill the time and take his mind off the ache in his legs.

"What's your name?" he opened.

"Pau."

"Pau? Hmmm. Okay, Pau, tell me about your family."

"There's just me and my mother."

He'd have to work at this conversation, the man told himself.

"So your father passed away?"

"Yes."

"No little brothers or sisters?"

"No."

There was a short lull.

"Oh yeah—how old are you?"

Pau lacked a ready answer.

"How old were you this year?"

Pau had to think about this. Around the time the bush clover were sprouting, his mother had told him he had turned twenty-two. But was it that spring or the one before? He had to say something, and finally he decided on twenty-two.

"Are you for real?" the other smirked, before Pau could answer. He studied Pau anew, and his eyes came to rest on Pau's legs. His three-quarter-length summer farmer's pants were rolled up above the knee, and with every step the veins in his calves bulged. Whatever his age, Brownbeard thought, he was certainly a grown man.

"A grown-up fella with hair in all the right places, and you don't know how old you are?" Brownbeard chuckled in disbelief.

The laughter, lingering in the void, sounded unnaturally loud in the remote backcountry. Brownbeard choked off the laugh.

They fell silent again. It occurred to Brownbeard as they walked along that he had survived battle but might never live to see his way out of these mountains, where idiots like this Pau lived.

Somehow they managed to cover a good seven or eight miles. Brownbeard had convinced himself they would have to give up, when finally they crested a ridge, and there on the other side of the valley were some houses—three in all.

Brownbeard sighed in relief.

"You can find your way back here, right?"

Without a word, Pau looked once in all directions. Then they returned to the others, who in the meantime had finished hollowing out the cave.

As soon as they had eaten more roasted acorns, the men set out. Beardless was left to mind the cave. Brownbeard tried to beg off, saying he was too tired, but the platoon leader put him at the head of the line. This was no time for fanciful thoughts, the leader told him. He ordered Pau to take his backrack.

After a few miles it began to get dark. But little light penetrated these woods anyway, and the men continued, their faces scratched by branches, occasionally sliding over short dropoffs. Brownbeard would insist on going in a certain direction, but after wandering for some time the men would have to resort to Pau to get back on route. The moon was almost a week past full, but the men found it quite helpful in finding their way.

Finally they arrived at what they thought was the ridge reached by Brownbeard and Pau. There on the hillside across the valley was a light that resembled a firefly. Where were the other lights? Had they come to the right place? After dropping toward the light, the man saw they had. Only one of the families had lit its pine resin lamp.

Pau realized the others were spreading out in the darkness. Snaggle Tooth was doing something—he was taking something out of that full leather pouch. As this thought registered in Pau's mind, a flame shot from the object and the sound of a shot reverberated in the night air. And then there was a flame and a roaring sound from the hands of the man with the rifle—a roar even louder than that from Snaggle Tooth's.

The single light went out, as if startled into darkness. But it was Pau who was most startled. His limbs trembled, and he felt dizzy. He could make no sense of this chaos breaking out in the gloom.

Doors were yanked open. "Don't move, or you're dead!" "Where's the rice?" "Corn and potatoes—that's all?" "Better than nothing—hand 'em over." "Don't move—I'll shoot!" "Oh god, somebody help!" Tangled figures in the dark. "The backrack! Where's the backrack!" Somebody rushed over and punched Pau in the face. "You idiot! Get over there and load up!" "Make sure you get a pot! And don't forget a kitchen knife!" "You got the salt?" "Grab the biggest guy here and make him carry this stuff!" From one of the houses came the muffled sound of a baby's cries.

The dried, coarsely ground kernels of corn were delicious cooked with chopped potatoes. The men gathered round the pot with chopsticks fashioned from small branches, and greedily devoured the meal. All they had to accompany it was salt.

"Hey, has salt ever tasted this good?" said Brownbeard, regaining some of his strength. Earlier, he had collapsed on the ground, the most exhausted of the men.

"Good or bad, maybe it's time you quit eating," Rifleman kidded him.

"Don't worry about me. You're the one who should take it easy. Keep shoveling down food on an empty stomach, and you'll get a gut-ache—then what?"

"Gut-ache?" the other snorted. "If I could eat my fill and die of a gut-ache—no regrets. You can write on my grave: "1951, October . . . what day is it, anyway?"

None of them knew.

"Well, well, what a life—can't even keep track of the days. Anyway, it must be October by now, so: 'Here lies Yun so-and-so, overate and died of a gut-ache, October 1951, who knows where.' How's that?"

"Knock it off!" the platoon leader said, shooting a fierce glare at the man with the rifle. It was a meager meal, but for the first time in days the men had filled their stomachs, and they all felt more energetic. Granted, they were stragglers from the main army and no longer kept strict discipline. Still, he was the platoon leader, and it wouldn't do to have his men shooting off their mouths. "I want you men to straighten up and not let your guard down," he said, trying once more to recoup his authority. Then he put down his chopsticks and rose, the first to finish his meal.

"Well, it's true—living in these mountains you can't keep the days straight," said Brownbeard when the platoon leader was out of sight. "We're going to end up dying here. And our pal here doesn't know how old he is—can you believe that?" he said, recalling the previous day's conversation with Pau. His jocular tone was a sign that full stomachs had given the men fresh life.

The scorched corn and potatoes at the bottom of the pot were left for Pau and the young man drafted as a porter. After the others had finished, Pau chewed the crisp food, his eyes returning again and again to the rifle. How could that metal contraption make such a roar? And to think you could drop a large animal with it. The more he thought about it, the more it seemed a frighteningly wondrous thing.

The man from the village sat hunched up staring off at the distant mountains. He made no effort to eat.

Rifleman suddenly jumped to his feet and hurried off in the direction where the platoon leader had disappeared. In a few minutes he was back.

"People are downright disgusting when they want something," he snorted. "First time there's food in my gut since god knows when, and I want a cigarette. And then it occurs to me: When our leader goes off by himself, he wants to steal a smoke. So I go and find him, and you know what—that's exactly what he's doing. He hears me coming, and he hides the butt just like magic. And he told me we smoked the last one yesterday. Yet I saw him just now with my own eyes. Damn— what a disgrace! At a time like this, one drag from a cigarette and I could die happy."

The others salivated, craving a cigarette, adam's apples bobbing. But there was little to do now except lie down in a warm, sunny spot, and before long they were all snoring.

Beardless was left with the job of tidying up and washing the pot.

Pau too sprawled out and fell asleep after gathering a load of firewood and a pot of water. Some time later, there was a piercing noise and he bolted up. Sleepy though he was, he was sure it was the same sound he had heard the previous night. The others woke up and looked around, then rushed toward where the sound had come from. Pau followed.

They found Snaggle Tooth standing with his back toward them. The man from the village was sprawled on the ground in front of him.

"He would have been a problem. It's best to get rid of someone like that on the spot. If he runs away, it's trouble for us; if we keep him, he's just an extra mouth to feed."

The man's limbs twitched, and then he was still. A pool of blood formed on the back of his muddy, traditional summer jacket, then spilled off to the side.

As Pau eyed the small metal contraption in Snaggle Tooth's hand, he couldn't help shuddering. It frightened him just as much as the longer weapon. Snaggle Tooth ordered him to bury the body, but even as Pau did this he couldn't stop shuddering.

That evening Pau spread dry grass in the cave and buried some coals off to one side. That way the men could save matches and at the same time ward off the chill.

During the night Pau was again awakened where he lay in the corner of the cave. After the events of the previous night and what had happened that afternoon, he realized, perhaps the slightest noise would awaken him now. He thought he heard someone rustling about, and a short time later he saw two figures leaving the cave. In the intermittent light from the moon, he could make out Snaggle Tooth and the young man who never said anything. Pau's heart dropped. Snaggle Tooth held the young man by the wrist. Wasn't that the small gun in his other hand?

Soon he would hear that frightening sound, Pau thought. But there was only the occasional chirping of insects along with the wind whispering in the trees.

Eventually the two of them returned. Pau was glad to see that nothing had happened.

The following night Pau again woke to the rustling sound to see Snaggle Tooth with his pistol leading the young man by the wrist outside the cave.

That night, the other men awoke as well.

"I want you men to straighten up and not let your guard down."

Pau recognized Rifleman's voice. He was mimicking Snaggle Tooth.

"That no-good. . . . Who does he think he is, anyway? I guess he figures as long as we're not going to get out of these mountains alive, he might as well do what he wants."

Pau couldn't understand the reason for these mutterings in the darkness.

After a while the pair again returned without incident.

The following day Pau discovered that the one who was led outside the cave each night was not a man but a woman. He had gone down to Trickle Stream to fetch water and had seen smoke rising. There, sitting beside a fire, clad only in underwear that clung to the skin, was the young soldier, arms and legs exposed. The soldier's washed clothes had been hung near the fire.

Pau was amazed that a man's skin could be so white. But then his eyes traveled to the soldier's chest. No way those things sticking out could belong to a man. The soldier's hair had been chopped off above the shoulder, but there was still no doubt in Pau's mind that he was looking at a woman. Pau quickly turned back, feeling he had witnessed something forbidden.

Should they stay where they were, or try something else? This was the question now facing the men. Rifleman was for moving on. Now that they'd recovered some of their strength, why not try to get closer to the main army? And they ought to leave while they still had food. Otherwise, they'd end up starving or freezing to death here in the mountains or in some hamlet unknown to the outside world.

The platoon leader thought differently. It was no use trying to find the main army, since the enemy probably occupied the area in between. Running off half cocked would only make a bad situation worse. Better to stay put here in the mountains and see what developed.

"So, how are we going to keep warm? And what are we supposed to do for food?" asked Rifleman.

"You call yourself a soldier? Listen, there's no guarantee we'd find the main army in a day or two. And after that, what are we going to eat? It makes more sense to stay here and raid the local villages. In the meantime, we wait for our boys to counterattack."

The platoon leader abruptly rose and left.

"Doesn't seem too concerned, does he?" said Rifleman. "But if an enemy patrol finds us, we're dead." He pulled the trigger of an imaginary gun. "I know what he's up to—he'll make a go of it here as long as he can keep us under his damned thumb."

In a burst of anger he snatched his rifle and rose.

That day, Rifleman shot a roe deer. For several days he had been leaving camp to roam the mountains. Carnal desire had possessed him, and he needed a release. That day too he had gone out roaming, and come across a roebuck.

Pau packed the carcass back to camp on his backrack, then dressed it out. The midsection was a mess of flesh and entrails. It reminded Pau of the corpse of the young man from the village.

Dinner that day was a feast.

"All we need now is some booze," said Brownbeard.

Rifleman snorted. "You actually remember what it tastes like? Tell me: Is it bitter? Is it satisfying? Does it burn your throat? I forgot what things taste like a long time ago."

He shot a furtive leer toward the young woman.

Again that night the platoon leader stole out of the cave with the woman. This time, the woman went in front without having to be led. She seemed resigned to the situation.

As soon as they were out of sight, there was a shot. The others crawled outside to find the platoon leader and the young woman standing there.

"What happened?" asked Rifleman.

"Damned thing."

The platoon leader motioned with his pistol toward the tree where the roebuck's head had been hung earlier that day. Then he explained: Outside the cave he saw something flashing in the dark. It was the roebuck's eyes, and they were glaring at him. He had felt as if those horns were about to charge him.

"Damned thing scared me," the platoon leader muttered again.

The next day the platoon leader ordered the men to boil up the head for eating. They could have the rest of the meat later.

It had been so long since they'd eaten greasy food, the men developed diarrhea.

Rifleman alone was unaffected. After breakfast he took his rifle apart and began to clean it.

Pau couldn't resist looking on. That metal contraption was the most wonderful thing. How could it produce such a roar? And where did it get the power to kill a man or a deer, just like that?

Rifleman was at work on the muzzle.

"Down to my last cartridge," he muttered. "Better save it for something that counts."

Brownbeard, who had left to relieve himself, reappeared.

Rifleman glanced at Pau.

"What's so interesting? Figure out how it works? All right, then, beat it."

Pau wanted to stay and watch how the contraption was put back together, but what could he do?

After Pau had left, Rifleman took a guarded look about him.

"Think about it—you ever heard of a deer's head getting a gleam in its eyes and charging someone?" he asked Brownbeard. "All they did was sparkle in the moonlight."

Brownbeard suspected his companion was referring to the previous night's incident. But what was he getting at?

"I'll tell you—he talks big, but he's gutless, isn't he?"

Brownbeard found himself nodding as his eyes met those of the other, whose whites seemed so large.

"So why are we tagging along after him? Why trust a chickenshit?"

Something's going to happen, Brownbeard suddenly realized.

Sure enough, that evening a shot rang out from the stand of firs. When the others ran over, they saw the platoon leader sprawled on the ground.

Rifleman strapped on the platoon leader's holster with its revolver, then transferred the map from the other's pocket to his own.

"Thought he was a deer," he mumbled.

A search of the platoon leader's pockets turned up a cigarette butt.

"Look at this—he's got a stash, yessir."

Rifleman collected every shred of tobacco from the pocket, rolled a cigarette, and savored it with Brownbeard and Knapsack.

Again it was Pau who buried the remains.

Night fell, and Brownbeard lit a pine knot lamp using the embers stored in the cave. He then thrust three twigs toward Rifleman.

"What's this?"

"We're drawing lots."

"Lots? What for?"

Brownbeard shot a knowing glance in the direction of the young woman.

"What do I need these for?" he snorted. He ripped the twigs from Brownbeard's hand, then took the woman by the wrist and led her outside.

During this time, the men had launched out twice in search of plunder, but had drawn a blank. Pau accompanied Knapsack the first time, Brownbeard the second. Each time, the men forged through the woods for five or ten miles, but saw nothing resembling a dwelling and returned emptyhanded. Pau, however, wouldn't lead the others to Flatland Village, where he went in the spring to barter for salt. On one of the forays his partner had turned in that direction, but Pau had redirected him by saying there were only cliffs that way.

Pau's thoughts turned to his mother. Despite his delight and a sense of wonder at having encountered so many people here in the mountains, their frightening behavior had made a deep impression on him.

Because he had left carrying a basket on his backrack, his mother might have guessed he had gone to Acorn Valley. Perhaps she had given up waiting and had gone there to look for him.

Pau climbed a tree near camp and called out toward home at the top of his lungs. "Hey!" The shout echoed once, and then again and again, finally trailing off in the distance. Again he shouted. But this time another voice interrupted before the shout trailed off.

"Who are you calling, you loony idiot? Get down from there!"

Rifleman was standing directly below him. He had drawn his revolver. It was so frightening, that object he held. Pau climbed down. He would have to wait to return home.

Some time later, as Rifleman was looking over the map, Knapsack rushed over, face etched with fear. He had seen someone.

"Was he alone?" asked Rifleman.

"Looked that way."

"Was he in uniform?"

"I think so."

"See a gun?"

"No."

Rifleman folded the map and returned it to his pocket, hands trembling.

The best they could do, they decided, was to keep the fellow in sight.

A short time later the stranger approached, and they saw he belonged to their unit.

Like them a remnant of a defeated company, he had come this way to scout the area and had heard someone shouting. His company was in the mountain country a few miles to the east, he reported. There were eight of them altogether.

Rifleman wasn't at all pleased to hear this. What if they asked him about the platoon leader? His heart sank. And what if one of the others ratted on him? He'd have to prevent his men from talking with the visitor.

"Happen to have any extra ammo?" he ventured when he was alone with the man. When he had strapped on the platoon leader's revolver, its cartridges were already spent. And when Knapsack had reported sighting the soldier, it had occurred to him that he had nothing to defend himself with in case the man was an enemy. It was this realization that had set his hands trembling.

"Are you serious? All we've got is our captain's revolver and a couple of rifles, and we don't even have enough for them. We're in trouble. I was hoping you had some."

To Rifleman's relief, the other didn't ask about the platoon leader. The man left after instructing Rifleman to keep his present position and await further orders.

But when the man was some distance away, Brownbeard ran after him.

A shiver ran down Rifleman's spine: He's going to rat on me! He decided then and there that if Brownbeard ever informed, he'd kill him—with his bare hands if he had to.

Brownbeard was grinning when he returned.

"Out of ammo, huh?"

"Yeah. I thought we had some, but it turns out the last cartridge went for that deer's head."

He handed Brownbeard the revolver.

"You might as well have it—better than nothing."

Then he snapped off three birch twigs and held them up with a flourish.

"Starting tonight we draw lots."

The same man returned the following day with orders to fetch the woman. After instructing Rifleman to maintain his position until further contact, he disappeared with the woman.

They had just boiled some of their meager stock of corn for breakfast. Suddenly there was an explosion and the roar of a jet zooming overhead. The three soldiers scurried into the cave.

Pau hid under a tree. He couldn't figure it out: That contraption that flew by—was it so scary even to these men?

That day, Pau left with Knapsack to look for habitations. They searched a good five miles to the northwest, but found nothing you could call a house. As usual, only the mountains were visible. Their lower halves were ringed with the stands of dark green fir and various pines, and higher up were those white birches along with thorny ash, basswood, and elm. The colorful maples, dotting the groves of broadleaf trees, had passed their peak and turned dark red. This wash of green, white, and red gradually faded in the distance, eventually dissolving into an indistinct gray.

They arrived at a ravine bordered by cliffs. For a short time now, a solitary bird had been circling in the blue sky. Though Knapsack knew full well the bird was a kite, a peculiar feeling came over him whenever its shadow grazed his head. On the battlefield, he had heard the deafening explosion of shells and seen jets fly directly overhead, strafing friend and foe alike. But there were moments when he had forgotten his terror, when he had acted involuntarily, empowered by a will he had never known before. Now, he was all alone; there was no one to depend on. How was it he had roamed the sickening fields of battle only to be driven to a place like this? Here he had no place to turn. There were only his fellow stragglers back at camp, and this idiot in front of him. And the surrounding mountains offered no relief; they merely existed, intimidating and aloof.

They walked seven or eight miles, again with no results, and it seemed they would have to give up and return home. But then off in the distance, in a secluded area at the foot of a mountain, there appeared dwellings—two of them.

It was past the usual dinnertime when they returned to the cave. After a quick meal they all set out.

The moon, near the end of its cycle, hadn't yet risen. There was only a sprinkling of starlight visible through the dark woods. The stars seemed closer here, as if they were just above the trees.

How long had they walked? Pau realized he could no longer see the stars scattered above the groves; something was draping them. Then he heard a breeze. But it was unlike the breeze that passed through the crowns of the trees. This one swept to the ground, and it carried rain. Drops of water fell from the leaves, chilling Pau's neck.

The men hunkered down together where the trees offered shelter. The sodden tree trunks took on a dull sheen in the darkness.

As Pau was resigning himself to spending the night there the rain stopped and he could once again make out the stars through the dark groves. The men set out. But the farther they walked, the more Pau worried that they were off track, for the cliffs he remembered from daytime were not to be seen.

Rifleman took to cursing him for losing the trail. Suddenly Pau came to a stop. Everyone strained to listen. Sure enough, you could hear a faint sound when the breeze died down. A dog was barking.

They moved forward, and as the barking grew louder Pau saw Rifleman take his rifle from his shoulder and tuck the stock under his arm;

Brownbeard took the smaller gun from its holster. And Pau witnessed almost the same scene that had unfolded elsewhere several nights earlier.

Now, though, there was no explosion from the weapon Rifleman held in his armpit or from Brownbeard's revolver. And before, a young man had been made to carry their plunder back to camp, but this time they took a young woman. In the darkness, the woman's screams pierced Pau's ears. Rifleman dragged her along.

Suddenly Rifleman shouted, and Pau heard a slap.

"Fucking bitch bit me!"

Rifleman, bitten on the hand, had lashed the woman across the cheek.

"Try that again, you cunt, and I'll shoot you."

From then on, there was only the sound of the woman's wailing.

Amidst all this, Pau realized that the biggest difference from before was the way he himself felt. That other time, he had trembled all over, felt dizzy, hadn't understood what was happening. But this time he didn't have to be punched in the face to load the basket of corn and potatoes onto his backrack. And while packing his load back to camp, he was composed enough to think about various things.

First of all, the rifle hadn't exploded with that frightening, deafening roar. That meant Rifleman must have used up his last bullet when he killed Snaggle Tooth. And the small gun hanging at Brownbeard's side hadn't made a sound, either. Didn't that mean it was out of bullets too? Rifleman's promise to shoot the young woman must have been an empty threat. If so, then there was nothing to be afraid of. He could return home.

Pau's thoughts turned to the young woman being pulled along. How old could she be, this girl who still hadn't stopped sobbing? He could tell at a glance from her height that she was probably physically mature.

He recalled what his mother had said one evening after his father had died, a time when Pau had gained a measure of perception. His father had been the son of an untouchable, she had told him. And no matter how much his father had liked her, they couldn't marry. His only choice had been to steal her away to these mountains, carrying her on his back.

The young woman finally stopped sobbing about the time the waning moon rose, and Pau could distinguish the black braids that fell to her waist. Steam rose from Pau's body where the cold rain had fallen.

After a meal of chopped potatoes and mashed corn, they sprawled out and fell asleep. Pau, off to the side, was soon snoring. The sun had already burst forth.

But one of the men only pretended to be sleeping—the man with the rifle. Eyes closed, he was absorbed in thought. The captain didn't yet know he had killed the platoon leader, but the story would come out sooner or later. And now that he thought about it, wasn't there a chance that the woman had told him? Under these circumstances, it was foolish to stay here. Earlier, he had felt he was at the end of his tether, and so it didn't matter what he did; when the end came, he would accept it. But now he thought differently. He would do anything to survive. But first he had to get out of these mountains.

Knowing the other men were sound asleep, he quietly rose and tiptoed toward the young woman, who was sitting by herself, hands covering her face.

The woman looked up with puffy eyes. Her lips began to quiver.

"Now there's nothing to be afraid of. I'll do right by you. You don't want to die here, do you?" And then, in a low, reassuring tone: "If you want to get out of here alive—hmm?—just do what I say—all right?"

The young woman's lips lost their color and continued to quiver.

"All right now, go over there and hide under that rock—go on. And then just do what I say. I'll take care of you."

He tilted her chin up and indicated a large rock among the trees, then took her arm, pulled her to her feet, and prodded her in that direction.

Seeing her set off reluctantly for the rock, he went to where Pau was lying and gently shook him awake. He had something to talk about, he whispered in Pau's ear; would he join him a ways off from camp with his backrack?

Pau was puzzled, but did as he was asked.

Rifleman stopped a short distance away, at an angle from the large rock.

"You've been a big help to us. I'll bet you'd like to go home."

Pau nodded.

"Well, I'm going to let you go home. And for all of your efforts, I'm going to give you my uniform. Why don't you get out of those rags and change into it? Then you can go."

His plan was to change into Pau's clothes, put on the backrack, and escape with the young woman. Pau, of course, was ignorant of this scheme.

"Come on, I'm serious. Your one and only chance to wear the uniform. It's my way of saying thanks. Don't think twice—just put it on, and off you go. And here's something else for you."

He set the rifle on the ground in front of Pau.

Pau broke into a wide grin, picturing himself changing into the uniform and putting the firearm to his shoulder. Then, embarrassed at this image of himself, he looked away.

Thinking Pau was refusing, the other became frantic. Don't tell me this asshole knows what I'm up to! He had to do something before his comrades awakened. Snatching the backrack's supporting stick from the unwary Pau, he hammered him across the shoulders.

Pau skidded backward, then toppled over.

Rifleman followed up with a glancing blow to Pau's head. But in his haste he had swung too early, and his momentum carried him off balance.

Pau removed the backrack and got to his feet. Gripping the frame, he lashed out wildly, back and forth. Wood cracked loudly on wood, and the supporting stick flew from Rifleman's hands.

The next instant, Rifleman found himself flat on the ground.

"Help! He's going to kill me!"

Rifleman's shouts woke Brownbeard and Knapsack, and they ran over. But Pau's murderous rage kept them at a distance.

Ignoring the blood streaming into his eyes, Pau looked down at the corpse of his opponent. Then he dragged the body by the legs out of sight around the hillside and sent it careening into a gorge.

"God, you're strong as an ox," Brownbeard flattered him when he returned.

Knapsack felt all his energy drain. An uncontrollable urge to urinate seized him, and he relieved himself on the spot.

That night Brownbeard lit a pine knot lamp from the embers of their fire, then held out two twigs to Knapsack, to see which of them would have the young woman.

Pau bolted to a sitting position. His eyes, bloodshot since daytime, blazed in the light of the flame.

"Gee, almost forgot about you."

Brownbeard snapped off another twig and held out all three to Pau. Pau slapped Brownbeard's arm aside, went to the corner occupied by the young woman, and led her outside by the wrist.

Brownbeard picked up the kitchen knife.

"Don't," said Knapsack. "Out in the open, you're no match for him. I thought he was just some stupid son of a bitch, but uh-uh. Instead, finish him off when he comes back."

Pau tugged the young woman along. He couldn't understand what was making him do this.

Suddenly he stopped. Sensing something, the woman tried to twist her hand free. Pau punched her in the shoulder, knocking her in a heap to the ground. Then he hefted her to his back.

Translated by Bruce and Ju-Chan Fulton

Kapitan Ri

Chŏn Kwangyong

A writer of the immediate post–Korean War period, Chŏn Kwangyong (1919–1988) made his debut in the newspaper *Chosŏn ilbo* in 1955 and flourished in the late 1950s and throughout the 1960s. He was also a noted scholar of early modern Korean literature and a professor at Korea's top-ranked Seoul National University. This strong and commanding figure is revered by generations of students, who recall his booming Hamgyŏng accent echoing down the halls of his school office building.

In 1962, Chŏn's story "Kapitan Ri" (Kkŏppittan Ri) brought him the coveted Tongin Literary Prize, established by the intellectual magazine *Sasanggye* to honor contemporary writers while commemorating a pioneer of modern fiction, Kim Tongin (1900–1951). The prize citation referred to "Kapitan Ri" as a work that "sets historical consciousness into bold relief as it also shows the possibilities of satirical characterization."

Chŏn Kwangyong was born in Pukch'ŏng, South Hamgyŏng Province, on March 1, 1919, a date that still stirs an emotional reaction in Koreans when they recall the millions who arose that day in unarmed rebellion against Japanese colonialism. By the time of Liberation from Japan, Chŏn was already twenty-six and had been educated in the Japanese-operated educational system. Then in 1947 he entered the Department of Korean Language and Literature at Seoul National University. A member of the first generation of Koreans to receive a college education in their own language, he graduated in 1951.

Having lived through these changing times and being embued with a strong sense of national pride, Chŏn Kwangyong was particularly well prepared to create the character Yi Inguk, M.D., who energetically collaborates with whatever power there is—Japanese, Russian, American. The biting satire of "Kapitan Ri" captures the feelings of those who, after Liberation from Japan, were sworn to "liquidate" the "colonial vestiges" represented by people such as Yi Inguk, M.D.

"Kapitan Ri" was first published in *Sasanggye* magazine in 1962.

Yi Inguk, M.D., emerged from the operating room and buried himself deep in the reception room sofa.

Dr. Yi lifted away his platinum rimless glasses and mopped his forehead. As the sweat on his back dried, fatigue began to sink into his body. Two hours and twenty minutes in surgery, removing an abdominal abscess. The patient had not yet recovered consciousness.

He would feel a presentiment the moment an operation was over, a revelation of the chances of success. But today, for some reason, he came out of it feeling leery.

He recalled the time he had set a record for the shortest abdominal operation since Japanese colonial days, when antibiotics weren't so advanced.

Appendicitis or circumcision—such surgery is a simple matter. It can be turned over to the young doctors and forgotten. But one cannot be so casual about major surgery. The patients feel that way, too. Most allow themselves to be hospitalized on the condition that the director himself operate. For Yi Inguk, M.D., this was a matter of pride, and he felt a real sense of pleasure in wielding the knife.

His clinic was in a neighborhood so busy and crowded that it seemed nearly every second building was another clinic or hospital. But this nameless modern facility actually waited in empty leisure for its clients, like a country shop between market days.

When he received his clientele—the overflow emergency cases passed on to him by a busy, first-rate university hospital—Yi Inguk, M.D., would take his time, exercising as much concern as each patient's appearance recommended. He was perhaps like an innkeeper who takes one look at a new arrival's clothing and instantly decides which room to give him or unhesitatingly turns him away without stirring from his seat.

The clinic of Yi Inguk, M.D., had two characteristics. The interior

was kept spotless, and the fees were at least twice as high as at any
other place. His examination of a new patient began with an inquiry
into his ability to pay, followed by questions about his disease. If the
patient didn't seem such a good prospect, the doctor would offer some
excuse. Not personally, of course—his nurse would show the person
out.

In all but the most serious cases, younger doctors conducted the
preliminary examination. The Director then had only to make a final
diagnosis—based on a judgment of the patient's physical condition and
economic status, which had been duly recorded on the examination card.

Except for very close friends and the socially prominent, there was
no such thing as credit here. Even admitting the little credit given, his
twofold diagnosis was the secret of his practice, the guiding principle
of thirty-some years of medical life that had seen neither penny lost
nor penny uncollected. Hence, his clientele had been mainly Japanese
during the occupation and now had to be among the ruling political
circles or the great business magnates to qualify at his door.

His daily routine began with an appearance in the examination
room, where his first act was to draw his fingertips along the window
frames or table tops and peer, with sunken eyes through rimless
glasses, at what he had found. If this inspection revealed any dust he
erupted in a thunderous rage, and the nurses faced another day of bad
temper from the Director. His regular clientele, however, were full of
admiration and respect for such spotless integrity.

This was Yi Inguk, M.D., who had fled to southern Korea during
the January Retreat in 1951, carrying only his black bag with a stethoscope in it. Then, as soon as Seoul was recovered, he had quickly rented a
room that he outfitted as a clinic. But now he had a two-story Western-
style building in downtown Seoul where land was extremely expensive. In addition to his own specialty, surgery, this private hospital also
offered departments of internal medicine, pediatrics, obstetrics, and so
on. While the profit and loss of each department was its own concern,
the directorship of the general hospital resided in his dignified person.

Yi Inguk, M.D., drew an eighteen-carat-gold pocket watch from his
vest and checked the time.

Two-forty.

Only twenty minutes until his appointment with Mr. Brown at the
American embassy. His watch had seen a lot of history and could tell

many tales. Whenever Yi Inguk, M.D., consulted it, he recalled one or another of the near-miraculous turns his life had taken. He had taken the watch when he crossed the thirty-eighth parallel as a refugee with only his black bag in hand. And now that he had replaced the old bag with a new one given to him by an American army doctor, the watch was the only remaining object that had escaped with him. It was, in a sense, his life's companion.

When he went to bed at night, he never placed it by his bedside or even left it in his vest pocket. He would always be sure to take it out and tuck it away inside the steel safe where he kept his registration papers, bank book, and other valuables. Indeed, he had good reason to do so. The watch was a prize of honor he had received on graduation from the Imperial University. His name was engraved on the back.

No matter what changes had swirled about him these past thirty-odd years, his watch had always shown him a constant face. It wasn't only his surroundings—hadn't he himself changed, too? The proud and rosy-cheeked youth in his twenties had somehow disappeared, leaving this graying man with deepening wrinkles. The Japanese occupation, imprisonment under the Russians, the Korean War, the thirty-eighth parallel, the American army—how many crucial moments had he faced?

Waltham. Seventeen jewels.

It was nothing short of marvelous that this watch could have managed to keep time through so many tortuous years. He would often look at the time only to find his ear drawn to the ticking of his watch, as if by habit. He would then begin to see, with narrowing eyes, a miniature of his bygone life. He couldn't escape the renewed vision he would find there of himself on the day he first put on the coat and tie of a gentleman in place of the familiar high-collared uniform and angular cap he had worn as a student.

Dr. Yi Inguk's thoughts turned to a letter he had tucked away in a drawer just before the operation.

His daughter, Nami, was in America. Her name had once been typically Japanese—Namiko. But he had dropped the "ko" for good when he filed his residence papers after Liberation, since such names had begun to sound awkward then.

Dear Nami, little Namiko! Thoughts of his daughter called back visions of the warm family circle of yesterday.

Nami, the charmer, the pet of the family, was now fully grown. Though it was natural for her to have left his side now and to live within a new affection, Yi Inguk, M.D., could not hold back the flood of loneliness that overcame him from time to time.

His wife had died in the wartime internment camp on Kŏje Island, and he still had no idea whether his son was living or dead.

Hyesuk, whom he had met again in Seoul, was his second wife. He strained to deny the difference the twenty years between them made, though it was a generation. But when he compared Hyesuk's resilient good health and firm, glowing skin with his own coarse and wrinkled flesh, there were times he felt the physical withering of age upon him.

Their year-old baby, with its remote, unclear future, was the only blood kin that Yi Inguk, M.D., had left by his side.

Yi Inguk, M.D., tore open the air mail envelope, his heart full of expectation and curiosity. This was the reply to his advice to think things over and not to leap to some sudden, irreversible decision.

Is that the way it's going to be, after all?

He slid the letter onto the table. The thought struck him that maybe this whole business had begun even before his daughter had left the country. It couldn't have been an accident. She chose to major in English at the school where the man had been a foreign visiting instructor. He must have found her the scholarship and then offered to be her sponsor. Of course. But hadn't he, her own father, encouraged this overseas study as being in keeping with the times?

And when the visiting instructor, a student of the East, had confessed he might like to marry a Korean girl, hadn't he actually given his unintended approval by suggesting it would be a boon to the instructor's studies? Shouldn't he have caught the hint? Yi Inguk, M.D., bit down firmly on the ivory mouthpiece of his ozone pipe and closed his eyes. He felt like a squanderer, angry and desolate.

A big-nose for a son-in-law!

His whole body shuddered with aversion at the thought, as if his blood had suddenly run backward.

That little vixen.

He coughed heavily and spat.

His thoughts leaped back to all the fuss they had made over Japanese-Korean marriages during the occupation. Then such things weren't the makings of slander and humiliation. Rather, they were thought quite natural by many, if not possibly even a mark of distinction. But, then, in his daughter's case . . .

He read his daughter's letter over again.

"Can love know any national boundaries?"

A cheap, time-worn platitude. Daddy had mastered all those fashions, too, when he was a student. Impertinence. Taking this fresh, preaching tone with her own father. Couldn't she be more open about it? So she, an only daughter, expects to experiment in international marriage?

"Anyway, since you said you could easily come overseas sometime, Father, I certainly want to hear your views before making any final decisions. However . . ."

So if Daddy doesn't go, she'll do as she pleases!

Yi Inguk, M.D., shook his head as he called to mind the laws of heredity for a first hybrid generation. A white grandson—the very thought disgusted him.

He picked up the discarded letter once again.

A large stone building on a landscaped campus and, in the background of the picture, boys and girls strolling in pairs; in the midst of this, his daughter and that foreign instructor standing side by side, smiling, with their arms around each other's shoulders.

Hmm. They certainly seem to be enjoying themselves.

He moaned and got up from the sofa. He had to hurry to avoid being late to Mr. Brown's. His anxieties were heightened as he thought how important the State Department invitation had become for him now.

He went back into the living quarters where his wife, Hyesuk, was waiting.

"Dear, it seems Nami has her heart set on getting married."

"Oh, really?"

Yi Inguk, M.D., quickly sensed the lack of any real concern in her voice. He was as careful as possible of what he said in front of Hyesuk about the children of his first wife. He really had to reproach himself for the atmosphere at home, which had been part of the reason for Nami's decision to study in the United States. Nami, of course, had never once called Hyesuk *Mother.* And Hyesuk, for her part, had quite fairly avoided asserting herself as a mother in front of Nami. Inexpressibly subtle and delicate feelings lay hidden in the relationship between Nami and today's mother, who was yesterday's nurse.

"I'm ready to help you in any way I can."

It was with these words that Hyesuk had opened up her heart to Yi

Inguk, M.D., when they had met again in Seoul. At first, Hyesuk did not know of his first wife's death; nor did Yi Inguk, M.D., pry into Hyesuk's marital status. Hyesuk soon quit her job at the university hospital and came over to the clinic.

For Nami, it was a revival of old affections, and she clung to Hyesuk as to an older sister. When Yi Inguk, M.D., found himself on the brink of a new marriage, thoughts of his daughter's reaction made him seek out her opinion first.

She had sympathy for the loneliness he felt. And she was quick to sincerely praise his choice of a wife, since she knew that he needed more attention than she alone could give and also that Hyesuk had actually been doing much to raise his spirits. But as time passed, Hyesuk and Nami became more distant, and Hyesuk began to feel that Nami stood in the way of a normal family life for herself and her husband.

Hyesuk had found it impossible at first to feel at ease with Yi Inguk, M.D., in her new role as his wife. But with Nami's departure, the birth of the child, and other things, she reached the point where she could just manage to be a wife to him. Yi Inguk, M.D., for his part, even learned to become a familiar, joking husband.

"She really seems to be getting serious about that foreign instructor."

Yi Inguk, M.D., avoided direct contact with his wife's eyes and repeated his words as if grumbling to himself.

"That can happen. I suppose she should do as she likes."

To Yi Inguk, M.D., her voice sounded as though she were talking about a stranger.

"Well, she's doing that all right, but . . . "

He clicked his tongue and couldn't continue.

He was aroused by the sight of his wife's young body as she gave her breast to the crying baby, who had just woken up. But at the same time he felt overwhelmed by an obsessive sense of guilt toward his daughter, Nami.

He still had some twenty years to wait before this child would be old enough to talk with as he could talk with Nami or his son, Wŏnshik. Come that day, he'd be an old man in his seventies. Modern medicine had extended man's life span and, except for things like cancer, even eliminated sudden death; still, a doctor couldn't guarantee his own life.

Didn't I let my wife die in front of my eyes as easily as I would let a bird take flight?

At any rate, he had to live until that child made it through college. Indeed, if he lasted long enough he'd have to see the boy through to study in the United States.

When he thought of things in that light, getting started early as a member of an American family did not seem to be such a bad idea. No question that they live better than Koreans do. It's just that it's difficult to keep from losing face with others.

So he mulled his problems over—whether he was consoling himself or simply resigned, he didn't really know.

"Dear, would you wrap that up for me?"

Dr. Yi Inguk's voice had taken a gentle turn.

"Wrap what up?"

His wife turned her head toward him, letting the child nurse undisturbed at her breast.

"That vase, there."

He pointed to an antique standing on his wife's dressing table.

"Where are you taking it?"

"To that Mr. Brown at the American embassy. I'm so indebted to him now."

Yi Inguk, M.D., carrying the package neatly wrapped by his wife, stepped out into the front hall. The evening paper had already been delivered.

No matter how you look at it, his survival had to be a miracle. The confused recollection could still whip up alternating feelings of fear and gratitude—so vivid that the event always seemed like yesterday to him.

Late August 1945. Strong emotions were sweeping over the world and churning up whirlpools as they spread. The dog days were nearly over, but the weather was as hot and sultry as ever. For some days, Yi Inguk, M.D., driven by feelings of anxiety and impatience, had found normal sleep impossible. He could only quiver with tension as he waited for the coming of whatever was approaching.

No sign was left of the many patients who used to come and go, and the once restless telephone now waited silently. All the rooms were empty and echoing, now that the last patient—a Japanese section chief from the provincial administration who had been ill with peritonitis—had been taken away.

The assistants and pharmacists had all given in to anxiety and left, saying they would return after visiting their hometowns. Only the Seoul-born nurse Hyesuk remained to watch over the empty clinic.

In the ten-mat tatami room upstairs, Yi Inguk, M.D., clad in Japanese breechcloth and kimono, could toss and turn no more. He finally threw aside his fan and got up.

He went into the bathroom. He scooped up cold water by the basinful and poured it over his head, letting it flow down the length of his body. A chill traveled down his backbone, and he felt lighter. But while he could wipe his body with the washcloth, he could not wash away the uncertain and oppressive disquiet in his heart.

He glanced out the window at the streets below. Swarms of people were still surging back and forth, engulfed in their own noise. From across the street, a poster pasted on the tightly closed iron doors of a bank appeared only as a square of white to him. But what they'd written there . . .

"Destroy Pro-Japanese and Betrayers of the People!"

All he could see clearly from where he stood were the red circles that marked either end of the slogan. He felt once more the shiver that had gone through him the previous night when he saw it for the first time. Yi Inguk, M.D., instantly turned his head toward the room again.

Why, they certainly wouldn't touch me.

He repeated this to himself as he picked up the fan again. But he had been made extremely uneasy by something that had happened while he was down there, looking at the poster. As he withdrew his intent gaze from the slogan, his eyes met those of that troublemaker Ch'unsŏk, who looked him up and down, sneering with that distorted look that could have meant contempt or delight, for all he knew. The unnerving image of that encounter had taken to attacking his memory without warning, like a spider web that entangles you in the dark of night.

As much as he tried to wipe that Ch'unsŏk out of his thoughts, the fellow would always be there, clinging like a leech.

It had happened six months before.

A critically ill patient was carried in from a prison, freed temporarily for treatment, they explained. The helpless youth was but a gaunt, emaciated frame punctuated by a pair of vacant eyes. He could hardly shift his body for the examination without help from the nurse.

As he moved the ivory tip of his stethoscope from the patient's chest to his back and tried to make out the sound of breathing through the rubber tubes, Dr. Yi Inguk's mind wandered to thoughts of the Last Judgment.

Should he be taken in? Should he be turned away?

A glance at the patient's appearance and at the clothing of the man who had carried him in easily revealed his economic status.

But this time something else disturbed him. Not only did it seem improper for him, as a government-appointed City Assemblyman, to admit this political criminal to a clinic patronized by leading Japanese officials; but he also feared that the monument of his good works, for which he was officially recognized as a model citizen of the Empire, could come crashing down overnight because of something like this.

As was his style, he weighed the facts and, in an instant, rendered an immediate and incisive decision. He gave only emergency treatment and sent the supplicant on his way with the very reasonable and proper excuse that there was no room for him at the clinic. He learned later from the nurse that the patient's house was in an alley across the street from the clinic. But since such things were common for him, he dismissed it as a trifle.

Then, just a few days earlier, caught up in the enthusiasm of the moment, he and Hyesuk had stepped out front of the clinic to watch the parade following a mass rally to celebrate Liberation. His eyes happened to meet those of a young marcher wearing the armband of the Self-defense Corps. He felt as if the young man were shooting sparks with those relentless eyes.

The bewildered Yi Inguk, M.D., had no idea of the reason for this until Hyesuk told him that the marcher was Ch'unsŏk, the political offender who had once been turned away from the clinic. Hearing this, he looked furtively from face to face around him and slipped back into the clinic. After that, he had avoided going out into the streets as much as possible, only to run into Ch'unsŏk again in front of the poster the previous night.

Suddenly a clamor arose outside. Yi Inguk, M.D., who had been lost in aimless reveries as he lay with his hands clasped behind his head, sat up and turned an ear toward the street. The commotion grew even louder. Unable to suppress his anxiety any longer, he rose and, squatting by the window, looked down into the street. Outside, the seething crowds were waving Korean and Russian flags as they raised great shouts of joy.

What could this be?

He cocked his head in wonder as he sank down to a sitting position. Hearing the sound of footsteps, he rose as someone came hurrying up the stairs. It was Hyesuk.

"I think maybe the Russian army's coming into town! Everybody's out there carrying on.

Yi Inguk, M.D., gave no response to Hyesuk's breathless report. He only blinked and sat back down. For some time now the radio had been predicting that the Russians would enter the city today. So it seems they're really here. For some time after Hyesuk had gone back down, Yi Inguk, M.D., sat there looking numbly out the window.

Stirred into action by a passing thought, he suddenly got up. He then slid open the door of a small closet. He reached deep into its recesses and drew out a framed Japanese document.

National Language Family.

He had completely forgotten about this award since taking it down and putting it away in the closet on the day of Liberation from Japan.

He opened the frame from the back and, removing the heavy vellum sheet, which looked like a restaurant license, carefully tore the document into such fine shreds that not one letter was left legible. This one sheet of paper could demonstrate how honorable his relationship with the Japanese was. An odd melancholy flashed through his mind.

Few of his patients had ever come from the groups that couldn't speak Japanese. Not only had he always spoken the national language in the clinic and throughout his social life, but he had also insisted on using Japanese exclusively at home, too. So unfamiliar had he become with Korean that he had found it awkward to express himself in it after Liberation.

His wife had contributed a great deal toward winning this award by her efforts to set an example for others. Even the children had done their part in maintaining the spirit. On the day of the award, the entire household celebrated the occasion as joyfully as it might a birth or another happy family event.

"You use the national language so faithfully that you must surely speak it in your sleep! How else could this honor have come to you?"

The sound of those complimentary remarks, made that day by the smiling officer from the local branch of the Citizens League for Total Effort, came floating back to him. Hadn't he at that moment even reflected on how fortunate it had been for him to have given his children a Japanese education from elementary school on?

He heaved a long sigh. He had just recalled with gratitude the helpful branch manager of the bank who had let him withdraw the entire balance in his savings account. What if he didn't have that with him now? He felt a chill creep down his spine. Whatever became of the government, as long as he had the cash in hand half the people in the city could starve to death before his family was touched. He mumbled to himself as he thought of the cashbox in the bedroom closet. Yi Inguk, M.D., mulled over his vague concern that, somehow, he had to survive, come what may.

The day around him grew darker.

As a distant rumble approached, the earth itself seemed to shudder on its axis. The crowds outside exploded into round after round of cheers. His wife came back in from the street.

"Dear, there's a tank unit in town, and the streets are just packed with people! Whatever are you doing here all alone in the house?"

"What am I doing?"

"Come out and see, dear! The *Russkis* are here!"

In the darkness he couldn't tell why his wife's voice seemed to tremble, whether from emotion or bewilderment. *Can women really be so silly and yet so fearless at the same time?* Yi Inguk, M.D., peered in his wife's direction across the dim room and clucked.

"Why, you haven't even turned the light on yet!"

His wife snapped the switch on the lamp. The brightness of the 100-watt bulb was too much for Yi Inguk, M.D.

"What are you turning the light on for?"

"All right, leave it off and sit in the dark, then. Come on now, come along outside!"

Yi Inguk, M.D., had no choice but to follow his insistent wife, feigning indifference as he went.

Blazing headlights dazzled the eyes of the onlookers as the endless column of tanks rumbled by. Yi Inguk, M.D., leaned against a wayside tree, avoiding the glare. The tanks rolled on slowly like a rising tide between two heaving banks of cheering, clapping, shouting people. The Russian soldiers, standing waist deep in the hatchways of their tanks, waved and called *"Urra"* from time to time.

Yi Inguk, M.D., stood staring blankly and awkwardly, unable to clap or cheer as he nursed the illusion that these foreign soldiers had nothing to do with him or his life. He glanced at the crowd around him, wondering if perhaps his behavior had attracted attention. But no one seemed to be taking any interest in him; all eyes were on the passing tanks as the onlookers cheered themselves hoarse.

What's to come of this?

He repeated this question, to which there was neither end nor answer, as he went slowly back into the house.

On the radio, the folksongs and marches were over now and the commander of the Army of Occupation was making a proclamation. Yi Inguk, M.D., sat down in front of the radio and brought his ear up close to the speaker.

The army guaranteed the lives and property of the populace, announced a strict prohibition on the possession of swords and firearms (which had to be turned in), and requested all citizens to remain calm and conduct business as usual.

He suddenly thought of the hunting rifle he kept in the bedroom closet. Would he have to turn it in? It was the newest model, a double-barreled British shotgun that bore the sweat of his own hands. Did he really have to give up this beloved treasure, which he had never once even loaned out?

Yi Inguk, M.D., turned the radio dial. What could they be doing in Seoul now? Same story there, too. If not folksongs, then marches, followed by speeches by someone or other from the Preparatory Committee for National Foundation.

How on earth was this all going to end? There seemed to be no relief from the anxiety this question stirred up in him. He had been calm and composed for two or three days after Liberation, but then, after the announcement of the arrival of the Russians, even those friends who used to pop in and out all the time stopped appearing. And he was growing less and less interested in the idea of running around to ask after them.

It wasn't until late at night that his middle school son and primary school daughter had come home, bursting with talk of the *Russkis* and their tanks, as if they had seen something quite colossal. Their father didn't seem at all interested in listening, but their stories flourished and multiplied as they shared them with their mother and Hyesuk.

Yi Inguk, M.D., had gotten up and slipped out of the room. He went upstairs to the tatami-matted second floor, where he tossed and turned alone. How were things going to work out? The future seemed to spread out before him like a vast ocean that he could never cross. His thoughts were a tangle of string that wouldn't yield up a free end—he could only stare dumbly at the ceiling, nursing vague hopes as if blowing on a dying tinder. Guilt or regret for bygone acts was simply beside the point.

Inside the car, Yi Inguk, M.D., opened up the evening paper he had taken from the house. After glancing over the headlines, he folded the paper back to have a look at the miscellaneous items on page three.

North Korean Students in Russia Defect to West Germany.

Type as large as the pieces in a game of go topped a foreign dispatch that monopolized a full column at the left of the page. It was accompanied by a picture as big as the palm of your hand. He pushed his glasses back up on the bridge of his nose, from where they had slipped, and strained to read the text. His eyes dug through the fine print as a vision of his son rose to his mind's eye.

It seemed to him that his son's study in Moscow was the direct result of his own insistence. But was there any other way to overcome the limitations of his social origins and ideology? It was the year of his son's graduation from high school, the year he entered medical college. Yi Inguk, M.D., then as now, was quite confident that he knew how to run his son's life.

"You'd better work hard on your Russian, young man!"

"What for?"

The boy's only response to his father's sudden and suspicious comment was a question.

"Now, Wŏnshik! There's no magic formula, you know. During the Japanese occupation you had to speak Japanese to get anywhere in spite of yourself. Today, it's Russian. Since a fish can't live out of water, he's got to think about surviving in the water, doesn't he? You've got to apply yourself to Russian."

The son didn't seem to be particularly inspired by his father's words.

"Here I've managed to pick up a smattering of conversation, even at my age. There's no reason why a youngster like you can't do it."

"Please, Father, don't worry about it any more."

The answer sounded convincing enough to him. But Yi Inguk, M.D., continued to speak with an expression of grave concern on his face.

"Do you think there's anything special about them, except for their big noses? If you can just speak their language well enough to get your point across—they're the same as all the others."

Yi Inguk, M.D., had finally decided on a Russian education for his son when he happened to obtain a letter of recommendation from one of Major Stenkov's powerful connections in the Party leadership.

"Dear, let's live quietly, the way others do. In a world like this it's safest to keep a low profile. Here we have just barely managed to escape the threat of death, and now you want to push our boy into the middle of that 'Raise the Red Flag' business. If you succeed in this, what will become of him?"

"Listen, now. You can't catch a tiger without entering his lair. Whatever comes of the world, let's get what we can out of it."

"You mean to send the boy all the way to Russia?"

"Well, no. But lots of other middle school children are bearing down on their studies right now, even though they can't go abroad yet. Even college students don't find it all that easy."

"But still, how can you be so sure about the future?"

"Don't talk nonsense. Once that boy comes back with his Russian education, we won't hear a peep out of all those people who like to jabber so much about me. Let's live again as we did before, second to no one."

He browbeat his wife into agreement—in spite of her worries over such a venture—and then went on to complete the arrangements for his son's Russian education.

Hmph. The son of that pro-Jap Yi Inguk got in where even the survivors of revolutionaries find it difficult! Just wait and see!

Full of hope, he crowed to himself, beaming with high spirits.

The Korean War broke out the following year.

The flow of reassuring letters from his son was cut off by the upheaval, leaving a silence that continued until the January Retreat. Yi Inguk, M.D., feared that the cause of his wife's death lay ultimately in the melancholy with which she had watched her only son being sent into the jaws of death.

He carefully read every last word of the newspaper dispatch. But there wasn't any reference to his son's case.

What's that kid dragging his feet for? Can't he get in with these people? When the times are changing, you've got to keep your eyes open and take the initiative. That featherhead!

He folded up the paper and rolled it tightly in his hands.

They say that dragons appear even from creeks, but this boy can't keep up with his old dad.

He clucked with disapproval.

He probably doesn't even know that the family has already defected to the south and is himself just hesitating. But news should have gotten that far by now—the meaning of our silence should have gotten through. He's always been too stupid and honest for his own good.

As he got out of the car he spat thickly on the pavement.

Doktor Ri, I will take the responsibility, I give you my guarantee. Send your son to study in our fatherland, the Soviet Union!

Stenkov's voice seemed to reverberate on his eardrums.

It was the day after the Self-defense Corps became the Public Security Corps. Yi Inguk, M.D., was taken into custody.

He knelt on the concrete floor—lips blue, legs numb, sides aching. This seemed to him the most painful experience he had yet endured in his life. But even worse, he was swept with fear of an approaching, unpredictable future. As he listened to the footsteps coming and going and to the torrents of abuse being heaped on him, it was beyond his power to lift his head, which drooped like a broken flower.

As time passed, thoughts he had forcibly suppressed began to creep back into his mind, one by one.

If I had only known it would be like this, I could have hidden somewhere or fled to the south right off. Who can help me now? Anyone who could protect me must be in the same boat or soon will be. The Japanese! That fortress I staked so much on has crumbled and left me defenseless. All the same, something might turn up.

That vague sense of hope had not wholly deserted him even at this crucial moment.

I was lucky at least not to have been caught up in the first round of people's trials. No one seems to know anything about what happens to the ones who are taken away. They say they're judged and executed on the spot. Three more days and I might well have left the city. But in the end it's all a matter of fate. No, not all. There ought to be some way—

"Hey you, Jap-lover! Lackey . . . ass-kisser!"

Startled by the sudden shouts, Yi Inguk, M.D., raised his head defensively. A youth in a spotless Japanese army uniform with an armband on the sleeve stood glaring down at him. It was Ch'unsŏk. Yi

Inguk, M.D., hadn't the strength to stare back. He could guess it all now. "This is the end for me," he murmured to himself.

"You doormat, son of a bitch!"

A Japanese army boot caught him in the ribs.

"Let's watch you die, dog."

Kicks landed all over his body, front and back alike. As an abrupt shock hit his spinal cord, Yi Inguk, M.D., collapsed with a scream of pain. He slipped into a stupor. He was hauled into a sitting position by somebody pulling at his shoulders but was unable to control his own body and fell over sideways.

"You pig! A bastard like you who sells out his own people and fatherland deserves to die in front of a firing squad. A firing squad!"

The voice sounded faint, as if it were deep within a dream. But he could manage no response to the words.

More time seemed to have passed. He became aware of a rustling sound in the front of his clothing and could hear a light metallic tinkle as he began to regain consciousness.

A hand covered with yellow hair was pulling at his watch chain. He instinctively grabbed for his watch pocket and stole a look up at the owner of the hand. It was a blue-eyed, closely cropped Russian soldier with a toothy, sheepish grin. The watch chain was in his hand. The doctor closed his hands with all his strength over the watch pocket of his European-style suit.

"Urgh. Yaponski!"

Anger began to show in the soldier's eyes.

"No, anything but my watch!"

But neither could understand the other, and their confrontation was only one of eye and hand. With a hand as large as a water scoop, the soldier flung Dr. Yi Inguk's arms aside and jerked the watch free. The chain broke and hung dangling from Dr. Yi Inguk's fingers—with only a large open ring at its end. The soldier went out.

Death and a watch.

Yi Inguk, M.D., repeated his lament over and over. He could only lie there calling forth again and again the picture of that soldier—not satisfied with the two watches on each of his wrists, he had to snatch away a pocket watch as well!

As packed as the prison cell was, the system of seniority by which old-timers outranked more recent arrivals was quite clear. Within about a month's time, Yi Inguk, M.D., had been gradually promoted from his original place over the toilet deep within the cell to a position two-thirds of the way up the seating order.

He spent his days in silence. The day after an informer among them had been released, the noisiest complainers in the cell were called out and then later sent back half dead. But when only one or two days more had passed, the atmosphere of the cell had returned to normal—complaining about prison and talking about food were the favorite pastimes.

But Yi Inguk, M.D., said nothing. Though, of course, he disliked divulging the details of his crime, he was heeding the advice given him in the old days by an informative acquaintance in the Japanese secret police that silence is the first commandment. He just spent his time diligently studying a Russian conversation book left behind by a student who had been released one night.

He often felt a stinging sensation up and down his back, and his sides were painfully stiff, a condition, he feared, that could easily turn chronic. The temperature in the mornings and evenings would drop extremely low. No matter how he tried to resign himself to these conditions, he could not suppress a feeling of anxiety over his health.

Even while studying his Russian conversation book, he listened carefully to the talk that went on every day inside the cell, never missing a word. Judging from what the others were regarding as heavy penalties for their cases, his crimes loomed monstrous in comparison. Secretly selling rice from a grain cooperative, seven years; pressing innocent citizens into the National Service Corps, ten years. They claimed their trials would lead not to emotional snap decisions but to judgments based on law. Still, what was law in these days of chaos? A momentary lapse could lead to the firing squad.

Pro-Japanese clique, betrayer of the people, refused treatment to anti-Japanese fighter, spied for Japanese imperialists.

These crimes were enormous. If judged and sentenced on all the counts they had listed against him during the investigation, he could easily get life imprisonment or even the death penalty.

He looked around the cell and heaved a long sigh.

In through a ventilating window just under the eaves fell a patch of sunlight no larger than a handkerchief. It lengthened into something like a bamboo measuring stick but soon thinned into a thread and quickly disappeared. The distant autumn sky he could see through the latticework of the vent brought back a host of forgotten memories. They stabbed at his heart.

An eternal separation from the outside world. He closed his eyes. His wife, son, daughter, Hyesuk . . . And when he came to the person of Yi Inguk, M.D., acknowledged authority in the field of surgery, he choked as his throat seemed to burn. He coughed dryly and swallowed.

What do they expect of a person, anyway? There's no other way out for the people of a colony. They had no place for you, no matter what your talent. Who didn't cater to the Japs at one time or another? Only a fool rejects the proffered cake. None of us is clean.

Now that Yi Inguk, M.D., had rationalized his behavior and vindicated himself a bit, he felt a sense of relief.

What's more, there was something he had caught in the expression on the face of a Russian adviser at his final interrogation two days earlier, something that offered a straw of hope. Of course, he couldn't be sure he wasn't fooling himself out of desperation.

What did they call the man? Something like Major Stenkov. The one with the wen on his face who peered across for a moment with that expression on his face as he repeated *"Doktor, Doktor,"* when the matter of occupation had been clarified. It seemed to presage a miracle of some sort.

Yi Inguk, M.D., opened his eyes with a start at the sound of moaning next to him.

The thin glow of the hallway light fell through the iron bars and cast a striped pattern across the interior of the cell. He looked up toward the ventilating window. It was still black outside, well before daybreak.

The stench of fresh excrement stabbed at his nostrils. One leg of his trousers felt damp. He touched the wetness and lifted his fingers to his nose. Definitely excrement. He was nauseated. It had come from the young man next to him, who continued to groan in pain. He took a long, careful look at the youth. His buttocks were thoroughly soaked.

Looks like diarrhea.

He rattled the barred door and shouted for one of the guards.

"What do you want!"

He could hear the thick voice of a guard just aroused from his sleep.

"Something's wrong with this man. . . . Look—come take a look!"

As the guard looked in between the bars, his face was nothing but a roundish outline, topped by a cap and brim, against the light. Yi Inguk,

M.D., had pointed in the general direction of the youth's buttocks and was now studying his raised fingers.

"This is blood. Blood!"

He had only now discovered the redness on his fingers and was crying out in surprise.

"He's passing blood. This boy's got dysentery!"

His loud voice carried the confidence of his professional knowledge.

"What? Dysentery?"

The voice outside didn't sound fully convinced yet.

"He's passed blood in his stool. Bloody diarrhea. . . . Take a look, here."

His voice climbed in pitch.

"Hmm. Bloody, you say . . . "

At the shouting, other inmates opened their eyes one by one and added their startled cries to the din.

"Dysentery. It's contagious. Dysentery's a contagious disease."

"What, contagious?"

The guard finally opened the door and came into the cell.

The patient was removed a while later, and the inmates raised such a ruckus trying to scrub away the mess that they were unable to get back to sleep again.

Two days later, two or three cases showing the same symptoms were discovered in another cell. As the days passed, the number of victims seemed only to increase. Yi Inguk, M.D., felt himself in the grip of a new menace. In these conditions, he estimated, nine out of ten would die if they caught the disease.

After supper, Yi Inguk, M.D., was called to the adviser's office.

"Comrade, for the time being you will treat patients in the first-aid room."

What sort of miracle was this? Like lightning from a clear sky. He doubted the interpreter's words. His eyes lit up as he stared first at the Russian officer, then at the interpreter, and back again.

"Do you understand?"

"Yes, sir."

Yi Inguk, M.D., struggled to mask the elation he felt and managed to answer with composure.

Like I say. The roof may fall in but there's always a way out.

He clenched his teeth to suppress any expression on his face that might betray him.

When Yi Inguk, M.D., saw the corpses being wrapped up and shipped out like so much cordwood, he felt as if it were his own doing. "Medicine is my mission in life," he would murmur over and over with strong feeling. He threw himself into the work of serving the patients assigned him. And these duties also happened to attract the particular interest of the Russian adviser with the wen on his face.

Not until much later did he finally learn that serious censure awaited those responsible for the death in prison of an ideological criminal like himself.

Yi Inguk, M.D., recognized by the Russian medical officer for his technical skill, was now allowed to continue his duties at the hospital itself. But still he had no knowledge of the final disposition of the criminal charges against him.

He vowed, however, to make the best of this remarkable opportunity. Even death itself could not deter him now. Shouldn't there be some way to work free of the invisible shackles that held him here?

While he treated his patients each day, his only thought was of the duck-egg-sized wen on Stenkov's left cheek. With such a deformity— for one could call it that, he thought—how could Stenkov have risen to such high rank without some powerful influence in the Party or particular heroism on the battlefield? No doubt about it. It seemed he would gain salvation if only he sank his teeth into that wen and hung on for dear life.

Yi Inguk, M.D., had progressed in his Russian to the point where he could exchange halting pleasantries when Stenkov came by on his occasional rounds. Though reading matter was generally prohibited here, Russian-language texts and Party histories were allowed as exceptions. Yi Inguk, M.D., nearly memorized his Russian primer, as if it were the key to his very life.

Several opportunities presented themselves around Christmas time, when the officers were having their holiday celebrations. A slightly tipsy Stenkov came by on his rounds. This time, Yi Inguk, M.D., promised himself, he would not miss his chance.

Several days before, a Russian officer had been hospitalized with acute appendicitis complicated by peritonitis. Stenkov came up beside Yi Inguk, M.D., as he was removing the stitches from his patient. He turned to the major and proposed, half in words and half in gesture, that he operate to remove the wen.

Stenkov responded enthusiastically with a volley of *khorosho*'s.

After that, he had a number of occasions to present his opinions in detail on the proposed surgery when they talked it over through an interpreter. Yi Inguk, M.D., was persuasively reassuring as he spoke confidently of having removed a wen for the Japanese mayor.

Didn't I lop that wen off neat as you please, even after Keio University Hospital said it couldn't be done?

Silently asking and answering his own questions as he went along, he prepared, with a gambler's heart, to stake his life on this one opportunity.

The Russian medical officer was brought in for consultation, and they conducted a number of preparatory examinations.

The day of the operation arrived. Yi Inguk, M.D., had them bring in all his own surgical equipment, with which his touch was sure.

Though three medical officers assisted him, it was Yi Inguk, M.D., himself who held the scalpel. These young field hospital doctors were no more than novices to him. In the course of the operation, he used them as he had used the assistants in his own hospital. The thought came to him that once the incision had been made the operating room became his absolute kingdom.

From time to time, however, the fact of the pledge signed just before the operation invaded his thoughts. In the case of failure, he would accept the firing squad.

Stenkov lay on the operating table looking tense though composed. It was not yet three minutes since the hypodermic needle, full of anesthetic, had pierced his spine.

The nurse continued to wipe away with a wad of gauze the drops of sweat that formed on Dr. Yi Inguk's forehead. Only the metallic clink of instruments and the sound of breathing cut through the oppressive silence of the room, which was illuminated by the rays of an intense overhead reflector light.

The operation was over sooner than anticipated. When Yi Inguk, M.D., removed his operating gown, his entire body was drenched with sweat.

On the day his recovery was complete and he was released from the hospital, Stenkov took Dr. Yi Inguk's hand in his crushing grip and roared as he squeezed.

"Kapitan Ri, *spasibo!*"

Dr. Yi Inguk's mouth fell open and he could only laugh. It was as if he had been released from a spiritual prison.

"Ochen, ocheno. . . . Ochen khorosho!"

Stenkov gave a thumbs-up gesture to express his high regard for Yi Inguk, M.D., and clapped him on the shoulder as a sign of praise.

The following day Stenkov called Yi Inguk, M.D., to his room. He offered his hand to the doctor in the first formal gesture of real courtesy he had shown him.

Can one confront one's enemy and manage such a complete conversion as this? Maybe even these yellow-tops are human, too, at heart.

"Starting tomorrow you may commute to work from your home."

Yi Inguk, M.D., gulped and sighed like a chimney that had just come unblocked. This time it was he who grasped Stenkov's hand.

"Spasibo! Spasibo!"

"But don't you perhaps have anything to ask of me? A favor, maybe?"

Yi Inguk, M.D., suddenly thought of his watch. But then he hesitated for fear that dragging that story in so abruptly here and now would actually seem rather shabby. Still, no matter what, he'd never lose his feelings for that watch. Yi Inguk, M.D., decided to reveal honestly all he felt about the watch even though there might be no chance of recovering it.

With the aid of an interpreter, he established what he could of the time and place and gave all the details he could recall of the theft. Stenkov listened tensely as he fingered the spot on his cheek where the wen had once been.

"Nothing to worry about, Doktor Ri. We do not condone such things in the Great Red Army. And even if something like that happened, it could only have been a misunderstanding of some sort. I will take responsibility and see that you recover your watch."

Yi Inguk, M.D., who was watching Stenkov closely, saw a serious and determined expression cross his face.

Have I blundered by bringing up this needless business, just when everything was going so well?

He tried to suppress the hidden feelings of misgiving and regret.

"Rest assured, Doctor Ri . . . ha, ha, ha."

Stenkov interrupted himself with his own booming laughter, leaving his implication in the air.

Yi Inguk, M.D., had been rescued from the brink of death and was headed home. He could still hear the interpreter relating Stenkov's exclamation.

Where did he ever learn to express himself like that in Russian?

The car pulled up in front of Mr. Brown's residence. The sight of the Stars and Stripes made Yi Inguk, M.D., think of the red flag he had received along with his watch the day it was returned.

Yi Inguk, M.D., was shown into the living room, and he had time to look around while he waited for his host to appear. Though he had called on Mr. Brown a number of times at the embassy, this was his first visit to the man's home.

His indebtedness dated back three years, to when his daughter had gone to the United States.

The bookcase along one wall was jammed with Korean historical works written in Chinese, such as the *Veritable Records of the Yi Dynasty* and the *Taedong Compendium of Private Histories*. The bookcase across the room held neatly wrapped sets of classic texts. On a desk, around a small gilt-bronze Buddha, a number of antique curios were grouped for display. In front of a twelvefold screen of ancient Chinese calligraphy stood a small wine table on which rested a patina-filmed white porcelain bowl, serving here as an ashtray.

All of these must have been gifts brought by various callers. Yi Inguk, M.D., felt his face suddenly flush at the thought of the Koryŏ inlaid celadon vase he had brought. Actually, he was giving it up with some reluctance. He really hadn't thought it reprehensible to send these things out of the country. Rather, Dr. Yi Inguk's main question was why a man would want so many of these things. Where was the value, the satisfaction, in having them?

As soon as Mr. Brown came in, Yi Inguk, M.D., presented his gift with a smile. When Mr. Brown had unwrapped the parcel a smile spread across his face, too. He thanked the doctor over and over, unable to conceal his pleasure.

"This is quite a valuable piece, indeed."

"Oh, it's really nothing, just an expression of goodwill."

A sense of relief became a flush of satisfaction as Yi Inguk, M.D., joined in Mr. Brown's pleasant mood. As he listened to the American's mixed English and Korean pleasantries, he felt suffused with a warm feeling of accomplishment.

"Dr. Yi, where did you learn your English?"

"I learned it during the Japanese period, in Japanese style. You know, '*Zatto izu ah katto*' for 'That is a cat' and so on."

"But your pronunciation is so good now. And your grammar's quite accurate, too. Standard English."

These words suddenly called to mind what Stenkov had said about his Russian.

It seemed to him that Mr. Brown, who said his ancestors came from England, didn't pronounce his "r" sounds fully.

"I have had a private tutor for some time now."

"Oh, is that so?"

Yi Inguk, M.D., felt a restrained pride in his linguistic abilities.

Mr. Brown disappeared for a moment toward the kitchen and returned with a tray of various foreign liquors.

"Do have whatever you wish."

As Yi Inguk, M.D., looked at Mr. Brown, the American's face was replaced by Stenkov's, who had seemed satisfied only when he could down his vodka in a gulp, not bothering with food on the side. The doctor, whose high blood pressure and general constitution forced him to moderate his drinking, only sipped at his scotch, warming his palate as he waited to hear what Mr. Brown had to say.

"Well, we've received notification from the Department of State."

Yi Inguk, M.D., could have leaped for joy but, subduing the rush of excitement he felt, instead extended his hand to shake Brown's.

"Thank you. Thank you."

It struck him that he was responding just as Stenkov had to him after the operation.

It seems my way of managing the world works even with the Americans, thought Yi Inguk, M.D., in high spirits. *True sincerity can move Heaven itself, they say.*

Mr. Brown, too, seemed particularly pleased as he caressed the celadon vase and refilled his whiskey glass.

"I am afraid I shall be asking you many favors concerning my visit to America."

"There's no need to worry about that. I'll write you a letter of introduction before you leave."

"Thank you very much."

"Our history may be short, but America is a wonderful place! I hope your visit will help to promote friendship and goodwill between our two countries."

"Thank you."

After promising to meet the next day for a hunting expedition into the Demilitarized Zone, Yi Inguk, M.D., left Mr. Brown's home. There was a spring in his step as he pictured the deep-blue barrels of his new, double-barreled English hunting rifle. Yi Inguk, M.D., was concerned for a moment over the condition of the patient he had operated on a while before, but that soon passed. New feelings of ambition and hope swelled within his heart.

It had been arranged with the responsible official at the Ministry of Foreign Affairs that, the physical examination now complete, his exit papers would be issued the day he received the State Department notification. He recalled Mr. Brown's comment that he could be leaving within a week's time if all went well.

So many people, fresh out of college with no particular clinical experience, carry on in that unseemly way as if they'd plucked themselves a star—all because they'd made a trip to the United States. Well, I'm going this time. Once I get back, we'll see!

Suddenly a vision of his daughter Nami and his son Wŏnshik came to him. He clenched his fists tightly, and his face tensed momentarily as if he were on the brink of a seizure. Then an odd smile passed across his face.

Hmm. I've lived among those warty Japanese, made it out of the grasp of those brutish Russians, and now the Yankees—could they be much different? Revolutions may come and the nation change hands, but the way out has never been blocked for Yi Inguk. There used to be so many who seemed to outdo me from time to time. I've made it through, but what about them?

He wanted to shout his heart out into the void.

Shall I drop by the airline office and look into the ticket situation?

With the custom-made California cigar clamped at a jaunty angle in his teeth, Yi Inguk, M.D., hailed a passing taxi.

"Bando Hotel."

The clear autumn sky outside the car window was bluer and loftier to Yi Inguk, M.D., than others might have realized.

Translated by Marshall R. Pihl

Seoul: 1964, Winter

Kim Sŭngok

Kim Sŭngok was born in Osaka, Japan, in December 1941, but returned with his family to Sunch'ŏn, South Chŏlla Province, upon Liberation in 1945. In 1960 he entered the Seoul National University Department of French Literature, then a hotbed of exciting young intellectuals who were soon to shake up a staid literary establishment. During his student years, Kim was a cartoonist for the *Sŏul kyŏngje shinmun* newspaper and published his first major story, "Practice for Life" (Saengmyŏng yŏnsŭp), winner of the 1962 Newcomers Literary Award sponsored by the *Hanguk ilbo* newspaper.

Soon after graduation Kim earned major recognition as the winner of the tenth Tongin Award for his "Seoul: 1964, Winter" (Sŏul, 1964 nyŏn kyŏul), published in *Sasanggye* magazine in 1965.

By accident of birth, Kim and his contemporaries belong to a generation that has a unique place in modern Korean history—a generation that has, indeed, earned a name of its own. Some speak of them as the *Hangŭl* Generation, in view of their post-Liberation education. In contrast with their fathers, who were taught in Japanese, and their grandfathers, who had studied Chinese, they were instructed in Korean using *hangŭl,* the Korean alphabet. Others call them the Liberation Generation, for the era of their birth, or the April 19 Generation, for their role in the student-led uprising that toppled the Syngman Rhee government on that day in 1960.

"Seoul: 1964, Winter" is a bellwether of a new generation. Kim

Sŭngok's youthful, modern vocabulary of high-frequency words is notable for its explicitness and its concomitantly rare use of the sensory language that had been an essential attribute of creative writing since the colonial period. He has a generational world view that is distinct from that of his predecessors, a world view revealed through his slangy and sardonic characters, who brashly and egocentrically reject the reality of life around them. The language and thoughts of these characters are those of a generation that has tumbled from the heady sense of victory gained in the student revolution to a distrustful frustration engendered by the Park Chung Hee coup in 1961.

Anyone who spent the winter of 1964 in Seoul would probably remember those stalls that appeared on the streets once it got dark—selling hotchpotch, roasted sparrows, and three kinds of liquor; made so that to step inside you had to lift a curtain being whipped by a bitter wind that swept the frozen streets; where the long flame of a carbide lamp inside fluttered with the gusts; and where a middle-aged man in a dyed army jacket poured drinks and roasted snacks for you. Well, it was in one of those stalls that the three of us happened to meet that night. By the three of us I mean myself, a graduate student named An who wore thick glasses, and a man in his mid-thirties of whom I knew nothing except that he was obviously poor—a man whose particulars, actually, I hadn't the least desire to know.

The chit-chat started off between me and the graduate student, and when the small talk and self-introductions were over I knew he was a twenty-five-year-old flower of Korean youth, a graduate student with a major that I (who hadn't even gotten close to a college) had never even dreamed of, and the oldest son of a rich family; and he probably knew that I was a twenty-five-year-old country boy, that I had volunteered for the Military Academy when I got out of high school only to fail and then enter the army, where I caught the clap once, and that I was now working in the military affairs section of a ward office.

We had introduced ourselves and now there was nothing to talk about. For a while we just drank quietly and then, when I picked up a charred sparrow, something occurred to me to say and so, after thanking the sparrow, I began to talk.

"An, do you love flies?"

"No, until now, I . . . do you, Kim?"

"Yes," I replied. "Because they can fly. No, because even while they can fly, they can be caught in my hand. Have you ever caught something in your hand that can fly?"

"Just a moment, now. Let me see." For a while he looked at me blankly from behind his glasses as he screwed up his face. Then he said, "No, I haven't. Except for flies, of course."

The weather that day had been unusually warm, and the ice had melted and filled the streets with mud, but as the temperature dropped again by evening, the mud had begun to freeze once more beneath our feet. My leather shoes were not solid enough to block the chill that crept up from the freezing ground. Actually, a liquor stall like this was meant just for people who thought they might stop for a glass on the way home; it wasn't the place to be drinking and chatting with the man standing next to you. This thought had just occurred to me when Four-Eyes asked me quite a question. *This guy's all right,* I thought. So I made my cold and numb feet hold on a little longer.

"Kim, do you love things that wiggle?" is what he asked me.

"Sure do," I answered abruptly, with an air of triumph. Recollection can give you this sense of satisfaction, whether you're thinking of something sad or pleasant. When the recollection is sad, your feelings of satisfaction are quiet and lonely, but when the recollection is pleasant, you feel a sense of triumph. "After I flunked the Military Academy exams, I stayed on at a rooming house in Miari with a friend who had also failed his college entrance exams. That was the first time in Seoul for me, you know. My dreams of becoming an officer were shattered, and I was really depressed. I felt as if I would never get over my disappointment. You probably know, but the bigger the dream, the more powerful is the sense of despair that failure gives you. The thing I took interest in at that time was the inside of a full bus in the morning. My friend and I would get through breakfast as quickly as possible and then trot up to the bus stop at the top of the Miari ridge. I mean, panting like dogs. Do you know what are the most enviable and the most marvelous things in the eyes of a young man from the country who's in Seoul for the first time? The most enviable thing is the lights that come on in the windows of the buildings at night—no, rather, the people who are moving back and forth in that light. And the most marvelous thing is a pretty girl standing beside you in a bus, not one inch away. Sometimes it's possible to stand so that you're not only touching the flesh of her wrist but even rubbing against her thigh. For this, I once spent a whole day riding around town, transferring from one city bus to another. Of course, I was so exhausted that night I puked, but . . ."

"Just a moment. What are you leading up to?"

"I was getting ready to tell you a story about loving things that wiggle. Listen for a moment. My friend and I would work our way deep into a full morning rush-hour bus like a couple of pickpockets. Then we'd stand in front of a pretty young girl who had found herself a seat. I would take hold of a strap and lean my head against my raised arm, a little dazed from running for the bus. Then I would slowly ease my eyes down toward the girl's tummy. I wouldn't be able to see it right off, but after a while when my vision had cleared, I could make out the girl's tummy quietly moving up and down."

"That up and down movement . . . that'd be her breathing, right?"

"Yes, of course. The tummy of a corpse doesn't move, does it? At any rate, I have no idea why it soothed and lifted my spirits so very much to watch that quiet movement inside a full morning bus. Really, I love that movement with a passion."

"That's quite a lewd story," said An in a strange voice.

That made me mad. I had remembered that story on purpose, just in case I got on some kind of quiz program on the radio and was asked, "What is the freshest thing in the world?" The others might say lettuce or daybreak in May or an angel's forehead, but I would say that that movement was the freshest thing.

"No, it isn't a lewd story, at all."

I spoke with an unyielding tone. "It's a true story."

"Why should there be a connection between being true and not being lewd?"

"I don't know. I don't know anything about connections. Actually, though . . ."

"But still, that motion—a 'movement up and down,' wasn't it? That certainly isn't wiggling. It seems you still don't love things that wiggle!"

We fell into another silence and were just fingering our drinks. *Sonofabitch. If he doesn't think that's wiggling, it's okay by me,* I was thinking. But then, a moment later, he spoke.

"I've just been thinking it over, Kim, and I've come to the conclusion that your movement up and down is, after all, one kind of wiggling."

"It is, isn't it?" I was pleased. "No question about it, that's wiggling. What I love more than anything is a girl's tummy. What kind of wiggling do you love, An?"

"It's not a kind of wiggling. Just wiggling, itself. All alone. For instance . . . a demonstration . . ."

"Demonstration? A demonstration? Then . . ."

"Seoul is a concentration of every sort of desire. Do you understand?"

"No, I don't," I replied in my clearest possible voice.

Then our conversation broke off again. This time, though, the silence lasted a long time. I lifted the glass to my mouth. When I had emptied it, I could see him holding his to his mouth and drinking with his eyes closed. I thought to myself, with some regret, that the time had come for me to get up and go. So that was that. I was thinking that all of this just confirmed what I had expected to begin with, and I was considering whether to say, "Until next time, then . . ." or "It's been enjoyable," when An, who had emptied his bowl, caught me by the hand and spoke.

"Don't you think we've been telling lies?"

"No." I was a little annoyed. "I don't know whether you've been lying or not, An, but everything I've said is the truth."

"Well, I have the feeling that we have been lying to each other." He spoke after blinking his reddened eyes once or twice behind his glasses. "Whenever I meet a new friend about our age, I always want to tell a story about wiggling. So I tell the story but it doesn't take even five minutes."

For a moment I'd thought I might understand what he was talking about, but now I wasn't sure.

"Now let's talk about something else," he began again.

But I thought it might be fun to give this lover of serious stories a hard time, and, what's more, I wanted to enjoy the drunk's privilege of listening to the sound of his own voice. So I started talking before he could.

"Of the street lights that are lined up in front of the P'yŏnghwa Market, the eighth one from the east end is not lit. . . ." As soon as I saw him getting confused, I continued with renewed inspiration. "And of the windows on the sixth floor of the Hwashin Department

Store, light was visible only in the three middle ones."

But now, it was I who was thrown into confusion.

Reason was, a startled look of delight began to light up An's face.

He started to speak rapidly. "There were thirty-two people at the West Gate bus stop; seventeen were women, five were children, twenty-one were youths, and six were elders."

"When was that?"

"That's as of seven-fifteen this evening."

"Ah," I said and began to feel discouraged for a moment. But then I bounced back in great humor and really began to lay it on.

"There are two chocolate wrappers in the first trash can in the alley next to the Tansŏngsa Theater."

"When was this?"

"As of nine P.M. on the fourteenth."

"One of the branches is broken on the walnut tree in front of the main entrance to the Red Cross Hospital."

"At a bar in the third block of Ŭlchiro Street that has no sign there are five girls named Mija, and they are known in the order they came to work there: Big Mija, Second Mija, Third Mija, Fourth Mija, and Last Mija."

"But that's something other people would know, too. I don't think you're the only one who has visited that place, Kim."

"Ah, you're right! I never thought of that. Well, one night I slept with Big Mija, and the next morning she bought me a pair of shorts from a woman who came around selling things on a daily installment plan. Now, there was one hundred and ten wŏn in the empty liquor bottle she used for keeping her money."

"That's more like it. That fact is entirely your property alone, Kim *hyŏng*."

He called me "older brother" as our speech conveyed our growing familiarity with each other.

"I—" We both began to speak at the same time. And then each yielded to the other.

"I, ah . . ." This time it was his turn. "I saw the trolley on a streetcar bound from West Gate to Seoul Station kick out bright blue sparks exactly five times while within my field of vision. The streetcar was passing by there at seven-twenty-five this evening."

"You were staying in the West Gate area this evening, weren't you, An *hyŏng*?"

"Yes, only in the West Gate area."

"I'm a couple of blocks up Chongno Street. There's a fingernail scratch about two centimeters long a little below the handle of the door to the toilet in the Yŏngbo Building."

He laughed loudly. "You left that scratch yourself, didn't you, Kim *hyŏng*?"

I was embarrassed, but I had to nod. It was true.

"How did you know?" I asked him.

"Well, I've had that experience, too," he answered. "But it's not a particularly pleasant memory. It'd be better, after all, for us to stick to things that we happen to have discovered and kept as our own secrets. That other sort of thing leaves a bad taste with you."

"But I've done that sort of thing lots of times and I must say I rather enj—" I was about to say I enjoyed it, but I suddenly felt a sense of disgust for the whole thing and broke off with a nod of agreement with his opinion.

But about that time something struck me as strange. If this fellow in the shiny glasses sitting next to me really was the son of a rich family and was highly educated to boot, why did he seem so undignified?

"An *hyŏng*. It's true that you're from a rich family, isn't it? And that you're a graduate student, too?" I asked.

"With about thirty million wŏn in real estate alone. That would be rich, wouldn't it? But, of course, that's my father's. As for being a graduate student, I've got a student ID card right here. . . ." As he spoke, he rummaged through his pockets and pulled out a wallet.

"An ID isn't necessary. It's just that there's something a bit odd. It just struck me as strange that a person like you would be sitting in a cheap liquor stall talking with a guy like me about things worth keeping to yourself."

"Well, that, all . . . that's . . . ," he began in a voice tinged with excitement. "That's . . . but first, there's something I'd like to ask you, Kim *hyŏng*. Why are you roaming the streets on such a cold night?"

"It's not my practice. I've got to have some money in my pocket before I can come out at night, you know."

"Well, yes. But why do you come out?"

"It's better than sitting in a boarding house and staring at the wall."

"When you come out at night, don't you feel something—a kind of fullness and abundance?"

"A what?"

"A something. I suppose we could call it 'life.' I do think I understand why you asked me your question, Kim *hyŏng*. My answer would
be something like this. It's night. I come out into the streets from my
house. I feel that I've been liberated, untied from any place in particular. It may not be so, but that's what I feel. Don't you feel that, Kim
hyŏng?"

"Well . . ."

"I'm no longer caught up, involved with all sorts of things—they're
left at a distance for me to survey. Isn't that it?"

"Well, that's a little . . ."

"No, don't say it's difficult. In other words, all the things that just
went grazing by me during the day stand stripped bare, frozen and
helpless, before my gaze at night. Now, wouldn't that have some
significance—looking at things and enjoying them like that, I mean."

"Significance? What significance does that have? I don't count the
bricks in buildings in the second block of Chongno because there's
some significance in it. I just . . ."

"Right. It's meaningless. No, there may be significance there, but I
don't understand it yet. You probably don't either, Kim *hyŏng*. Why
don't we just go find out together sometime? And not fake it, either."

"I'm a little confused. Is that your answer, An *hyŏng*? I'm lost. All
of a sudden this 'significance' and all . . ."

"Oh, I'm sorry! Well, this would be my answer. That I come out on
the streets at night simply because I feel a sense of fullness and close-
ness." Then he lowered his voice.

"Kim *hyŏng*, it seems you and I came by different ways to get to the
same point. Even supposing this might be the wrong point, the fault
isn't ours." Now he spoke in a bright and cheery voice. "Say, this isn't
the place for us. Let's go somewhere warm, have a proper drink, and
call it a night. I'm going to take a walk around and then go to an inn.
When I happen to go roaming the streets at night, I always stay over at
an inn and then go home. It's my favorite plan of action."

Each of us reached into his pocket, about to pay the bill. At that
point, a man addressed us. It was a man beside us who had set his glass
down and was warming his hands over the coal fire. He hadn't come in
so much to drink as to warm himself at the fire, it seemed. He had on a
fairly clean coat and his hair, slicked down in modest fashion, glistened here and there with highlights whenever the flame of the carbide
lamp fluttered. Though his background wasn't clear, he was a man of

about thirty-five who had the look of poverty about him. Maybe it was his weak chin, or maybe it was because the edges of his eyelids were unusually red. He just spoke in our direction, not addressing himself to me or to An in particular.

"Excuse me. But would it be all right if I joined you? I've got some money on me," he said in a listless voice.

From the sound of that listless voice it seemed that, while he wasn't necessarily pleading to go along, he dearly wanted to. An and I looked at each other for a moment, and then I said, "Well, friend, if you've got money for the booze . . ."

"Let's all go together," An added.

"Thank you," the man said in the same listless voice, and followed after us.

An's expression indicated that this wasn't what he'd planned on, and I, too, didn't have pleasant premonitions. There had been a number of occasions when I had enjoyed myself in the company of people I'd met over a glass of wine, but they usually didn't ask to join the group in a listless voice like that. To make a go of it, you've got to come on lustily, wearing a face that bubbles over with good cheer.

We poked along the street, looking here and peering there, like people who had suddenly forgotten their destination. From a medicine ad pasted on a telephone pole a pretty girl looked down at us with a desolate smile that seemed to say, *It's cold up here, but what can I do about it?* A neon sign advertising *soju* on the roof of a building flashed enthusiastically; beside it, a neon sign for medicine would go on for long stretches and then, as if it had nearly forgotten, would hurriedly flash off and back on again; beggars crouched here and there like hunks of rock on the now hard-frozen sidewalks; and people, hunched over intently, quickly passed them by. A wind-whipped piece of paper skittered over from the other side of the street and landed at my feet. I picked it up and saw it was a handbill pushing some beer hall's "Service by Beauties—Special Low Prices."

"What time has it gotten to be?" the listless man asked An.

"It's ten before nine," An answered after a moment.

"Have you two eaten supper? I haven't eaten yet, so why don't I treat?" the listless man said as he looked at each of us in turn.

"I've eaten," An and I replied simultaneously.

"You can eat by yourself," I suggested.

"I guess I'll skip it," the listless man answered.

"Please. We'll go along with you," said An.

"Thank you. Then . . ."

We went into a nearby Chinese restaurant. After we'd sat down in a room, he kindly asked us again to have something. And again we refused. But he offered once more.

"Is it all right even if I order something very expensive?" I asked in an effort to make him withdraw the offer.

"Yes, anything you want," he said in a voice that was now strong for the first time. "I've decided to use this money up, you see."

I felt sure the man had some scheme in mind, but still, I asked for a whole chicken and some liquor. He gave the waiter my order along with his own. An stared at me in disbelief.

It was just about then that I heard the low moans of a woman coming from the next room.

"Won't you have something, too?" the man said to An.

"No." An refused curtly in a voice that seemed sobered.

We turned our ears to the moans in the next room, which were quiet but growing more frequent. From a distance came the faint click-clack of streetcars and the sound, like flooding water, of rushing automobiles. And from somewhere nearby we could hear the occasional ringing of a buzzer. But we in our room were wrapped in an awkward silence.

"There is something I would like to explain to you," the good-hearted man began. "I would be grateful if you would listen a while. . . . During the day today, my wife died. She had been admitted to Severance Hospital." He looked searchingly at us but without sadness in his face as he spoke.

"Oh, that's too bad." "I'm sorry to hear that." An and I offered condolences.

"We were very happy together, my wife and I. Since my wife couldn't have children, we had all our time to ourselves. We didn't have a lot of money, but whenever we came by a little, we'd enjoy traveling around together. We'd visit Suwŏn when the strawberries were in season and take in Anyang for the grapes. In the summer, we'd go to Taech'ŏn and then visit Kyŏngju in the fall. We'd see movies and shows in the evenings whenever we could."

"What illness did she have?" An asked cautiously.

"The doctor said it was acute meningitis. Though she had had acute appendicitis once and also acute pneumonia, she got over them all right. But this acute attack killed her . . . now she's dead."

The man dropped his head and mumbled to himself for a while. An poked my knee with his finger and gave me a look that said, *What do you think? Shouldn't we get out?* I felt the same way, but just then the man raised his head and resumed his story. So we had to stay put.

"My wife and I were married the year before last. I had met her by accident. She once said her family lived somewhere in the Taegu area, but we never had any contact with them. I don't even know where her family home is. So I had no choice in the matter." He lowered his head and mumbled again.

"You had no choice in what?" I asked.

It looked as if he hadn't heard me. But after a moment he looked up again and continued with eyes that seemed to beg our pardon.

"I sold my wife's body to the hospital. I had no choice. I'm only a salesman, selling books on time payment. I had no idea what to do. They gave me four thousand wŏn. I was standing by the fence in front of Severance Hospital until just before I met you two gentlemen. I had been trying to figure out which building had the morgue with my wife's body in it, but I couldn't. So I just stood there and watched the dirty white smoke coming out of the chimneys. What will become of her? Is it true that the students will practice their dissection on her, splitting her head apart with a saw and cutting her stomach open with a knife?"

We could only keep our mouths shut. The waiter brought dishes of sliced pickled radishes and onions.

"I'm sorry to have told you such an unpleasant story. It's just that I couldn't keep it inside me. There's one thing, though, I'd like to discuss—what should I do with this money? I'd like to get rid of it tonight."

"Spend it, then," An quickly replied.

"Will you two stay with me until it's all gone?" he asked. We didn't answer right away. "Please stay with me," he said. We agreed.

"Let's blow it in good style," he said, smiling for the first time. But his voice was as lifeless as before.

By the time we left the Chinese restaurant we were all drunk, one thousand wŏn of the money was gone, and he looked as if he were crying with one eye while laughing with the other. An was telling me that he was tired of figuring out a way to escape, and I was mumbling *I got the accents all wrong, damn accents!* The street was cold and empty, like a ghost town you might see in a movie, but the sign was still flashing diligently and the medicine sign had shaken off its lethargy. The girl on the telephone pole was smiling, telling us, *Same old me.*

"Where shall we go now?" the man said.

"Where shall we go?" An said.

"Where shall we go?" I echoed.

But we hadn't any place to go. Beside the Chinese restaurant we had just left was the show window of a men's clothing store. The man pointed toward it and then dragged us inside the shop.

"Let's see some neckties. My wife is buying them for us," he bellowed.

Each of us picked out a mottled-looking one, and six hundred wŏn was eliminated. We left the store.

"Where shall we go?" the man said.

We still had nowhere to go. There was an orange peddler outside the shop.

"My wife liked oranges," the man cried and bounded over to the peddler's cart where the oranges were laid out for sale. Another three hundred wŏn was gone. While we were peeling the skins off the oranges with our teeth, we paced restlessly up and down.

"Taxi!" the man shouted.

A taxi stopped in front of us. As soon as we had gotten in, the man said, "Severance Hospital!"

"No. That's useless," An quickly exclaimed.

"Useless?" the man muttered. "Where, then?" There was no answer.

"Where are you going?" asked the driver in a sullen voice. "If you haven't any place to go, then get out."

We got out of the taxi. We still hadn't gone more than twenty paces from the Chinese restaurant. The scream of a siren rose from the far end of the street and came closer and closer. Two fire engines roared by us.

"Taxi!" the man screamed.

Another taxi stopped in front of us. No sooner had we gotten in than the man said, "Follow those fire engines!"

I was peeling my third orange.

"Are we on our way to see a fire now?" An asked the man. "We can't. There isn't enough time before curfew. It's already ten-thirty. We should find something more amusing. How much money is left now?"

The man rummaged through his pockets and pulled out all the money. Then he handed it over to An. An and I counted it together. There was nineteen hundred wŏn in large bills, a few coins, and several ten-wŏn notes.

"Good," said An as he handed back the money.

"Fortunately, there are women in this world who concentrate on showing off what it is in particular that makes them women."

"Are you speaking of my wife?" the man asked in sad tones. "My wife's characteristic was that she laughed too much."

"Oh, no. I was suggesting that we go up to see the girls in the third block of Chongno Street," An said.

The man gave a smile that seemed to show contempt for An and turned his head away. By then we had arrived at the scene of the fire. Thirty wŏn more was gone. The fire had broken out in a ground-floor paint shop, and the flames were now billowing out the windows of a hairdressing school on the second floor. We heard police whistles, fire sirens, the crackling of flames, and streams of water crashing against the walls of the building, but there was no sound of people. The people stood as if in a still-life painting, reflecting the blaze with faces as red as if overcome by shame.

Each of us took one of the paint cans rolling around at our feet, set up, and squatted on them to watch the fire. I was hoping it would burn a little longer. The *School of Hairdressing* sign had caught fire, and flames began to lick at the *dressing*.

"Kim *hyŏng,* let's go on with our conversation," An said.

"Fires and such are nothing at all, not worth the bother. Only thing is that tonight we have seen ahead of time what we would have seen in tomorrow morning's newspapers. That fire isn't yours, Kim *hyŏng,* it's not mine, and it's not this man's. It's just our common property now. But a fire doesn't go on forever. Therefore, I find no interest in fires. What do you think, Kim *hyŏng?*"

"I feel the same way." I gave him the first answer that came to mind. I was watching the *Hair* catch fire.

"No. I was in error just now. The fire is not ours, the fire belongs wholly to the fire itself. We are nothing at all to the fire. Therefore I find no interest in fires. What do you think, Kim *hyŏng?*"

"I feel the same way."

A stream of water struck the burning *Hair.* Gray smoke billowed out where the water landed. Our listless friend suddenly leaped to his feet.

"It's my wife!" he shrieked, eyes bulging, as he gestured toward the glowing flames. "She's tossing her head back and forth. She's tossing her head, crying that it'll crack with the pain. Darling!"

"The pain was caused by meningitis. Those are just flames carried in the wind. Sit down. How could your wife possibly be in the fire?" An said as he pulled the man back down. Then he turned to me and whispered quietly, "This guy's giving us quite a show."

I noticed the *Hair* flickering where I thought the fire had gone out. The stream of water splashed it again. But their aim was off, and the stream wavered back and forth. The flames licked nimbly at *of*. I was hoping they would catch on to *School* as well and that I would be the only one among all the spectators to have seen the sign burn all the way through. But then, just as the fire was becoming a living thing to me, I suddenly withdrew my wish to be the only one.

From where we were squatting, I had seen something white flying toward the burning building. A pigeon that fell into the flames.

"Didn't something just fly into the fire?" I turned and asked An.

"Yes, something did," An answered and then turned to the man. "Did you see it?" he asked.

The man was sitting, speechless. At that point, a policeman sprinted over toward us.

"You're the one!" the policeman said, grabbing the man with one hand. "Did you just throw something into the fire?"

"I didn't throw anything."

"How's that?" he shouted at the man, making as if to strike him. "I saw you throw something. What did you throw into the fire?"

"Money."

"Money?"

"I wrapped some money and a rock in a handkerchief and threw it into the fire."

"Is that the truth?" the policeman asked us.

"Yes, it was money. This man has the strange belief that he'll be lucky in business if he comes to a fire and throws some money in it. Perhaps you could say he's a little odd, but he's just a small-time businessman who wouldn't do any harm," An answered.

"How much money was it?"

"A one-wŏn coin," An answered again.

After the policeman had left, An asked the man, "Did you really throw money into the fire?"

"Yes."

"All of it?"

"Yes."

For quite a while we just sat there listening to the crackling of the leaping flames. After a time, An spoke to the man.

"It looks as if we finally used the money up, after all. Well, I guess we've carried out our promise to you, so we'll be going now."

"Good night, sir," I added in parting.

An and I turned and started to walk away. The man came after us and grabbed each of us by an arm.

"I'm afraid to be left alone," he said, trembling.

"It's almost curfew. I'm going to go find an inn," An said.

"I'm headed home," I said.

"Can't we all go together? Just stay with me for tonight. I beg of you. Please come along with me," the man said, grabbing and tugging at my arm as if it were a fan. He was probably doing the same to An.

"Where do you want to go?" I asked him.

"I'm going to get some money at a place near here, and then I was hoping we would all go to an inn together."

"To an inn?" I said as I counted the money in my pocket with my fingers.

"If it's the cost of the room you're worried about, I'll pay for all three. Shall we go together, then?" An said, addressing himself to the man and me.

"No, no. I don't want to cause you any trouble. Just follow me a moment."

"Are you going to go borrow money?"

"No, this money is due me."

"Somewhere nearby?"

"Yes, if this is the Namyŏng-dong area.

"It certainly looks like Namyŏng-dong to me," I said.

With the man in the lead and the two of us following, we walked away from the fire.

"It's much too late to go collecting debts," An said to him.

"Yes, but I've got to collect it."

We entered a dark back alley. After turning several corners, the man stopped in front of a house where the front gate light was lit. An and I stopped some ten paces behind him. He rang the bell. After a while the gate opened, and we could hear the man talking with someone standing inside.

"I'd like to see the man of the house."

"He's sleeping now."

"The lady, then?"

"She's sleeping, too."

"I really must see someone."

"Wait a moment, please."

The gate closed again. An hurried over to the man and pulled at his arm.

"Forget about it. Let's go."

"That's all right. I've got to collect this money.

An walked back again to where he had stood before. The gate opened.

"Sorry to trouble you so late at night," the man bowed and said, facing the gate.

"Who are you, sir?" came a woman's sleep-filled voice from the gate.

"I'm sorry to have come so late, but it's just that. . . ."

"Who are you, please? You seem to have been drinking, sir."

"I've come to collect an installment on a book you've bought."

Then he suddenly broke into a near scream, "I've come for a book payment." Now he rested his two hands against the gatepost and, burying his face in his arms, burst into sobs. "I've come for a book payment. I've come for . . . ," he continued in tears.

"Come back tomorrow, please." The gate slammed shut.

The man continued to cry for quite a while, mumbling, "Darling" now and then. We waited, still about ten paces away, for the crying to end. After some time, he came stumbling over toward us.

The three of us, heads lowered, walked through the dark alleys and back out onto the main street. A strong, cold wind was blowing through the deserted streets.

"It's terribly cold," the man said, sounding concerned for us.

"It is, rather. Let's go find an inn right off," An said.

"Shall we get one room for each of us?" An asked, as we went into the inn. "That'd be a good idea, wouldn't it?"

"I think it'd be better for us to share the same room," I said, thinking of the man.

The man stood vacantly, looking as if he wanted only for us to arrange things. He also looked as if he had no idea where he was. Once inside the inn, we felt the same awkward confusion of not knowing what to do next that strikes you when you leave a theater after the show. The streets seemed narrower and closer than the interior of the inn. All those rooms, one after the other, that's where we had to go.

"How would it be for us all to take the same room?" I repeated.

"I'm exhausted," said An. "Let's each take a single room and get some sleep."

"I don't want to be alone," the man muttered.

"It'd be more comfortable for you to sleep by yourself," An said.

Each of us headed for one of the three adjoining rooms indicated by the houseboy. Before we separated, I said, "Let's buy a pack of cards and play a hand."

But An said, "I'm completely exhausted. If you want, why don't you two play?" and went into his room.

"I'm dead tired too. Good night," I said to the man and went into my room. After filling in a false name, address, age, and occupation in the register, I drank the water the bellboy had left and pulled the quilt up over my head. I slept a sound, dreamless sleep.

The next morning An woke me early.

"That man is dead," An whispered in my ear.

"Huh?" I was wide awake.

"I just took a look into his room, and he was dead, sure enough."

"Sure enough?" I said. "Does anyone else know?"

"It doesn't look as if anyone else knows about it yet. I think we'd better get out of here right away—no noisy complications."

"Suicide?"

"No doubt about it."

I dressed quickly. An ant was crawling along the floor toward my feet. I had a feeling the ant was going to climb my foot, so I quickly stepped aside.

Outside, hail was falling in the early dawn. We moved away from the inn, walking as quickly as possible.

"I knew he was going to die," An said.

"I hadn't the least suspicion," I said, telling the truth.

"I was expecting it," An said, turning up the collar of his coat. "But what could we do?"

"Nothing. We had no choice. I had no idea," I said.

"If we had expected it, what should we have done?" An asked me.

"Fuck! What could we do? How were we to know what he wanted us to do?"

"That's it. I thought he wouldn't die if we just left him alone. I thought that was the best way to handle it."

"I had no idea that man was going to die. Fuck! He must have been carrying poison around in his pocket all night!"

An stopped beneath a scrawny roadside tree that was gathering snow. I stopped with him. With an odd look on his face, he asked me, "You and I are definitely twenty-five, aren't we, Kim *hyŏng*?"

"I definitely am!"

"I definitely am, too." He nodded once. "It frightens me."

"What does?" I asked.

"That 'something.' That . . ." His voice was like a sigh. "Doesn't it seem we've become old?"

"We're barely twenty-five," I said.

"At any rate," he said, putting out his hand, "let's say good-bye here. Enjoy yourself," he said as I took his hand.

We separated. I dashed across the street where a bus was just stopping for passengers. When I got on and looked out the window, I could see, through the branches of the scrawny tree, An standing in the falling snow pondering something or other.

Translated by Marshall R. Pihl

The Boozer

Ch'oe Inho

Ch'oe Inho (b. 1945) first came to public notice in the 1960s when several of his short stories were selected in competitions sponsored by the *Hanguk ilbo* and *Chosŏn ilbo* newspapers and by *Sasanggye* magazine (in 1963, 1966, and 1968, respectively). But he was not fully launched into his writing career until 1970, when, fresh out of the air force, he published "The Boozer" (Sulkkun), a story he had written some years earlier, in *Hyŏndae munhak* magazine. He briefly commented on this story when it appeared as the title work in a 1987 collection of his representative works.

> I wrote "The Boozer" in 1966—so that would be when I was a sophomore at Yonsei University. It took several hours to write out in a corner room at my sister's house, but it wasn't until 1970 that I got it published in *Hyŏndae munhak* magazine. This is the piece that gave me a royal sendoff in writing and brought favorable comments from many people.

Ch'oe Inho has continued to be an extremely popular writer whose work ranges from his morbidly fantastic "The Boozer" to a 1987 collection of sardonic anecdotes about the adventures of a college boy and girl, *Parade of Fools* (Pabo tŭl ŭi haengjin). He is a witty man whose penetrating humor sometimes tempts him to write more for the audience than for the art, but whichever way he inclines, he is a master of his craft.

Perhaps because of his wit, he refuses to take people at face value—he doesn't accept what they want him to believe. As critic Chŏng Hyŏngi has observed, Ch'oe Inho looks beyond the human facade into what makes people who they are, "turning them inside out and indicting them for what they've lost." This can make for fun and games if the objects are the cartoon-like characters Pyŏngt'ae and Yŏngja in *Parade of Fools,* but Ch'oe Inho can also be gravely serious and still penetratingly witty as he dissects drinkers and crawlers in the dark mosaic of "The Boozer."

A small boy's head poked into the tavern.

"Good evening."

The small boy pretended to know the boozers sitting by the door. Most of the boozers didn't pick up on him but, as luck would have it, one man looked his way.

"Look. . . . Hey, look! Get a load of the kid!"

The man's discovery offered plenty of food for conversation just as the drinking snacks were about to run out.

It took a bit of effort for the boozers, already drunk on rotgut and heated to their pickled brains by the coal briquette sizzling in the stove, to recognize the kid who appeared with the wintry draft through the open door.

"What'd the kid say?"

The drunken gaze of half a dozen men came to rest on the boy in rags. Their gaze flustered the boy and he prepared to leave, edging queerly away like a child caught picking through a trash can. The boy was extraordinarily ugly.

His head, covered with ringworm scars, was as messy as a tattered poster board; and the little hand that crooked out of a Chinese-style sleeve was so coated with grime that it glistened like a bullet casing.

"Hey, sonny! How's about a drink with us?" asked the man who had discovered the boy. He tempted him with the liquor bottle.

"I don't want it."

Suddenly the boy yelled out, as if he would burst into tears, "I came to get my father!"

"I know. I know, kid," the same man responded. "I know you're here to get your father. We know everything there is to know." The man chuckled. "Grown-ups like us really know it all. Hey, isn't that right, fellas?"

The man puffed himself up as he sought agreement from his friends, who were beginning to show an interest in this peculiar child. Just then, one of his friends joined in with a noisy guffaw, sounding like some comic doing a two-bit con man.

"Yeah, when you get to be our age, there's nothing you don't know! Hey, kid, do you know why the world goes around?"

"I don't know."

"It goes around to get a drink. Remember that one, kid. The world goes around to get a drink! Get it?"

"Yes."

"Want me to teach you another one, bright-boy?"

The first man, teetering, looked down at the boy.

"Why does a dog lift one leg to piss?"

"I know that one!" The boy laughed obsequiously. "If he lifts both legs he'll fall over!"

"Right. You're our bright-boy, all right. A real whiz kid—never forgets what he's taught!"

"What's your father's name?" another, unfamiliar man asked the kid as he broke up a fried bean cake with his chopsticks.

"It's Kuk Sŭnghyŏn. Kuk Sŭnghyŏn."

The kid's face suddenly lit up, as full as a page from an encyclopedia. He was moving like a toy soldier.

"Why, you'd know him! He has a great big mole over one eye. He always smelled like onions, and he always went around with cloves of garlic in his back pocket. And, they said he always cried when he drank."

"Why are you looking for your father?"

A man in black dyed U.S. Army fatigues, who had silently drained his shot glass, cut the boy off.

"Ah, ah . . ."

The boy instantly stared off into space with a dramatic look on his face.

"Mother is dying."

Before anyone realized it, the boy had sidled well into the tavern, where the warm air was circulating. Above the face of the extraordinarily ugly boy, the light of a thirty-watt bulb was doing a fair job at illumination; and the brume rising from the fish roasting on the coal briquette made a whitish blur of the tavern, like a smoke screen spreading.

"I saw her throwing up blood a little while ago and came running out. My father told me, if Mother looks like she's going to die, he'd be at this tavern tossing down *soju* and I should come here."

"Your father is . . ."

The man who had discovered the boy lit up a snipe and gave an empty laugh.

"He left. Really left is what."

"He left? Did he say where to?"

"He said if you come, to send you over to the Pyongyang House. Wasn't that it?"

The boy's body was like the works of a Swiss clock, full of life and strangely small. The US ARMY tag shining like an insignia on the urchin's chest presented a comical sight, and his face shone like velvet. And he was dressed in so many layers of clothing that he had the unnatural look of a crustaceous insect.

"Then I'll go over to the Pyongyang House."

The boy wavered briefly. A momentary shadow of loneliness flickered in his face—the kind of thing you often see in boozers when they leave a tavern after finishing their last drink. Whereupon, the man who had first called to the boy filled an empty shot glass with *soju* and slid it toward him.

"One for the road, bright-boy!"

"I'm not drinking. I've got to find my father."

"For all you know, he might have left the Pyongyang House for another place."

"It doesn't matter—I can find him. I'll look all night."

"Even if your mom dies in the meantime?"

"If I can just find my father, everything'll be okay. My father's different from you people. Father may be a boozer, but there's nothing he can't do if he sets his mind to it. You know, once he took copper and made it into gold. Gold!"

Unnoticed, the boy's hand had slipped out of its Chinese-style sleeve like a larva from its shell. Lifting the drink as deftly as a marketplace pickpocket, he downed it neatly. The shot glass had been filled to the brim, but the boy downed it without spilling a drop, like a master at sleight-of-hand. Perhaps swept with feelings of sufficiency, the youth popped a chunk of pickled radish into his mouth with a satisfied look.

"Think you'll have a cigarette, too, kid?"

"Please don't make fun of me."

The boy tugged at his jacket collar a moment and then went into a crouch. He had the very alert and agile look of a trained sprinter just about to take off, having wound his back up tight as if it were made of some fibrous and elastic material.

"Please don't forget. My father's name, I mean. Kuk—Sŭng—Hyŏn. But even if you see him in a tavern later on, don't tell him about the *soju*. Really!"

The stuporous boozers sent the boy on his way with their vacant gazes. A desolate chill, like the thin light of dawn, grazed the boy's face. And then the boozers, now heavily drunk, began to curse their families, curse their wives, curse their eldest and second-born sons, their lives, their hopes for the future, their lousy salaries, anything at all that lives and breathes, and they cursed themselves, as well.

The cold winter wind blew in, kiting a newspaper through the marketplace alley. Like sandy dust that billows over the desert, it raked the boy's face. The boy mumbled to himself as he walked along, hands stuffed into his pockets. Since about dusk he had already dropped in at five taverns and had the luck to knock off at least seven drinks. In that time he had consumed several kinds of booze. He'd put down rotgut *soju,* beery *makkŏlli,* and even some refined *yakchu.* That should have been enough for a hungry heat to rise in his throat and his life to leave his head for parts unknown. Nevertheless, the boy wanted more, as if his stomach were still empty. He was probably good for half a dozen more drinks yet before he found his father.

The wind whipped harshly from one end of the market to the other. Winter was snickering everywhere. Streetlights shone sky-bright overhead, and somewhere in the distance a cat yowled. In the deserted street of the market old awnings flapping in the wind grazed the boy's face like specters. Fortunately, as his tipsiness fired into a rush, the boy's small body began to generate heat like a hotplate switched on.

Oh, my goddamn head!

In a moment the boy felt like his head was far too heavy for his body. It suddenly seemed unfair that he had to go around carrying this unwieldy head.

The Pyongyang House was at the end of the marketplace. It cast warm, sweet light out into the empty marketplace street. The boy tiptoed quietly to the window to see if he could spot a familiar face inside. Because, if there was no one familiar there, he wouldn't be able to drink any more and he wouldn't be able to meet up with his father.

Fortunately, though, he recognized two of the drinkers inside. The boy dropped to his heels and began to curse himself a moment in the open air.

Goddamn booze.

Like a skilled and practiced boozer who decides he'll lay off this time for sure and then suddenly looks hesitant and old, the boy's little face was grazed by shadows of momentary depression, sorrow, and regret. But, as soon as he saw the transparent shot glasses gleaming on the tables on the other side of the window and heard the raucous banter of the laughing boozers, the boy's ugly face underwent a startling change. Assuming the pathetic expression of a penitent jailbird, he slowly took hold of the tavern door. The latch was familiar to his hand.

"Good evening," he said, sticking his head inside and glancing around.

But only the barmaid looked his way.

"Your father left, kid. Said he was going to the widow's tavern."

The boy looked vaguely up at her.

"That's for sure, kid."

Only then did the boozers seated inside take notice of the boy. A whiskered man laughed hugely. He always laughed when he was drunk. He laughed even when he told the story of how his wife had died during the war after she got hit by a bullet that opened up an air hole in her stomach. And he even laughed as he told how he had to live alone nowadays. And he laughed even when he said he'd kill himself before he turned fifty. It looked for all the world like the man knew only how to laugh. He had made his living sneaking into the station yard and making off with coal. Once he was caught by the watchman, who messed him up enough to rearrange the shape of his face, but he kept on laughing and drinking, saying he'd drink through his nose if his mouth got too swollen. He was a peculiar man who seemed both a little short-changed and yet blessed with personality to spare. At any rate, the boy was more than grateful that they had discovered him before they got too drunk to recognize his face.

"Hey, when I see a kid like that, I tell you, heh-heh-heh, I think of my dead kid, you know, heh-heh-heh. He was just that size, I mean, heh-heh-heh. He took after me and so he was good-looking and really smart, you know, heh-heh-heh. He was the kind of kid who would have been a big shot when he grew up, I mean, heh-heh-heh."

And there was another man who was totally different, who clammed up like a mute when he got drunk. He was a man with mottled tattoos on his forearm below a rolled sleeve who would sit still and speechless and then throw his knife. The boy had occasion just once to see the man's smile. The boy had opened the door of the Pyongyang House and said his "Good evening." The next instant he saw something slice through the air like a fish scale, whiz past his face, and bury itself in the doorjamb not a hand's span from his head. It was the man's knife. It served in place of the right hand he had lost in the war.

"Heads up, little shit!" the man shouted from where he sat. "See my right hand, how sharp and swift it is!"

And he smiled a curious and foamy smile. That was the smile.

He carved wooden dolls for a living. The previous year the boy had watched the man carve toy soldiers with his good left hand. Stripped to the waist, carving his dolls while the hot midsummer sun blazed outside his dugout, he would suddenly fling his knife in the direction of the distant wooden wall. Even now the boy remembered that summer day vividly—when he was suffocated by the maddening smell of sweat and felt a vague hostility well up as the shine of the earth, hot like oil at midday, showed in through the open doorway and he heard the metallic whine of the knife that flashed in flight and the firm, dry sound it made when it cut through the air and then sank into the wooden wall above the heart or above the genitals of a childishly drawn male figure.

Though the man had said to the boy in a low, intimate voice, "Hey, kid, how's about pulling out that knife and bringing it here?" the boy was well aware that the man did not like him. Naked contempt glimmered in the man's eye whenever he looked at the boy. Then, not long ago, when the boy had been passing by on the street, the man stuck his head out of his workplace and enticed the boy in a small voice. Bottle in hand, he was already dead drunk.

"Hey, kid. Wouldn't you like to have a little drink together? An eye-opener, you know."

Just as the boy stepped into the man's dugout, incautious and sweetly smiling, the man's left hand—on his one remaining arm—closed in a stranglehold around the boy's throat. As it began to tighten on his throat with fearsome power, the boy sank his teeth into the hand with all his might. As soon as the man loosened his grip, he fled out to the main street. The boy, in spite of himself, had cried then like a fool. For a while after, they did not run into each other in the tavern. So today was the first time they had met since then.

"I came to find my father."

The boy directed a tinny voice across to Whiskers, not looking in the direction of One-Arm.

"Saw him, heh-heh-heh. I saw him just a while ago. And that's not all. Heh-heh-heh. I even had a drink with him, heh-heh-heh."

"Mother.... My mother ..." The boy gestured as he spoke in a choked voice. "She's dying. I saw her throwing up blood and came right out."

The boy edged nearer to the table. His little long eyes were well bloodshot by the hotly rising rush of liquor, and a weepy discharge was gathering in them. In the middle of the table waited pellucid rotgut *soju*. The bottle, just uncapped, was filled to the very top.

The boy knew the taste of that *soju*. And he was well aware of what would happen to him after one more drink of it.

Whenever a shot of that rotgut washed the inside of his ever-insatiable mouth he knew just how much more dense his life was going to get.

The boy sat down at the very end of the long bench. Whiskers, biting off a mouthful of yawn, stretched with his arms flung out.

"You probably won't find your father tonight."

"I can find him," the boy concluded decisively. "I'll find him, all right."

"Heh-heh-heh. Well, if you don't find him today, there's always tomorrow."

"Oh, no. I have to find him today. Mother is dying. Just now I saw her throwing up blood and came running right out. She threw up dark red blood from her mouth and lay down. She said to me in a little voice to go find Father and bring him home. If I just find Father, Mother can get better."

The boy seized the perfect moment and, neat as you please, picked up a shot glass from the table. And then he smartly emptied it into his mouth.

"My father may be a boozer but he's different from you people. See, he even took copper and made it into gold. You know, gold!"

The one drink loosened him up. Like the last drink you toss off when it's time to part, this one made him happy. He picked up a pair of chopsticks and, beating out a rhythm on the table, began to sing:

In olden days, olden times, long long ago,
There lived a man who had a pretty daughter.
He put a notice on the bank above the village levee:
If you'd be a son-in-law who's good at song and drink,
Then come along and let us put you to the test!

Whiskers showed little sign of surprise and laughed soundlessly inside his whiskers like a sheep eating paper. One-Arm was scowling with fish eyes at the ceiling. He looked like he would sit that way for days on end if no one interfered. Seeing his opportunity, the boy reached out, grabbed the *soju* bottle, and poured himself another drink.

"My father always cried when he drank."

No one listened to what he was saying. Whiskers didn't laugh this time. Somewhere a stray cat yowled, and from a height, fatigue and sadness descended heavily upon them. The boy picked up the drink that he had poured himself and, as he eyed the men around him, lapped at it with the tip of his tongue. The barmaid puffed on her cigarette as she stared in his direction from time to time, studying the strange conjunction of three drinkers. By this point, the boy had flushed red as a beet and started to hiccup.

"I've got a funny question for you. Do you know why a dog lifts one leg to piss?"

"Nope."

"If he lifts both legs he'll fall over . . . kerplunk!"

The booze had made itself felt throughout the boy's body and he had given himself up to drinking games in a state of intense satisfaction. Everything began to pass in front of his eyes. He picked up the chopsticks again and beat out a rhythm on the table as he launched into a rowdy song.

Once upon a moonlit nignt
  a balding bachelor came visiting.
Fiddle, fiddle, fiddle—
  your long-necked fiddle sounds so good.
But the looks of you—
  you look so ugly I can't stand it.

This little boy, who was drinking booze and drumming on the table in a corner of a tavern as market closing time drew near, may have been small in physique. But, each of his gestures was skilled, and he exuded a strange aura that suggested he meant to play out his string all the way. When the boy had finished singing he quietly stuck his tongue way out and began to extinguish the cigarette he was now smoking. He took on the air of a circus boy doing magic tricks as the hot ember of the cigarette died on the surface of his tongue with a sharp hiss.

That's when it happened. As if suddenly waking up, the one-armed man went for his knife. In a flash he had taken aim at the boy's throat. The boy looked up dumbly at him. The man's eyes were glistening sickly and, below his curling lips, a white laugh was shining meaninglessly.

"Hey boozehound! You little shit!" the man yelled. "I'm going to snuff you, nice and easy."

The boy thought of defying him but realized that his tongue couldn't help him now.

"Don't move, little shit!"

In the man's hand, the flashing knife was taking a bead on the boy's throat. The boy felt a light pang coming to the area of his throat and heard the sound of grieving for an easy life.

Goddamn throat.

The man's hand was cocked way up, like when the P.E. teacher signals a start. Between his fingers, the knifeblade sparkled like a tiny bird. Then, in an instant, the knife sliced down through the air. Friction sounded lightly in the air as the boy caught sight of a spark flashing like flint in the man's moving hand. Next the boy watched the man collapse onto the table as his hand thrust itself into his own chest. The boy came flying out of the tavern like a bullet.

Stupid asshole.

The street was dark. The wind blew in every corner and the sky had a translucent leaden color. The cold was very, very familiar to the boy. The boy always had to struggle with this cold—whenever, wherever.

The market street was already completely empty. Steamy white vapor was escaping from below his nose and melting away into the darkness. The hiccups hadn't stopped and, luckily, he was still alive. It seemed he had drunk more than usual; all the same, he hadn't over-done it. He stood close in front of a cold wall and unbuttoned himself. Since he was dressed in as many layers as he could manage, it was difficult to rummage around inside that incubator. While he peed, he began to sing in his tinny little voice.

Once upon a moonlit night
  a balding bachelor came visiting.
Fiddle, fiddle, fiddle—
  your long-necked fiddle sounds so good.
But the looks of you—
  you look so ugly I can't stand it.

He knew well where it was he was going to go. He had never forgotten his route, no matter how drunk he got.

What could Father be doing while Mother is heading to her death?

He gazed up at a sky that looked suffused with dark dye. He had little hope of finding his father but, nevertheless, the boy could not surrender his last stronghold.

He began to totter. At the end of the market street a drunk lay sleeping where he had laid himself down. The boy approached slowly and peered into the drunkard's face, then began to rifle through his pockets. The boy went about his task without hesitation while thinking the man would probably freeze to death before daybreak. His outer coat pockets were empty. Out of the left pocket came a few cigarette butts and a half-eaten piece of pollack, and out of the right pocket, just two streetcar tickets.

The boy then began to search the man's inner coat pocket. When the feel of paper money met his fingertips, the boy's breathing turned rough and he extracted two notes. With these still in his hand, he set off again. His heart began to leap in anticipation of more drink. With these two paper bills, he could have a couple more shots of cheap *soju*. And he knew well the effect they would have on him, these two shots of *soju* that he would drink fair and square, without groveling. He knew, too, that wings would sprout painlessly from his sides and make him light as a bird.

The boy knew of a tavern that stayed open late. But, since it was closing time now for most of those places that stayed open late, the boy began to run. The sound of the boy's footsteps resonated across the frozen ground. The tavern he had in mind was already closed.

At the gate of the darkened tavern, he stifled his breathing and sniffed like a cat at the odor of liquor that seeped out through cracks around the door. His hair flew in the wind and his body hunched up. He thought a moment about what action to take and then began to rap on the glass window with determination. The window pinged like cracking ice. Crystals of white frost had blossomed on the glass. The boy would rap a while and then strain to listen, rap a while and tilt his ear. Each time he listened, he heard the sound of cold and distant wind. After a while signs of life appeared inside, and finally someone came up to the window. The person on the inside began to scratch at the frost. After a bit, a hole the size of a coin opened up and through the hole appeared someone's gaze.

"Good evening."

The boy gave his courteous greeting. Whereupon, a cubby window opened and the disheveled head of a barmaid appeared.

"He's not here. Your father didn't come here."

"I know." Cold, the boy rubbed his hands together. "That much I know."

"Then what are you up to? How come you're not in bed?"

"This time I don't need my father."

The youngster quickly but clearly made a decision. He moved the muscles of his face but they turned into a tearful look. His hoarse voice sounded like a goose crying at the setting sun.

"Auntie. I came for a drink."

His eyes were pleading to be believed.

"Are you crazy, child?"

"Just two shots. And I have the money, too."

The boy held the money up to show the woman.

"Really, I want to get drunk. I know how much I can hold. Two shots, only two, and I'll sleep well—no dreams. If I stop at this point, it's no better than having nothing to drink and I won't be able to fall asleep, you see. . . ."

The boy smiled like a freshwater fish. A handful of light from the kitchen cheerlessly crossed his face. The woman's face showed a moment's thought and then she opened the door for him with that abruptness these women often seem to use. The boy wobbled into the tavern and the woman, yawning, stepped into the kitchen and brought out a bottle.

The boy plopped down at a table in a swirl of cold air. The woman poured a drink, and the boy set the shot of cheap, kerosene-smelling *soju* on the table in front of him and steadied his breathing for a moment. The image of the seated youngster confronting his drink in the gloom was indeed somehow solemn. Each time the decorously seated figure reached for the shot glass, the weak light—dappling him like white mottling on the wings of a tiger moth—made him look like a youth sowing seed. As soon as he had finished the drink, he tapped his fingertip lightly on the table. The woman lifted her bottle and filled the shot glass generously full.

"My father cried when he drank. But, as you can see, I don't cry."

The crying of a child sounded from the inner room. But the woman ignored it. The child would cry and then stop of its own accord. The boy lifted his glass again and drank it down with a hand that trembled like someone with the palsy. That had been a very brief pleasure.

"Auntie. Please don't die before I grow up. Grit your teeth and bear it."

In the doorway, the boy bowed. As the woman closed the door, she shouted something.

"Good-bye. And don't come back!"

The boy was now walking like a wind-up toy that had run down. He knew well where he was going to go. He turned onto a sloping road. The shell of a collapsed house loomed like a beast in the dark. Inside, a stray cat yowled. About this time every night, that cat yowled in the lightless ruins, in those ruins where rusted reinforcing bars wove a netted sky.

Up on the slope, the wind was still more fierce. He was making his way up the sloping path with his hands thrust into his pockets.

At the top of the slope stood the orphanage. The lights were out and, by now, the children would be sleeping with their bodies rolled as tightly as possible into little balls to ward off the cold. One kid would be grinding his teeth in his sleep and another, as he did every night, would be fretting for fear of the dark.

Ah, ah . . . on this dark night . . . where is Father, really?

He staggered for a moment. But he wasn't one to get so drunk that he forgot where the dog hole was in the barbed wire fence through which he had slipped out.

He was concerned for a moment whether he could crawl safely through the velvet darkness into the bedding still warm with his body heat, without getting caught by the governess. But he put himself in the care of his typical easygoing optimism—a peculiarity of boozers.

From the bottom of the slope blew a wind laden with the smell of cold dust. He sniffed at it like a hunting dog and set his teeth as he decided, *I'll be finding Father tomorrow for sure.*

Translated by Marshall R. Pihl

A Dream of Good Fortune

Hwang Sŏgyŏng

In many ways, Hwang Sŏgyŏng embodies the theme of exile. Hwang was born in 1943 in Manchuria and lost his father at an early age. His family moved in 1945 to Hwanghae Province in what is now North Korea, and in 1949 to the Yŏngdŭngp'o district of Seoul. In 1950 the family fled to the city of Taegu after the outbreak of the Korean War. Hwang's interest in writing developed early, and in 1954 he was selected for a nationwide children's literary contest. Also during that year he briefly ran away from home—the first in a series of pilgrimages that has marked his life ever since. Though an honor student at Seoul's prestigious Kyŏngbok High School, he was not satisfied with school life and in 1962 was expelled. The same year, one of his stories was entered in a new writers contest sponsored by *Sasanggye* magazine. In 1964 he enrolled in Sungshil University; he eventually graduated from Tongguk University with a degree in philosophy. Also in 1964 he was jailed for political reasons. In prison he met labor activists, and on his release he worked for a time at a cigarette factory and at several construction sites around the country. In 1966 he enlisted in Korea's Blue Dragon marine unit and served in the Vietnam War; he was discharged in 1969. He made his literary debut in 1970 in the *Chosŏn ilbo* newspaper with the story "Pagoda" (T'ap), based on his experiences in Vietnam. In 1976 Hwang moved to South Chŏlla Province. His report of the violent government suppression of demonstrators in that province's capital city of Kwangju in 1980, *Beyond Death, Beyond the Darkness of*

115

an Age (Chugǔm ǔl nǒmǒ, shidae ǔi ǒdum ǔl nǒmǒ, 1985), was suppressed by the Chun Doo Hwan regime. An unauthorized, and widely publicized, trip to North Korea in 1989 resulted in his political exile from South Korea. He now lives in the United States.

Hwang's life has given him unquestioned legitimacy as one of the outstanding representatives of a group of authors who came to prominence in the 1970s through a body of work marked by a vigorous concern with social issues. His own fiction blends an idealistic vision with realistic, often gritty depictions of the working class. Good examples are "Far From Home" (Kaekchi, 1971) and "The Road to Samp'o" (Samp'o kanǔn kil, 1973). Among his major achievements is the ten-volume novel *Chang Kilsan* (Chang Kilsan, 1984). "A Dream of Good Fortune" (Twaeji kkum) first appeared in *Sedae* magazine in 1973.

1

A roof-tile factory with an evil-looking smokestack stood alone on a sprawling, denuded hillside, looming above the housing sites spread about the reddish-brown earth. The sun was setting, and the sparks soaring from the smokestack gradually began to glitter in the murky sky. Simple frame houses and squat huts were clustered here and there amid the undeveloped land at the foot of the hill.

Nearby, Kang pulled his cart past a depression beside the back wall of a chemical factory. Great heaps of rubbish were reflected in the grayish waste water that always collected there. Kang wore only a sleeveless T-shirt, tattered corduroy jodhpurs, and a perforated straw hat pulled down over his forehead. These clothes must have been picked from rags, and even the looks of their owner were worn and faded, like streamside pebbles parched by a drought. Kang looked like someone who had popped out of an ancient, yellowing photograph. He had the grizzled hair of a fifty-year-old, but his gait was dignified and his shoulders were solid from years of shouldering weight on a pole.

Kang hauled his cart through a tangle of rusty galvanized-iron lean-tos built by the Reconstruction Corps—that was what they called the ragpickers these days. Half a dozen men were busy sorting through the rubbish heaps, separating the jumble of paper, bottles, broken glass, wooden boxes, and tin cans into piles. Those who had just returned from their scavenging had unfastened bamboo baskets from their shoulders and were pouring the contents onto the heaps.

Boss, an older ragpicker who headed this branch of the Reconstruction Corps, was directing the work. He wore a field jacket whose pockets hung to the sides like ears; a reservist's cap was thrust down almost to his nose.

"Hey—get anything?" Kang greeted the man.

"Just get back?" Boss replied offhandedly.

"Get anything? Shit—I might as well try to find a middle leg on a woman," wisecracked a younger ragpicker next to him.

Boss looked askance at the other. "Tell that to your old man, asshole, and see what he thinks." He wiped his nose with one of the cotton gloves he was wearing.

Kang merely coughed instead of joining the banter.

"Unless I swipe something, the best I can come up with is stuff like this," Boss replied to Kang.

Kang somehow looked quite content, Boss felt. Judging from his greeting, he must not have made out too badly that day. "How about buying me a drink? You look like you made some money."

"Not enough for all the legwork I do." But then Kang opened up. "I got some wire."

"How much?"

"Fifteen pounds or so."

Kang made three or four hundred wŏn a day at most. Sometimes the neighborhood kids sneaked him useful items from home, and there were days when petty thieves who had hit the jackpot but lost the services of their fence would sell to him. In such cases Kang would inspect the surroundings, quickly exchange taffy or cash, and make his getaway. Nothing was more certain than a trip to the slammer if he were unlucky enough to be caught. Today he had worked a good deal on some electric wire from a suspicious character, then resold it. And that wasn't all.

"Take a look inside, pal." Kang pushed aside a wooden taffy tray and a plastic bag of popcorn.

Wondering what treasure was there, Boss craned his head into the cart, then jerked it back. "That's an animal, isn't it?"

The gray legs of a dog protruded from a sack.

"You bet! Big as a calf."

"A shepherd! Yeah, he's no runt, is he? What did you do, cozy up and knock it over the head?"

"Come on—I got it from the owner. Everything's aboveboard."

The dog had a fine coat. Boss gave the tail a tug, but couldn't budge the heavy animal. He was about to touch its ears when Kang subtly deflected his hand with the taffy board. Boss clicked his tongue, reluctant to withdraw.

"Just what the doctor ordered. The Dog Day before this, we ended up with squat."

"But you'll have to chip in," said Kang.

"What a great guy! All right, I'm good for some booze. But only if it's safe to eat—I don't want to croak, you know."

Kang surveyed Boss from head to foot as if he had said all he was going to say, then gave his cart a push.

"Okay, I get the message," Boss said fretfully. "It won't kill us. I can roast the hair off it, so be sure to give me a holler."

"You'll bring a bucket of *makkŏlli*?"

"I just said I would. Quit your worrying."

Kang nodded deliberately. "Good enough."

Every time Kang thought about what was under the taffy tray, his heart throbbed like that of a young woman at her first marriage interview. Plump and heavy as a man in the prime of life, the dog was almost too handsome to eat.

Boss still couldn't believe it. "What a find! It's not easy to see a dog during Dog Days."

"Still wondering how I got it? Well, I'm coming down in front of Kangnam School and this woman gives me a shout. I figure she has some scrap iron or something, so I follow her . . . ."

They had gone to a veterinarian's. The dog had been run over by a car. Its injuries weren't fatal, but both its hind legs were broken and there was no doubt it would be lame. The woman asked the vet to give the dog a shot to put it out of its misery, and within a short time it had spread its legs wide and was gone. The problem was how to get rid of the bulky beast. The vet wanted it disposed of immediately, but the woman had decided to bury it in some sunny place. It wasn't quite right to put it in her garden, she said, but then she couldn't just throw it in the garbage can either. What's more, she'd have to travel some distance to find a hill or an empty lot suitable for burial. Meanwhile, the woman's daughter was whining over the animal. It was then that they heard the clanging shears heralding the approach of a junk dealer. The woman had all she could do to soothe her daughter while asking Kang to take the dog and bury it.

"Man, I'm telling you, with its tongue hanging out and its legs spreadeagled it looked just like a tiger. I was drooling the whole time, but they probably never dreamed I might have other plans for the dog."

Suppressing a feeling of triumph, Kang had loaded the dog into his cart. And as if that weren't enough, the woman had given him a full three hundred wŏn for his trouble. It wasn't just a stroke of luck but a veritable windfall. While the daughter cried and the woman breathed a sigh of relief, Kang had to grit his molars to contain his excitement, which was causing his nose to twitch. Once out of their sight, he had looked inside the cart to see just how big the dog was.

"I don't get any meat these days, so my psoriasis is acting up," Kang continued. "Every day, skin flakes off like bits of rice. You know, I'd been thinking a stray mutt would be just the thing to eat to build up the old constitution."

Boss listened with a look of wonder and admiration. "Sounds like the gentleman who ran it over deserves all the credit, and not the lady."

"That's a fact. It wasn't rat poison and it wasn't a fit; it was a gentleman in a car hitting a big fat dog. He did right by us."

The two men were of one mind, and their laughter came easily.

Kang had received not only a healthy day's earnings but the three hundred wŏn as well. He had then thrown down a couple of shots of rotgut at a bar, indulging himself in his achievement. It was on his way home from the bar that he had met Boss.

"Okay, see you in a bit."

Kang exultantly pushed his cart into a neighborhood whose rows of dwellings could hardly be distinguished from the garbage heaps along the cement embankment about a foot and a half high that bordered a broad open sewer. Almost anyone who saw him could have guessed how his day had turned out. His dignified gait, his head held erect, his cart rolling lightly along, the jaunty angle of his hat, and the first question he asked anyone he met—"How'd you make out today?"— left no doubt that his day had been the best.

An old man who lent money at daily interest emerged from the public toilet. The head of the neighborhood association had raised black goats there until the previous year, but he'd never made any money at it. His goatpen was now a hut used as the neighborhood toilet.

"You're going to be a grandfather." The moneylender stood with both hands stuck inside the dirty pajama bottoms he was wearing.

"What are you talking about?" Kang asked.

"Misun's back."

"That little tramp!"

"Hard to recognize her. She's with child, you know."

Kang could only click his tongue in irritation. A few days earlier, his wife had been sobbing over a letter from Misun. He knew what this moneylender was like, and was not unaware of his habit of toying with people. Even so, this news galled him to no end. He was about to say, "She's not my girl anymore." But this was too hardhearted, and his face prickled with shame.

"What a pain in the ass! ... As far as your money's concerned, you'll get it whether the bitch is dead or alive. Talk to my old lady about it."

The old man was somewhat agreeable today. He had given up trying to find out if Kang intended to pay him back, but now there seemed to be hope.

"Misun's the one who started it all. Now that she's back, no problem."

"I agree," said Kang. "I'll leave the whole thing up to you."

"Listen to what she says. You'll see I've been telling you the truth. And the parents have to take some of the responsibility."

"But I had nothing to do with it."

Not satisfied with this, the old man shot a piercing look at Kang and his cart. "Her stomach's just like a watermelon," he chuckled. "I'll bet it's twin boys."

"Damned slut!"

Kang gave the cart a shove and entered an alley lined with low piles of bricks. The houses sat low enough to reveal their tarpaper roofs held down by rocks, and the slanting sheets of light green plastic that served as vents and windows. Beyond the other end of the alley was the neighborhood's single water pump and—an old custom reflecting the residents' rural origins—plots of vegetables being cultivated in the undeveloped land: scallions, cabbage, corn, and such. Most of the other workingmen had returned home, washed up and changed, and found a spot among the empty lots to squat and take in the breeze. Kang exchanged cursory greetings with a few of them.

Kang's boy saw him, left his playmates, and dashed over. "Dad— Uncle's back. And he brought Misun."

Kang removed the taffy and popcorn from the cart, then hoisted the dog. The children gathered, and there was a stir among the scattering of grownups. Kang, noticing his boy clinging to the taffy tray, punched him in the back.

"Little bastard!"

Kang turned toward his house, which was already dark. There was usually a response to his arrival, but today all was quiet.

Stamping in vexation, the boy heaped abuse at his father's back: "Dad's a sonofabitch! Dad's a fucker, a fucker!"

Ignoring this, Kang toted the dog into his kitchen and set it on a shelf. The wooden plank bent under the weight.

One fellow, perhaps designated by the neighbors, stuck his head in. "How about if we get a fire going?"

"Okay," Kang readily replied.

Kang entered the family room and just missed stepping on his wife's stomach. She was lying on the floor with a thin sheet pulled over the top of her head. Kang turned on the light and stared at his wife's body in its white shroud.

"What's eating you so early in the evening? How do you think I feel after pounding the pavement all day long?"

"Spare me—I'm not in the mood."

"Great! Just lying there like you've gone nuts."

Not wanting to aggravate his wife, Kang swallowed an urge to bark at her some more. But just then his boy, sitting astride the doorsill, started whining.

"Little son of a whore! You want to die?" Kang shouted.

The boy burst into tears.

"Well done," Kang's wife murmured from beneath the sheet. "What a way for a father and son to behave. The simpleton—is he whining because he can't shove anything more down his gullet?"

"That's right, bitch. And your two kids are real charmers too."

Kang's wife peeled off the sheet and lurched upright.

"If you had a thousand mouths you still wouldn't have anything worth saying. When have you ever tried to be a father to them? When? Have you ever? I'm so ashamed in front of others I could die. A man of your age still going after sex. . . . I know, why bring it up now, but who knocked me up so I had to get married again? How old was I when I had that kid? How many others did I get rid of? Tell me."

"Woman, you really are something! Like mother, like daughter. . . . So, Misun's back?"

"Why did I ever get myself into this? What a silly broad I was. . . ."

The sliding door to the back room rattled.

"Damn family," Kang growled. "I ought to burn this mother down. . . ."

At last the door slid open. Sure enough, there was Kang's brother-in-law in a dandy suit and a neat tie. He rose and emerged, hunched over.

"Hello, Brother-in-Law. Please calm down. The others will hear."

"Oh, the whole neighborhood knows." Losing his temper, Kang punched his knee over and over. "It's natural for kids to make their parents worry," he said to his wife, "but there has to be a limit. Why did that slut make up a story, borrow money at daily interest, and then take off? That's what gets me. We've gotten used to the moneylender bugging us, but if I say one word about Misun coming back home with her belly sticking out, you get bent out of shape. I'm a father, with a reputation like anyone else—a father!"

"Good grief. Well, how admirable. Father who can't bring any money home, if you were the outside of a cabbage, at least I could boil you and make soup."

"Sister, you stop too," said her brother. "As the Bible says. . . ."

Here we go again, Kang thought indignantly. His boy turned pale and was about to run off when Kang grabbed his wrist and said in an overly plaintive tone, "Let's go outside. Father'll give you some taffy."

Kang's wife gave a deep sigh that became a trembling sob, then threw herself down again. Her brother, seating himself squarely, began praying in a deep, encouraging voice.

"Almighty Jehovah, we in this family beseech you to cleanse us of the worry and suffering that dwell among us. May we sin no more in your presence, Father. Although she who went away has just returned and our family has come together again, we know not how to thank you. Instead, we feud and forget your kindness. Heavenly Father, though we struggle in poverty and anguish on this earth and know not heaven, show us the way; include us in your ranks on judgment day. We who are about to stand in the presence of heaven, we sinners . . ."

"Cut it out! 'Sinner, sinner'—it makes me sick. These days the King of Kings is getting on my nerves."

Kang's brother-in-law flinched at this outcry but didn't stop.

" . . . we sinners, every one of us, will repent and become faithful;

we will praise the glory of the Lord. We know that our unhappiness comes from our sins. We ask of you, bestow perpetual grace on Kŭnho, who is working the night shift at the factory, and on the head of this household, and bless the life Misun is bearing. . . ."

A choking sound came from the other side of the sliding door. Kang's wife became still. The prayer continued.

"Oh God, make us all your children. We beseech you once more, save us from the burning brimstone of hell, and allow us to live, with the Lord's favor, in truth and hope. We unworthy sinners, lacking any merit, pray in the name of Jesus Christ. Amen."

This talk of sinners, heaven, and hell seemed to have suddenly filled the room with a sweet, languid sorrow and expectation. Behind the sliding door Misun felt the tension drain from her chest. But her mother couldn't avoid feeling she herself had somehow been treated unfairly. Her uncle, still sitting piously, leafed through his Bible, its pages marked through and through with a colored pencil, and read to himself.

The old clock on the wall struck eight. Next to it, mounted in a frame, were several photographs fading with age. And beside them was a calendar, brought home by Kŭnho, advertising a cosmetics company. The current month showed a woman in sheer underwear with her legs coyly spread. On a low desk stood such books as a Japanese primer, a dog-eared economics text, a Chinese historical romance, Andrew Carnegie's autobiography, and a volume titled *The Secret of Success*. On top of the worn-out, old-fashioned bureau was a portable hi-fi that Kang's wife turned all the way up whenever she was in the mood. The songs from the old days, performed on an electric organ, sounded to her like rice gruel boiling in a pot. It was something Kang had given her as a present rather than turning over to a second-hand shop.

But now Kang's wife was in no mood for music. She hated Misun to death, yet pitied her, realizing in retrospect that as her mother she was entirely to blame. The evening breeze felt chilly, so she pulled the cord from the vented window in the ceiling and it banged shut. She heaved another sigh. Her expression was much more composed now; by nature she was hot-tempered but cooled off easily. Though she was almost fifty, the skin on her face was taut and she had kept her figure.

"It's all my fault. I lost my head and got married again—to an old halfwit," she said to herself with a sigh of grief.

It was in the city of Ch'ŏnan that she met Kang. Her first husband had been lost in heavy seas off Taebu Island—her previous home—

and she had settled in Ch'ŏnan shortly thereafter. Finding it difficult to raise Misun and Kŭnho as a single mother, she had taken to selling rice cakes filled with bean jam on the trains, using a nook at the station to avoid the security men. Kang, still brawny, handled freight at the station. Before they knew it, this rice-cake vendor and freight hand had caught each other's eye. Having been two-timed once, Kang had lost heart with women. But even though he was not your usual bachelor, he couldn't help falling for this widow who had kept her charms. It was long before their child was born that they had moved to Seoul. Though arriving empty-handed, Kang knew how to provide, and the family had quickly adapted to their new life.

Absorbed in these thoughts, Kang's wife called her daughter as mildly as she could.

"Misun, come over here."

Misun, barely replying in a voice that seemed to retreat rather than project from her throat, squatted hesitantly at the threshold of the back room, her head sunk squarely on her chest.

"What's the plan? Have the baby just like that?"

Misun fingered the hem of her skirt without answering.

Her mother repeated the question, lifting Misun's chin, but the girl's head drooped again as soon as she let go.

"It's not going to work. Let's talk with your brother, and then tomorrow we'll go to the hospital." Looking at her daughter's slender face and swollen abdomen, she wiped away tears with her fingers. "It's not six months yet—there has to be a way out."

Misun's head snapped up. "I don't want to."

"Then what are we supposed to do with a kid and no dad?"

"It's got one."

"So where is he? He ought to be right here explaining the situation and asking permission to get married, or if the timing isn't good, then asking us to wait awhile. Fat chance we have when you come crawling in with a big belly like a mangy dog. When Kŭnho sees that, he'll blow his stack—he'll kill you."

Her brother, still looking through his Bible, broke in.

"Sister, how could you kill a healthy, living baby?"

"Don't you butt in. The things that come out of that mouth of yours. . . . You know what it's like for us to make ends meet."

Her brother tried to change the subject.

"Was I ever surprised when Misun showed up. I couldn't get her to tell me anything—all she did was cry. But I did get the impression that they lived together before they split up."

"Did you split up with the guy? What happened?"

"He went in the army. He said he was going to learn how to drive, and we could get married when he got out."

"What if it was somebody besides him?" her mother asked.

"Oh, I don't know," Misun said, brazenly ignoring her mother's feelings. "He's got a good personality, but he's lazy."

Her mother gave her a rap on the head and heaved a deep sigh.

"There's no other way. We've got to settle this. If you don't want an abortion, then write this creep and make him own up."

"Mom, he's not some knight in shining armor."

Her mother spoke half to herself: "Before we do anything else, we're going to get you out of this mess."

"All right, if you can find someone who'll accept the baby, then I'll marry him."

Kang's brother-in-law slapped his knee. "Terrific! Thank you, Lord."

"Oh, be quiet!" said Kang's wife. "My guts are so torn up I could die."

Misun was now completely philosophical: whatever happened was fine. A few tears dribbled out, and that was all. In truth she looked less dejected than her mother. "I'll do it your way."

"Oh, how wonderful. Crazy bitch!"

Her mother tried to make a rough estimate. It looked as if the wedding would come to thirty or forty thousand wŏn, no matter how she worked it. And there was the twenty thousand Misun had borrowed at daily interest when she ran away. To make good on the debt and then pay for a wedding would easily require fifty thousand wŏn. In addition, someone had to provide for Misun until she was able to go back to work at the wig factory. But the immediate question was, who would want this young thing for a wife? As soon as one cause for concern disappeared, a new one cropped up.

"This is going to be quite a project.... What happened to that money you borrowed, anyway?" she asked Misun.

"I took out a room. And the ten thousand that was left . . . I blew it the month after he went in the army."

"You should've gone to hell instead. Then I'd feel better."

They needed money—that was the bottom line. Kang's wife tried again to calculate how much Kŭnho would bring home that month. Since he'd put in a lot of time on the night shift, he'd probably make at least fourteen thousand. What if they could get by on barley and wheat flour on the money Kang brought home? And they'd have to rent out the back room. But there was no guarantee that events would tally with this scenario. As for blood relatives, there was just her brother. If he could help out with ten thousand for the ceremony, how proud of him she would be! She picked up her brother's Bible and shook it in front of his nose.

"Eating comes first, then Jesus and all the rest. You think you can save the world by locking yourself up in that mountain chapel for the rest of your days? I wish you'd make a clean break with them, so you could get your hands on some money."

"Sister . . . now what's wrong with my being there? It's the least I could do after God helped me get over my mental problems. And starting next month I'll be in charge of the chapel and get thirty thousand a month to live on."

"That's what I like to hear! I'll lend it out at high interest. And how about ten thousand for the wedding?"

"I'll bring that up with the evangelist."

"Good luck! And I suppose the next thing you'll tell me is that it's your turn to get some of the money those people donate who go there to bow and pray—those sinners with heavy hearts and the ones who have such a tough life."

"You'd be surprised. The financial situation at the chapel really is better these days."

As soon as Kang's wife had made up her mind about her daughter, her worries seemed to ease. Although the family was pinched from day to day and occasionally in danger of breaking up because of its poverty, the five of them managed to survive. There's always a way . . . things will work out somehow. She had made a vague decision to go through with a wedding, but that child inside Misun was more worrisome than anything else. A baby without a dad? No way.

"I've never had money to live on—only deception," she mumbled to herself as she stepped down into the kitchen.

2

A bonfire blazed in the field across the sewer ditch, fed by apple boxes split by Kang's neighbors. In the pitch darkness where one day a factory would stand, the flames shot up to reveal weeds head-high among piles of rubbish. Humming and chuckling could be heard amid the stir of the men gathered about the fire. As soon as the flames had come to life and the fire had stopped smoking, they had strung up the dog and begun singeing off its hair. When you have fire, liquor, and meat, it's only natural that you'll give fresh life to a gathering. And these men chuckled and swapped jokes like a bunch of mischievous country boys who had just stolen some chickens. The womenfolk watched this cheerful group with satisfaction, for their men were usually irritable and dispirited in the evening. The women remained on the far side of the ditch, but the impetuous little ones had crossed over and were hanging around in clusters among the grownups. Their faces and naked chests flickered crimson, and the smell of scorched fur filled the fireside air.

In groups of half a dozen or more, the men made a point of thanking Kang. Since they had all contributed toward the bucket of *makkŏlli,* no one felt like a deadbeat waiting for the meat. Water was boiling in the iron kettle brought by Boss. The dry wood crackled, and fat ran from the skin of the dog, now stripped of its fur and black as coal. The men talked about the neighborhood that had sat until this day below the roof-tile factory, occasionally looking apprehensively at the flat expanse where not a dot of light could be seen.

"We're pretty lucky, aren't we?" said the gray-haired, bespectacled head of the neighborhood association. "The people at the district office say that since our neighborhood's been here more than ten years, they'll compensate us. Anyway, there shouldn't be any problem before next year."

"I sure hope not," said one of the other men. "After all, most of us came here to put in the foundation of that factory. That's how this neighborhood got started."

"So when they do tear down our neighborhood," the headman continued, "they'll pay fifty thousand wŏn per household."

"Damn—that's not too bad," the other replied.

"Come on, pal, don't let the booze go to your head. You think fifty thousand is enough for that imperial palace of yours?"

"Well, I guess not. . . . Yeah, it's an imperial palace to us, all right."

The loud jangle of a bicycle bell sounded behind them. A tall, well-built man with several wooden tubs piled on the carrying rack of his bicycle came alongside.

"Looks like you boys planned on counting me out of this one."

"Tŏkpae—you're just in time. How about the liquor peddler treating us to some drinks, huh?"

"Yeah, take the night off from that booze stand of yours and get some nourishment into you."

Tŏkpae propped the bicycle against the inside of his thigh. "How'd it turn out?" he asked the headman. "Did someone say each household gets fifty thousand?"

"I'm not sure when they'll tear the houses down, but I think we're safe for this year. Just remember—I've been busting my ass on this." The headman patted himself on the chest.

Tŏkpae thought for a moment as he whisked away the sweat streaming down his forehead with the back of his hand.

"What about a case like this: I'm thinking of renting out one of our rooms. When it's time for us to get out, would the tenants get fifty thousand too?"

"You'll have to work that out in advance and get it down in writing."

"Could you help me out? They're coming tomorrow, and you're the only one I can count on."

"You need a witness? Okay—but you'll have to treat me."

"No problem."

"Hey, Tŏkpae, we've got an empty room too, you know," said Kang, who had been thinking of every possible way to pay off Misun's loan. Despite wrangling with his wife, he felt remorse over Misun's predicament. It was a fact that he had never shown any affection to Misun and Kŭnho. "You meet a lot of people on the street. Why don't you find someone for us, too?"

"Let's wait and see," Tŏkpae replied. "The people who're coming tomorrow might know someone."

"What kind of work do you suppose these guys are going to do?"

"What do you think? Anyone who's looking for a place around here is up from the countryside putting in for factory work—remember?"

"Yeah, I suppose so."

"Considering the room, I ought to be able to get twenty thousand from those hicks," said Tŏkpae.

"Listen to this guy! . . . I suppose you're not a hick?"

"Cut it out. I've been drinking city water for six years now."

"And you still don't know your way around town. You think this here isn't the sticks? Let me tell you something, buddy—this is the boondocks."

Tŏkpae turned away from the boisterous joking, pushed off on his bicycle, and passed by the field. The traces of furrows made the road bumpy. Every time the wheels caught on something Tŏkpae cursed to himself: "Scummy, idiot bitch!"

He couldn't help being in a foul mood, for his wife had told him to go home and cook more noodles for the liquor stall. This meant business was good these days, but wasn't it a fact that the goddamned broad didn't have an ounce of foresight? They'd taken a beating on that tub of sea cucumbers she'd bought: the things had turned bad and she'd had to toss them. Ditto with half the sausage. She knew that the people on the night shift always ordered noodles, but just the same she'd come up short.

Tŏkpae crossed the sewer ditch on a plank bridge connecting the cement embankments and walked his bicycle onto a broad asphalt street that stretched right and left. In both directions were bright streetlights and a row of factories. The solitary sound of machines filled the empty street. The liquor stall was at the edge of the ditch where the factory buildings and an abbreviated commercial area came to an end. Inside the stall were seats fashioned from logs and boards.

"Where the hell have you been?"

While Tŏkpae was parking his bicycle behind the stall his wife began ticking off a litany of grievances.

"We just lost a couple of parties, you know. . . . Did the big one go home?"

"I didn't see him."

"What did I tell you! I'll bet he's got his eyes glued to the TV in the comic book shop again. . . . Just wait till that little bastard shows up."

Innocently clicking his tongue, Tŏkpae set down the tubs of noodles with a thud and went inside the stall. A man who had been swilling *makkŏlli* held up his glass in greeting. He was a peddler of transistor radios who stopped by every evening for a drink.

Tŏkpae responded with a nod. "Well, look who's here," he said uneasily. "That old lady of mine is getting carried away."

"Life has a way of doing that to people."

"I couldn't have put it better myself. Making a living is one big headache."

"I'll bet I walked thirty miles today, and that's no lie," the peddler said with a sigh. He stroked his sparse beard. His face was always melancholy. Though his expression was less somber now than several months before, it was still a bit gloomy. That spring he had been released from prison. It was no big deal, he had said, but according to the gossip of the people across the ditch, he had been jailed for sticking a knife in his deranged wife.

Tŏkpae hoped the peddler wouldn't drink too much that evening. He was quite familiar with the lethargy and insecurity that dwelled in the faces of the men who had lost their jobs, and he knew that when the peddler grew excited he would sometimes crow about his days as a clerk. Realizing the peddler lived in the neighborhood that had been leveled that day, Tŏkpae became completely ill at ease. And today of all days the snack plate was empty except for a couple of deep-fried morsels. He chopped up some baby octopus and set it on the plate.

"You must be tired," Tŏkpae said to the peddler. "Maybe you ought to hustle on home."

"Well, I guess I could . . . but it's so godawful hot I think I'll take it easy here."

"Was there some trouble in our neighborhood today, honey?" Tŏkpae's wife asked.

Tŏkpae elbowed her, at the same time nonchalantly offering the peddler a cigarette.

"Trouble?" the peddler asked laconically.

"Uh . . . let's see . . . oh yeah, everybody had to line up for water—boy, it's been dry," said Tŏkpae.

As if she had just remembered something, Tŏkpae's wife untied her apron, grumbling all the while.

"Damn brats. . . . You mind the place, okay?"

"Just forget about them, huh?"

"They don't study like I tell them to. Every day it's the TV or the comics—I'm sick and tired of it. And they're always getting into the money box."

Tŏkpae sighed. "Educating the kids takes a lot of effort," he told the peddler, who was calculating some of his customers' monthly payments. "I'm trying every way I can to get the big one through school so he can get a desk job. . . . I only went to middle school, and look at me."

The peddler smiled.

Tŏkpae's wife rushed out shouting, "When the factory kids come, check the account book and get what they owe for last month's rice cakes. I'll be right back."

"Hey, woman!"

Just as Tŏkpae was going out after her, an old man entered the stall and ordered a bowl of noodles and broth. Tŏkpae had no choice but to return. The man toted a folding chair and a whetstone worked by a crank. Probably sharpens knives and scissors, Tŏkpae thought. While Tŏkpae was preparing the noodles, the old man looked over the various rice cakes. After a while he took out some coins and counted them several times.

"How much for one of those sticky ones?"

"Ten wŏn. A couple will fill you up more than plain rice. Sticky rice is the best thing if you can't get a square meal."

"Okay, I'll take one."

"Excuse me, mister," said a young man of about twenty in a thick, husky voice. He had bushy hair and wore a gaudy shirt.

"Hey, it's Kŭnho. What's up?" Tŏkpae said casually.

"Oh, not much—just out for a snort. Can you get me a drink?"

"Looks like you've done some snorting already," Tŏkpae said disapprovingly. Only then did he discover that Kŭnho's left hand was completely bandaged. "What's wrong with your hand? Aha, been in a scrap."

"Huh? Oh, this. . . . Yeah, I went a couple of rounds with somebody."

"Nice boys who think about their mothers avoid that sort of thing. . . . Looks like your sister came back, young fella."

Kŭnho hesitated as he was reaching for the kettle of *makkŏlli*.

"Who?"

"You know who . . . Misun."

Kŭnho scowled, then shook his head roughly. For a moment he looked down vacantly toward his feet. Then, regaining his composure, he drank a glass of *makkŏlli*.

Tŏkpae served the old man his noodles and turned to the peddler. "How much do you make in a day?"

"Oh, maybe a thousand wŏn."

"Hey, that's not bad."

"That's on a good day. It's a different story during the rainy season and when it gets hot."

"I know, I used to be a salesman myself. This time of year, why don't you try parasols or something? You know, if you sell them on credit, the housewives get jealous of each other and snap them up one after the next."

"Parasols! They went out with straw shoes. Different things are in fashion now."

"Yeah, I guess times have changed. Would you believe I made two million wŏn selling them?"

"You must have felt pretty flush."

Tŏkpae couldn't help tossing down a glass of *makkŏlli*. "Fuck it. . . . Who the hell would've thought I'd end up like this?" Tŏkpae spoke over Kŭnho's head, which was still bowed as if the young man were mulling something over. "Two million, honest to god. . . . I'm telling you, once I started making money I couldn't think about anything else."

In a tone of exaggerated wonder, the peddler chimed in: "It's shit luck—that's all it is. Grab it, and you make so much money it's scary." He spoke like someone who had also made millions in the past.

"You made two million—in cash?" the old man asked Tŏkpae.

"One fell swoop, hot off the press."

"How long did it take?" asked the peddler.

"Just one summer." Tŏkpae grew animated. "At first I was hustling by myself. Then I gave my cousin and my brother-in-law in Taegu a piece of the action. If only I'd quit while I was ahead and set up a nice safe business. . . ." Tŏkpae struck himself on the forehead. "I just wish I'd known about the tastes of Seoul people. I come up here to Seoul, and you know what? I really did try to think things out. In business you've got to use your head. I had the capital, I had energy to burn, and when I stopped to think about it I realized that practically every house in Seoul has some old folks in it. Now if a gentleman wants to go out for a walk he needs a walking stick, right? So I sank all my money into walking sticks. I figured I could sell them in front of the temples and playgrounds. I had more than a hundred of them carved every day—even hired some kids and sent them out. Ah, what an idiot I was. . . . I can't figure this friggin' city out. The old folks didn't show up, and so the damn walking sticks were no better than kindling— that's the story."

"It sounds to me like you *didn't* use your head," said the old knife sharpener, who had been drinking his noodle broth. "If you want to know what an overnight fortune feels like, you'd better think like a thief. But for hicks it's the land that comes first. Walking sticks—that's what somebody from the countryside would dream up. I've got two kids, and if I don't work like a dog I can't get by in a big city like this."

All this talk had made Tŏkpae expansive. He was cranked up and felt like drinking his fill. Already he had finished half a kettle of *makkŏlli*.

The long hair of a young woman swept inside the canvas curtains of the liquor stall and then withdrew. Voices chattered outside.

"There's a lot of guys in there."

"So what? Is eating something to be ashamed of?"

Tŏkpae quickly followed the voices outside. Some factory girls on their way to work had stopped by for a snack. They all looked about the same age.

Well, well, thought Tŏkpae. Look at the little clams. He ushered in a cute, demure-looking one in pigtails.

"Come on in, girls. I'll whip up enough noodles to feed the whole bunch of you."

"You got rice cakes too, right?"

"You bet—all kinds. And I know how to make 'em tasty."

"Gee, those hands of yours are filthy."

"Knock it off. I'm always dipping them in water."

"Mister, when's the last time you took a leak?"

"Come on, I do my business with my hands behind my back."

While the banter continued, Tŏkpae went in through the canvas curtain behind the girls, a smile of satisfaction filling his reddish face. As the girls stepped inside, the cramped liquor stall swelled like a distended ball.

First the girls threw down a bowl of noodles apiece. Then they had some rice cakes and began to jabber.

"Hey, I've got a problem. I'm short on money again this month."

"Are we ever going to finish being apprentices and get to be regulars? I think I'm going to quit."

"We can't go back home now. You girls think you can?"

"If we stick it out for a couple of years, we'll at least pick up some job skills."

"Are you kidding? If that kind of work is a skill, then so is cooking rice and making love."

"Well, they are . . . if you can sink your teeth into a rich one."

"I could go work in a bar, or else latch onto some guy who doesn't know better."

"A factory boy?"

"No way. Even after ten years the best they can do is foreman."

The knife sharpener put his tools in place over his shoulder and went out grumbling: "God. . . . What in the world is it with these crude bitches? Don't they know how to keep their place with men? Ought to be ashamed going around at night cussing like that. If it was my girl I'd break her. . . ."

The girls cried out in alarm. Tŏkpae, putting a finger to his lips and gesturing with the other hand for the girls to relax, kept an eye on the old man as he left.

"Elderly men are all like that. They just think about the old days, or else they think they're back in the countryside going out for a good time."

"The old man might have been right," said Kŭnho, who had stopped drinking and become lost in thought.

"What!" said one of the girls.

"Don't get me wrong. I'm not saying you ladies did just like he said, but . . . frankly speaking . . . in this screwed-up area anyway, all someone has to do is sweet-talk the ladies and they put out. Isn't that right? I mean—"

"Look here, who do you think you're—"

"I'm serious!"

"Put out? Put out what?"

"Fix me up with a boyfriend, will you, mister?" one of the other factory girls said to Tŏkpae.

"How about me?" Tŏkpae replied. He looked around bleary-eyed at the girls, who were becoming more and more flippant.

A girl who was spitting out particularly trashy remarks answered coquettishly, as if she had been waiting for just that moment: "You're too old—I don't think you'll do."

"Anyone here who can pay our rent for us?"

"I'd rather have someone pick up our tab here."

Kŭnho interrupted in a voice just high enough with liquor: "Fuck! Now listen to me—*I've* got some money. So how about a date? I heard the Na Huna show's in this part of town."

The factory girls looked put off, as if their pride had somehow been injured.

"What time is it getting to be?" asked the demure one with the braided hair, who looked the oldest.

"Low-life bitches, you're ruining the mood," growled Kŭnho.

Tŏkpae made a flamboyant gesture and looked at his watch. "Ten to nine."

"Those of us who're off work tomorrow let's go see Na Huna," said Kŭnho.

The girls grew sullen at this. "Why don't you move on?" the cheeky one spat.

Someone outside called for Tŏkpae, and there was a glimpse of a policeman's cap and uniform. Tŏkpae's face suddenly tensed and he went out. The girls started jabbering again.

"Hey, last night that short little guard who gives us a body search every day tried to get me to go play badminton with him. I wonder what he thinks he can see at night."

"You know Myŏngja, the one who started working in Manufacturing the month before last? These days she's short on money, so she takes business trips to an inn. Then she comes to work and makes like she's so prim and proper. Well, one of the girls tells her she saw her coming out of an inn, and then she gives her a poke, like she knows what's going on, so Myŏngja takes her into the bathroom and starts bawling and begging her not to say anything."

"Kim, the engineer, says he's going to Japan pretty soon for technical training."

"That's the first thing he says to every good-looking girl in the office—it's the way he gets women."

"I wish I could learn some Japanese too and go to the main office."

"The likes of us can't even get near people from the main office. . . . That Miss Pak who works for Inspection—the skinny one, you know? I hear she's shacking up with the big wheel himself—Watanabe, or Waribashi, or whatever you call him."

"*Toyota-no, Honda-no, skoshi, Tokyo-no, sayonara,*" said Kŭnho, who was feeling cocky among all the cackling girls. And then without warning he broke into a boisterous song:

Ŏlsshigusshigu, here we go!
Chŏlsshigusshigu, here we go!
Where are we going to bury the wretch who never, ever
    saw Seoul?
In front of Seoul Station we'll bury the wretch who
    never, ever saw Seoul.
Factory boy, beggar boy, here we go!

The girls covered their ears, but Kŭnho, brandishing his bandaged hand, raised his voice to a howl as if he were the neighborhood tough guy:

In front of a college we'll bury the wretch who never,
    ever studied.
In front of Myŏng-dong we'll bury the wretch who
    never, ever spent money.
In front of a hotel we'll bury the wretch who never,
    ever went dancing.
In front of a comic shop we'll bury the wretch who
    never, ever read books.
In front of some yodelers we'll bury the wretch who
    never, ever went hiking.
In the red-light district of Chongno we'll bury the
    wretch who never, ever got married.
In Mugyo-dong we'll bury the wretch who never, ever
    went drinking.
In front of a chapel we'll bury the wretch who never,
    ever had a day off.
In front of a Western-style house we'll bury the wretch
    who never, ever rode in a car.
In Vietnam we'll bury the wretch who never, ever had
    chocolate.
In a rice pot we'll bury the wretch who never, ever had
    rice.
Factory boy, beggar boy, here we go!

Then, playing the part of a listener, he exclaimed, "God, it's noisy! Hey, beggar boy, I'll give you a coin. Now get lost!"

As Kŭnho began to repeat the song, Tŏkpae's head poked into the stall. "Hey! Will you be quiet? Don't you have any sense, boy!"

The girls stampeded outside to see what was happening. Tŏkpae, his hand on the back of his neck, was nodding continuously while the policeman admonished him in a low voice. Tŏkpae's wife approached as she was herding home their kids, faces puffy with sulky expressions. Having become the focus of so many eyes, the policeman lost interest in what he was doing. He gave Tŏkpae a couple of pats on the back and then crossed the street at a snail's pace.

"How much did he shake you down for?" Tŏkpae's wife asked, scowling at the policeman's back.

"Two thousand," Tŏkpae said dispiritedly, his shoulders sagging.

"God, there goes three days' business."

As if all of this were the children's fault, Tŏkpae's wife roughly jabbed them in the chops. They began to scream as if they were dying. Tŏkpae hurled his apron to the ground.

"Maybe I should feed 'em rat poison . . . or sell the whole goddamn bunch to the Chinaman," he muttered. "See, bitch? The cop knew I was looking after the place, so he came around and stuck out his hand."

While Tŏkpae and his wife were thus preoccupied, the girls slipped away one or two at a time. After arguing some more, Tŏkpae finally realized they were gone. He looked inside the stall and out, then set off down the street toward the factory, but he lost the girls at an intersection. He paused and caught his breath.

"What a shitty day! That woman always has to be bitching about something."

There was a flash of red beneath a utility pole on the other side of the street at the entrance to a dim alley lit up by a streetlight. Gotcha, thought Tŏkpae, his temper flaring. He ran straight over, and as he entered the alley he heard soft footsteps ahead of him. He drew nearer and nearer to the sound.

"Hey! You think you can run away from me?" he roared.

The girl stopped running but continued slowly down the alley. Then she came to a halt and looked back apprehensively. As Tŏkpae came up beside her she cringed.

It was the demure one. Tŏkpae grabbed her hand before she could say anything.

"Damn girls! If you don't pay you've got to leave something behind. . . . Come on, we're going to the police station right now!"

The girl squirmed backward, trying to huddle in a ball.

"You've got it all wrong, mister," she pleaded. "One of the other girls said she'd pay, but she ran away on us."

"No excuses. Pay up!"

"I'm telling you the truth. I'll give you the money for sure on payday. Have a heart, just this once. I have to get to work."

As he yanked her toward him Tŏkpae had a fleeting urge to let her go—it's only a lousy hundred wŏn, he told himself. But then this kind of thing had happened all the time in the early days of his neighbor-hood: the one who was fleeced was always the one who had shown others a good heart.

"If you don't have any money, you'll have to leave me something. You've got a watch, don't you?"

"No. I pawned it a few months ago, and I haven't gone back for it yet."

"Where do you live?"

"Over in those prefabs—building three."

"Let's get over there."

The girl's tone and gestures of supplication stopped. Shaking off Tŏkpae's hand, she set out ahead of him. The road to the factory ended and they passed through a market. Tŏkpae relaxed, knowing he could see the girl's red T-shirt ten yards away, and the girl, apparently decid-ing that one attempt to escape was humiliating enough, didn't look back once. They zigzagged down a narrow, muddy alley among the prefabs, which looked much more attractive than Tŏkpae's neighbor-hood, and entered the girl's building. Twenty families appeared to be living under that one roof. Both sides of the long hallway were lined with sliding doors, and from the rooms came the sounds of drunken rowdiness and the racket of men and women singing. The girl un-locked a door, stepped inside, and turned on the light. Tŏkpae couldn't quite bring himself to follow her in; his chest began throbbing.

"Come on in. This is all I have," the girl said, kicking aside a synthetic quilt lying in a heap on the floor. Two pots, two bowls, and some toiletries were lying on an overturned box that had once con-tained packets of instant noodles. Hanging on the wall were some shabby clothes, a photo of the singer Nam Chin with his shirt open at the chest, and a mirror; there was an ashtray on the floor. Feeling somewhat awkward, Tŏkpae sat down across the doorsill and lit a cigarette.

"You know, I didn't plan things this way, but that was pretty cheeky what you did."

The girl pouted and then with a knowing smile looked hard at Tŏkpae, but without making eye contact.

"Now that you've stopped me from getting to work on time, why don't you take the quilt and go."

"Well . . . maybe that's not necessary."

Tŏkpae's eyes traveled to a small piece of paper tacked to the wall.

Existence

Though life deceives you, my beloved,
    don't be sad or angry.
If days of sorrow are patiently endured,
    then days of joy are soon to come.
The present may be sad,
    but if the mind dwells in the future,
    then all is momentary.
And what has passed is what is yearned for.

Sea gulls and clouds appeared below the poem. Not bad, thought Tŏkpae; these kids must know something. Somehow he was reminded of the times he had wandered around by himself, and without really thinking about it he moved well inside the room.

"I'll . . . just . . . talk some and then go."

The girl sat uneasily with her back against the wall, singing a song about bygone days and an uncertain future.

"There's a saying that the hardships of youth are more precious than gold," said Tŏkpae. "But if you learn some job skills and eventually get married, then what's there to worry about?"

"Marriage? Oh, come on. . . ."

Tŏkpae liked the way she scowled.

The girl stretched her legs comfortably and punched down her short skirt, which she had gathered between them.

Tŏkpae anxiously tried to keep his eyes from straying to her white thighs.

"So you're going to get old and die all by yourself? You're in the prime of life—"

"Mister, as long as you're going to give me a break, could you do something else?"

"What's that?"

"Take care of our rent? I'll pay you back next month—promise. I've been sick this month and had to miss a whole week of work, so you can see I'm in the hole."

"You think I'm not playing with a full deck, or something?"

Tŏkpae was sitting so that the two of them faced each other. The girl undid her braids, and with fingers spread, pushed her hair back again and again. She looked much more feminine and mature now.

Tŏkpae wiped his sweaty palms on his knees and gulped.

"Good lord, how can a man's smell be so strong in a girl's room?"

The girl glanced up at the men's clothes hanging on the wall. "Three of my friends live here too."

"This room's a coffin. I'll bet it's like cordwood when the four of you lie down."

"We'll always be friends and nothing else—we made a pledge."

The girl raised her wrist to display two ink dots made with a needle to seal the promise.

Tŏkpae nodded. "Looks like you could switch off with each other when you lie down—you know, man, woman, man, woman."

"Okay, mister, now I get it. You didn't come here to get the price of those noodles. . . . At any rate, you got something up your sleeve." The girl lifted her arms and stretched.

Tŏkpae began inching his way toward her.

"You know, as far as family life is concerned . . . I haven't had any luck either."

The girl groaned. "Your heart won't stand it. Will you take the quilt and go right now?"

She subtly drew up one of her legs and piled her hair against the side of her head.

Until now Tŏkpae had been sobering up, but all at once he felt flushed with liquor.

"All I know is I lost money today—dammit!"

With the tip of his foot he jerked the door shut.

3

"Awk—awk—awk, byoo-tee-pool Sun-day, awk—awk—awk, byoo-tee-pool Sun-day."

Staggering along much like the peddler, Kŭnho kept repeating these few bars of a Western pop song that had caught his ear. He cared not that he knew only the one stanza. Every forceful, staccato "Awk!" lifted his spirits.

"It's the moment," he told the peddler. "We have to live for the moment."

"You bet! My place for another drink."

The peddler hoisted his load of radios higher on his shoulder, made a fist, and shook it resolutely in front of Kŭnho.

Kŭnho waved him off. "Uh-uh," he said, rapping his chest with the palm of his good hand. "I got some money today. Money . . . as much as a guy could want. There's a place called the Ch'ŏngju House down an alley near the neighborhood market. What do you say we drop by and give the girls a squeeze? Awk—awk—awk, byoo-tee-pool Sun-day. . . ."

The two of them stumbled past a tangle of barbed wire outside a row of warehouses that belonged to an appliance factory. Some muscular men clad only in shorts were loading boxes onto trucks. The women reporting for the night shift stood in line having their work cards validated. A siren sounded from the factory, and a pair of girls who looked like sisters ran by, gripping each other's hand. There were no streetlights beyond the path to the warehouses, and Kŭnho and the peddler could scarcely make out their feet in the darkness.

"How much do you make, anyway?" the peddler asked.

"Me? Shit . . . three hundred twenty a day."

"You talk pretty big for that kind of pay. I thought—"

Bristling, Kŭnho stopped, produced a thick envelope from his shirt pocket, and shook it in front of the peddler's nose. "We're not talking about pay. Take a look at this." Like a boxer, Kŭnho proudly raised the hand with the huge bandage. "It's a mess, isn't it? But it's a godsend, I tell you."

"What's this? . . . You been in a fight?"

"Fuck! You think I go around beating up on people? I had an accident. So I got pissed off and had a few drinks, and now I can't tell if I'm in a good mood or a bad mood."

"So they gave you money to get it treated."

"But I don't know whether it's too much or too little. Anyway, I lost three fingers, right in a row."

"Three?"

"Yeah. Thumb, index, middle. . . . Three in a row, bye-bye. So, don't I have a reason to treat?"

"I can't drink on that kind of money. Let's go to my place," said the peddler in a soft voice. He placed his arm under Kŭnho's.

Kŭnho briefly held his ground.

"Let's go to my place instead. I've got my own room."

"But didn't Tŏkpae say that runaway sister of yours came back?"

"Ah, that bitch! I could kick the shit out of her and it wouldn't satisfy me. I might just throw her out—no problem. You watch me—

the minute I see her I'm going to grab her by the scruff and give her a thrashing."

A gurgling sound interrupted this furious outburst, and Kŭnho hunched over and vomited at his feet. The peddler patted him on the back. Kŭnho, squatting in a heap, stuck the fingers of his good hand in his mouth and continued to throw up.

"Listen, fella—a woman's life can be hell if she hooks up with the wrong man."

Kŭnho hawked and spat, shook his head, and stood up with a sigh.

"Come again?"

"I said we ought to have a little sympathy for women."

"Yeah, I know. I heard you served time on account of a woman."

"No, I got mixed up in a labor dispute. Actually, I was one of the guys who stuck with management."

"Doesn't matter what side you're on. . . . If you get caught up in that stuff you get hurt."

"I acted like a peacemaker, but what I really wanted was to finagle some money from both sides so I could start my own business." The peddler clicked his tongue. Bit by bit his voice softened, as if it were retreating inside him. "It was a shitty thing to do."

"What's wrong with trying to make some money?"

"You live a little longer . . . and you'll find out. Are you happy you got yourself a pile of money for your hand?"

Kŭnho stared at his bandaged hand as if for the first time. It's only a bit of bad luck, he thought. And it's better than no money at all.

"Supposing I wasn't, what could I do about it? It was my fault."

"How much did you get, anyway?"

"Ten thousand apiece, so thirty thousand wŏn."

Kŭnho was told he would also be treated at no cost at the factory infirmary and receive an extra month's pay. It wasn't as if the higher-ups had been completely cold and calculating, Kŭnho was thinking. At any rate, he wanted to show the peddler that his spirits weren't that low.

"The doctor said drinking would do me in, but he was just trying to scare me. It's hard without booze when you're feeling as weird as I am."

The two of them arrived at the embankment along the sewer ditch. The peddler walked silently in front, head bent forward. Kŭnho did something extravagant: he bought two packs of Milky Way cigarettes and gave one to the peddler. They stepped onto the embankment.

"You ought to call it quits and get some sleep," said the peddler.

"Uh-oh, what's this? Backing out on me?"

"It's not that." The peddler quickened his pace. "I'm just saying go home and get some rest. Hell, we'll have another chance."

"What a bummer."

Kŭnho shot forth a long belch.

Transferring his load to the other shoulder, the peddler gazed across the sewer to the dark expanse where his neighborhood should have been. "Strange," he murmured to himself. "Is the power out?"

"I want to tell you I'm glad I got to know you. I mean it. Let's get together once in a while for a snort. . . . Awk—awk—awk, byoo-tee-pool Sun-day . . ."

"I'll see you at Tŏkpae's place. Where you headed?"

"Our house—over there at the foot of the embankment."

"Looks like they've got power . . ."

"What a bummer. No shit."

"Okay. See you later."

The peddler crossed the sewer ditch.

Kŭnho continued along the embankment. The insects grew still at every "Byoo-tee-pool Sun-day."

Kŭnho worked for a Japanese company in the woodworking shop of a factory that produced radio and television cabinets. All day long he cut plywood, veneer, or synthetic resins to a standard size, using an electric saw. That day he had started work at six in the evening. After he had cut about two hundred pieces of six-by-twelve plywood, word had come from Quality Control that the standard was off by a fraction of an inch. With a tape measure Kŭnho had laid out the new dimensions on a piece of stock. Next he had set this piece on the saw blade, preparing to make a new model. As usual, he had then stepped on the starter switch. "Ow!" Blood sprayed over his work clothes. A co-worker pulled him back. It wasn't the pain but rather the tingling chill in his left forearm, as if it had been struck by a sledgehammer, that he couldn't stand.

"Is that you, Kŭnho?"

It was his mother. She was sitting next to her brother on a straw mat spread out on the embankment. The two of them were enjoying the evening breeze.

Kŭnho remained standing. "Hi, Uncle," he said bluntly. Then, addressing his mother defiantly: "I heard Misun came back."

His mother nodded.

"Don't say anything," his uncle told him.

"That bitch—I'm going to . . . "

Kŭnho brushed past them and was about to step down from the embankment when his mother grabbed his forearm.

"Pretend you don't know. Things are working out okay now. . . . So, you've been drinking again."

"What's working out okay?"

"This fellow who might marry Misun was just here talking with us. He said he'd go over and see her."

"Ow—God, that hurts! Hands off, huh?"

Only then did Kŭnho's mother discover his bandaged hand.

"Well, isn't this nice. First you go out drinking, and then you get into a brawl, and now look at you. . . ."

"What kind of guy is this would-be bridegroom?"

Kŭnho's uncle rose and dusted off the seat of his pants. Well aware that his nephew always regarded him with displeasure, he spoke in a slightly self-conscious tone.

"Uh, what's his name . . . the one who heads up the Reconstruction Corps."

"You mean that old fart Yi, the one who's always acting like a big shot?"

"You'd never know it from looking at him," said Kŭnho's mother, "but I understand he makes an awful lot of money from second-hand stuff."

"Are you kidding? He's nothing but a fucking ragpicker. Mother, we were brought up in a decent farming family. Did you raise Misun to give her to some son of a bitch who's no better than the dirt under my feet? She's not like you, Mother. She's pure—pure!" Kŭnho said, indirectly criticizing his mother for remarrying. The liquor had loosened his tongue.

"Now you be quiet, boy. Pure? I wish. But she's not—she's . . . "

Clutching his forearm, Kŭnho squatted on the embankment and sighed through pursed lips.

"This throbbing is driving me crazy."

"Are you hurt bad?"

Kŭnho lit a cigarette and sank into thought: at this point, beating up his sister would only make him feel worse rather than less disappointed. He felt more and more resentful toward his mother.

"What does Misun have to say about all this?"

"Who knows? They're probably talking to each other right now."

Kŭnho shook his head and spat. He was quivering with emotion.

"Shit, what a low-life family."

"Something's gotten into you."

"Starting tomorrow, I'm not working."

"Now don't tell me you got fired. Wasn't it a fight?"

"I had an accident. I'll get my pay, same as always, so don't worry. And . . . "

Kŭnho produced the thick envelope and thrust it toward his mother.

"Take this and hold onto it. Don't let the old man know. And don't spend it unless you know what you're doing."

His mother took the money out of the envelope and glanced about uneasily.

"What's all this money for?"

"It's thirty thousand wŏn."

"Thirty . . . thirty thousand. . . . Where'd you get it?"

"From the company—I had an accident at work."

"My oh my—bless us. Thirty thousand wŏn at a time like this! You know, I didn't worry all that much—I knew there'd be a way out. This is wonderful!"

"And this throbbing is killing me. Maybe I need another drink."

While Kŭnho was rubbing his wrist, which had started to swell, his mother counted the money, holding the bills in front of her nose and folding them over one at a time. Murmuring could be heard from across the sewer ditch, and the bonfire was visible.

"What's going on over there? An ancestral ceremony?"

His mother remained absorbed in counting.

"Drinking," his uncle said, clicking his tongue.

"Say, there's only twenty-eight thousand. . . ."

"Oh yeah—subtract two thousand for the drinks."

"Two thousand! What have you been swilling? If you'd come right home you could've drunk for free and had your fill of dogmeat."

"Dogmeat? Where'd they get their hands on a dog?"

"Your father got one as big as an ox. There's enough for a dozen big men to gnaw on all evening, and then some."

"Instead of bringing home money—he ought to be ashamed."

"It's no skin off my back if you don't want to eat."

Kŭnho was about to express further dissatisfaction with Kang, but gave up. As people say, even a worthless husband is better than a filial son.

"So Misun and that guy are the only ones at home now?"

His mother pleaded with him to understand. "Yeah. Go on over and say hello. See how things are going, and try to keep the ball rolling."

Kŭnho became noticeably less testy. He clicked his tongue. "As far as I'm concerned," he muttered, "if Misun turns out okay, I'll be happy. But I'm not going to butt in. This is the bitch who was screwing around and ran away, and she's not going to listen to anyone this time either. Nothing left to save for her husband. She's just a pain in the ass. Are you really serious about this marriage?"

"Why not?" said his mother as she stuck the money in her waistband. "Since he mentioned it first and he's already following up, I'd just as soon be done with it. If they want to get married in the next few days, fine."

"There's going to be gossip. Selling off a pregnant girl—that's what they'll say."

"Now look you—are we supposed to take you seriously when you run off at the yap like that?"

"I can guess what you'll use that thirty thousand for."

"So, you're going to feel sorry for yourself if we put that money toward the wedding? Isn't she your only sister?"

"Sister, I don't think that's what Kŭnho meant. He said it because he's proud to be helping out."

Uncomfortable with this flareup, Kŭnho's uncle gently prodded his sister.

"Dammit!" Kŭnho shouted as he picked his way down the embankment. "That money cost me three fingers, that's what!"

"Well, well, a brat who couldn't care less about his sister. So you got hurt—you can get it treated. When the family's threatened like this, we all have to make some adjustments and get through it the best we can. Now look—if you're going to act like the servant who became chauffeur, then who needs your help?"

Kŭnho scuttled across the sewer ditch toward the field where the dogmeat was supposed to be.

His mother poured out more invectives, but then tears of remorse began to trickle from her eyes. Before long she was unburdening herself to her brother, telling of her years selling rice cakes to support the two children.

"Well, like I said, you'll find peace if you believe in the Lord," said her brother as he patted her rhythmically on the back.

"I guess I'd better visit one of those Jesus temples before I get any older."

"Now that's more like it."

They rolled up the straw mat and headed home. The men and children had long since departed for the field, and the neighborhood was perfectly still. The women were sleeping here and there on mats along the paths.

The two of them stopped in front of the kitchen and peeked inside the house. They heard the gravelly voice of Boss as he made his case before Misun.

"Even wild geese fly off together, so why can't two lonely people like us try to make a go of it? In my thirty-five years I've been through every hardship you could imagine, and I haven't blinked once. But I haven't met a woman who suits my fancy. Heh-heh. Now I don't look at life in terms of black and white. When I heard you came back, that opened up some old wounds and I got angry.... But I made up my mind. It's forbidden fruit all right, but who cares whose baby it is? I'll be the dad and we'll bring it up together."

Boss seemed intoxicated by his own glibness.

"I may not look like much, but I've got an Eagle hi-fi and thirty LPs worth of tunes from the old days.... I've got a cinder-block house that I built with my own hands, and we'll lay in a little old TV and a mother-of-pearl wardrobe."

Kang's wife prodded her brother firmly and nodded.

"Look at that. Now if Misun will just answer him, the wedding'll be in the bag. Goodness, I've never seen a man propose that fast—like lightning!"

Misun said something in a low voice, and then Boss could be heard chuckling.

"Fine and dandy. I've got a big announcement to make to the neighbors, and then I'll be back."

The door rattled open as if it were about to fall from its hinges, and Boss's broad, smiling face, flushed with satisfaction, popped out.

Kang's wife, standing nearby, grabbed his wrist. "What'd she say?" She now addressed him less formally and politely.

"Mother-in-law, I may not be much to look at, but I want you to know, back in the old days I was quite the man. Now you can just rest easy. I made her melt like taffy in the summer sun. It's not easy for a godforsaken old bachelor to find a wife."

But from inside came a distressful sniffling. It was impossible to tell whether Misun was crying with joy, or with relief that there was a way out.

"Now hush up!" shouted her mother. "Just sit tight and count your blessings."

"Well—I'm in the mood for a drink. I'll be back."

Breaking into another meaningless chuckle, Boss hurried off toward the field.

The drinking party was winding down, and most of the men were pleasantly drunk. Some were dancing in nimble leaps, others reeled off songs. Sparks shot from beneath the nearly empty stewpot. Kang was about to finish a second heaping bowl of dog soup. Kŭnho lay snoring on the bare ground where he had sprawled out after shouting one last chorus of "Byoo-tee-pool Sun-day." Buckets and aluminum bowls were tumbled about the stewpot—it was a lavish scene, resembling a family ancestral ceremony.

Boss made a deep bow and prostrated himself before Kang.

"Please accept this greeting from your son-in-law," he said gallantly.

The revelers simultaneously came to a halt and gaped at the two of them.

"What's this all about, pal?"

Boss uttered his meaningless chuckle, rose, and offered Kang half a bowl of slightly stagnant *makkŏlli* from the bottom of the bucket.

"Sorry to surprise you like this. Misun and I decided to get married. Father-in-Law, I offer you this drink."

"Well, looks like we'll be drinking every day for a while."

"In any event, we've got something to celebrate tonight," said another, slapping his knee.

The head of the neighborhood association came forward:

"Let's not forget who saved our neighborhood. Remember, I've got what it takes to make a case to the authorities."

"We've had dogmeat, booze, a good time all around. . . ."

"So—Misun's going to have a husband, and you there—you don't have to sleep by yourself anymore."

You could feel an extraordinary vitality everywhere in the field. The men sang, danced, and squabbled drunkenly until the fire went out and the iron stewpot grew cold. At last, weary and exhausted, they found their way back in ones and twos to their cramped rooms, which had cooled in the night air. Those passed out were dragged away or led off with a supporting arm by family members. Kǔnho remained face up on the ground. The embers lingering in the fire glowed near his feet.

Misun, dressed in her slip, crossed the sewer ditch. Her stomach protruded, but she looked like a little girl as she skipped smartly from one stepping stone to the next. She reached her suffering brother, who was moaning listlessly, and gently shook him. A fellow drunk to the gills passed by on the embankment singing a song.

Translated by Bruce and Ju-Chan Fulton

Winter Outing

Pak Wansŏ

Until the age of forty, Pak Wansŏ (b. 1931) had not revealed her literary talents; rather, she had married and raised five sons and daughters. But with the publication of her debut work, *Bare Tree* (Namok), in 1970 she emerged as a leading writer, and has since produced more than seventy stories and novels. "Winter Outing" (Kyŏul nadŭri) first appeared in *Munhak sasang* magazine in 1975. She has received both the Korean Writers' Award (1980) and the prestigious Yi Sang Award (1981). Some twenty-five collections of her work have been published.

Her language, enriched by the skillful use of irony and metaphor, implies much about the characters and their world with a minimum of authorial intervention. Like many Korean writers of fiction, Pak spends more time on people and their attitudes than on physical description. While using objective description to establish a physical setting, she conveys most of her information through the language of her characters and, in her first-person narratives, the attitude of her narrator. We are told less about how things *appear* to the narrator and more about how they make her *feel*.

In "Winter Outing," for example, the world of Seoul, and the artist's studio that is evoked in the opening section, comes across to us as cold, cerebral, impersonal—one from which the narrator seems emotionally distant. This sense of alienation continues through her arrival at the hot springs, growing more striking and intense until it culminates in the icy harshness of a frozen lake and the unpopulated alleys of a shuttered resort. Her relief is almost palpable as she discovers the inn and the warmth of its proprietor and engages in meaningful human interaction for the first time in the story.

In a brief essay about "Winter Outing" that appeared in *Hanguk munhak* magazine in April 1986, Pak Wansŏ remarked that the pivotal character, Grandmother No-no, was based on a real person, the great-grandmother of a young girl from Chŏlla Province who once worked at the author's house. The story was like so many that came out of the Korean War, particularly from those districts that changed hands day and night. "We heard innumerable heartrending stories of good and simple people who had managed to survive only at the cost of mental trauma of one degree or another," Pak said.

"When I first heard of that head-shaking grandmother I was so very struck that I couldn't get her out of my mind. Not only did I find myself drawing extremely close to that grandmother but, before I knew it, I was actually gaining solace from her."

Before slipping into the bath and indulging myself in the pleasant sensation, I began to wonder selfishly whether this hot-spring water was the real thing or not. The shower and the two faucets labeled hot and cold, attached to the ordinary tile bathtub in this deluxe room at a second-rate inn, weren't the least bit different from what you would find at any cheap bathhouse. Just where, I wondered, is the proof that the hot water pouring from this faucet marked with a red circle is not just heated city water but rather hot-spring water that has gushed up out of the earth?

It wasn't that I had some rare chronic disease that required me to soak in the water; nor had I come here expecting some sort of power in the water, as touted by those who go on about such things. Actually, I was looking for an excuse to feel more sorry for myself. From the outset, the journey hadn't held portents of pleasure. It was a journey that seemed to have started off wrong, and I was of a mind to let it end up in total disaster.

Though not commercially popular, my husband was an artist of some standing who clung tenaciously to his own rather peculiar artistic outlook, for which he had made his name and gained critical recognition. Owing to preparations for his third one-man show, he had been spending several nights at his studio. Things were at the point where I would occasionally bring him food out of concern for his health or he would drop by the house only to change his clothing. The previous day, too, when I was downtown, I had bought some sliced beef and dropped by the studio. Our married daughter was there, modeling for my husband. This was quite a surprise to me since people almost never appear in my husband's paintings. I had thought he enjoyed painting only natural scenes and animals in highly simplistic or nursery styles. And this painting of a human figure was utterly different from my husband's usual style. It was dreadfully detailed, vivid, and realistic. Whether an exact likeness was appropriate was secondary; what concerned me most was the sudden loathing I immediately felt. It was as though I were looking at a portrait into which he had moved her soul. Even more sickening was the curious air exuded by model daughter and artist father. A soft, warm, and satisfying rapport between a loving father and daughter—that I can understand. But there was something more than father and daughter to their secrecy. It was plain to see that they wanted their intimacy for themselves. Though the two of them welcomed me quite politely, I felt like I was being kept at a distance.

Our daughter, now three years married and her first child just over a year old, was seated upright on the sofa with a prosperous and elegant beauty quite unlike that of her maiden years. As I was admiring my daughter in her prime, I was struck with a blinding, shocking realization. Right! It was just about that very age! My husband's separation from his first wife in the confusion of the war took place when she was as old as our daughter was now. Moreover, this daughter was not my own, but had been born to my husband and his first wife. Daughters always resemble their mothers and there was no question that my husband recalled through his daughter the appearance of his wife when he left her behind in the North. Though I was considerably younger than that woman, I was the one, now growing old and ugly, at my husband's side, while that woman lived within my husband's heart, glowing with our daughter's present youth and beauty. As I realized this, I felt jealousy raising its viper's head. To accommodate a woman's jealousy, there generally must be a hank of hair for her to grab. But, at this moment, whose hair could I grab? I had no choice but to seem ordinary and restrained—a difficult and painful task. Insistent feelings of jealousy gave way to a sense of utter disappointment, as if I had lived my life so far in vain.

I had thrown myself energetically into the task of living, but. . . . To have pitied and then loved and then even married this unknown painter of insecure occupation, twelve years older than me, who had left his parents and wife behind in the North and come south as a penniless refugee with a baby daughter on his back; to have smoothed away the distress of this womanless man and motherless child and to have loved them and waited upon their needs these years now seemed, to my chagrined eyes, more like a lost labor. The more I mulled over this feeling of having lived vainly, deceived, the more I felt disgust and let it show in the grimace on my face. My husband and daughter asked solicitously if I were feeling all right. I answered that there were some things distressing me and that I should like to get away and knock around by myself for a while.

"All alone, in the middle of winter!" More than just surprised, my husband was nonplused. It had been bitterly cold for several days. Through the studio window, I could see the skeletal roadside trees and sparsely peopled, frozen sidewalks below. I was suddenly overwhelmed with emotion at the sight of winter in this dismal city. Now my talk of a trip, proffered only as a complaint at first, came back to me invested with a realistic feeling. I made up my mind on the spot that I would get out of town. More than wishing to leave Seoul or to get away from my husband's side, I wanted to cast aside like worn-out shoes this life I had fashioned so perseveringly and to live free and unfettered. As if the bleak winter day outside had taught me that my life had been a complete waste, I suddenly felt an unreasoning yearning for the winter scenery of some distant place. Not caring whether my husband and daughter would be suspicious or surprised, I agitated to leave immediately.

"Well, I guess there's a time for even you to be temperamental!"

With that degree of understanding, my husband gave me a generous travel allowance, while advising me that I would best go to a hot springs since it was winter. I left my husband with the mentality of someone who had just discovered that a cherished treasure was a fake and, as a first reaction out of disgust, tossed it aside.

I went to Onyang by the most convenient means. No sooner had I stepped from the express bus into the unfamiliar street than I was seized by the cold and a feeling of loneliness. The unfamiliarity of the scene before my eyes brought me to the brink of tears. My mood of unfettered freedom was no match for the alien and unwelcoming streets of the hot springs. It seemed most unlikely that I would settle into such a mood. Only my body had ventured forth. In the face of this

I smiled grimly as I realized I was tied to patterns of living which had long since permeated my being. Having my generous travel allowance, I headed toward the tourist hotel but then, turning on my heels, found a cheap, second-rate inn. As is my habit when buying sesame oil, I seriously questioned whether their hot-spring water was the real thing. Nevertheless, I took one bath after another despite the inevitable enervation, as if I were saving the cost of a public bath against the room charge at the inn. I was disgusted the next morning by their breakfast tray, in spite of its fifteen side dishes, as if I had been bored by such food for days on end. It was actually only my second meal there. I felt like I had been away from home a long time, but in fact I had spent no more than one night away. This realization saddened me to tears.

An errand boy at the inn came to ask whether I was leaving or whether I would stay another day. I felt as if the boy would feel sorry for me if I said I was staying, and so I told him I was leaving right away. Having packed my small overnight bag and emerged on the street, I felt like I had been driven from the inn by that boy, just as I had been driven from the house by my husband and daughter. The cold here was every bit as severe as it was in Seoul. The lowering sky and harsh wind were well suited to my bitter ruminations on my feeling of fraudulence at having lived wastefully thus far.

The streets of this small hot-springs town were not very extensive. Though I made the rounds of the place a dozen times, it didn't take even an hour. I dropped into the tourist hotel and had a cup of coffee. If I was to pretend to my husband that I had stayed at the tourist hotel, then I ought to have some idea of what the interior is like, I thought. Across the street from the hotel, I caught sight of a bus terminal. Antiquated buses, posted with the names of unfamiliar destinations, were turning over their tired motors as the passengers were being called. I saw a way out of my plight. Grabbing anyone I could find, I asked if there weren't some scenic or historical spots worth visiting nearby. The bus girl jumped down from a bus which had just begun to leave and, before I had a chance to say anything, swept me up like so much baggage. I stumbled aboard and found a seat. With less than a dozen passengers, the interior was deserted. The vinyl seat was as cold as a slab of ice.

"Where are we headed?" I asked in an apprehensive voice as the bus gathered speed.

"I'm to let you off at the lake, right?" the bus girl announced, as if I had at some point asked her to take me as far as the lake.

"Lake?"

"Yes, the lake. It's the only place around here that has any good scenery. Except for winter, we have all sorts of passengers going there!"

Less than five minutes later, the bus girl demanded my fare and, saying we had arrived at the lake, shoved me off the bus. There was, indeed, a lake there. Solidly frozen, surrounded by a low, bare mountain, it looked gloomy and opaque, as if the sullen sky had simply sat down on the spot. Then, all of a sudden, a jealous wind licked fiercely at the icy surface of the lake and swept up toward me, slapping my cheeks heartlessly like a whip. I hastened to reboard the bus. But it had already left for the next stop, leaving only dust in its wake. Close to tears of utter defeat, I first of all hurried to the lakeside shopping area to escape the harsh wind. A rather large signboard reading *Pleasure Park* hung high above the arched entrance to the shopping area, suggesting the prosperity it enjoyed in any season but winter. But now the shutters on the restaurants, tearooms, variety shops, and gift shops were tightly closed and there was no sign of habitation. There were only faded signs rattling dismally with each gust of wind, worsening my feeling of desolation. Several open-air Ping-Pong tables lay coated with frozen snow and layer upon layer of dust; it made a miserable sight, like filthy bedspreads scattered about. There seemed not a single occupied building. I felt so helpless I could only wish it were just a dream. I made one tour of the shopping area and again confronted the frozen lake spread out before me. Although it was impossible to launch a boat on a lake that was frozen solid, it was also impossible to throw oneself in to drown. This did not seem the least fortunate; rather, I thought it fearful.

I went searching recklessly into yet another alley. And, indeed, at some distance down this otherwise lifeless alley I could see a house with a tidy front and an open gate with a sign that read *Lodgings*. Spent coal briquettes were stacked by the main gateway and, within the courtyard, white laundry hung frozen to a clothesline, twisted into queer shapes. In a trembling voice I called for the innkeeper. A presentable woman in her fifties emerged from the main building, smiling a warm welcome. Upon seeing her I relaxed as if I had come to my own house and, indeed, wished I were a child for whom she would care. This woman had about her a most uncommon ambiance. There was something about her that seemed to wrap me in protection, warm and good and generous like quilted clothing. I felt as if something I had forgotten for a very long time had made its way back to me.

"I was hoping to thaw out some before moving on. Do you have a warm room available?"

The woman promptly led the way to one of several guest rooms in the front wing of the house and slipped her hand under a taffeta quilt that was spread over the warmest spot on the heated floor. It seemed warm enough, but she was troubled by the chilly drafts. Sorry for the trouble, I asked the woman if I really looked all that cold. I was moved to laughter, but my frozen cheeks would not form into a smile of their own accord.

"Yes, you look just like an icicle. For heaven's sake, let's go into the family room! The floor is all warmed up and we have a heater there, too."

And so, with unreserved sisterly affection, she led me into the main building. In addition to the heater, a curtain had been hung around the inside of the family room, making it as dim and cozy as the interior of a cave. At first I thought there was nobody else in the room, but as my eyes became accustomed to the gloom, I could see an old lady decorously seated at the warm end of the room. The desiccated old lady, looking like a mummy draped with clothing, stared at me without expression and shook her head to the left and right. Since her behavior signaled disapproval, I hung back, awkwardly. But the woman insisted on drawing me to the warm end of the room and, there seating me, put my hands under the quilt which the old lady had spread to seat herself. The old lady's lips smiled a little. But she did not stop shaking her head. The woman told me that this was her mother-in-law and then said to the old lady that I was a guest whom she had invited into the family room since I was so cold. And with that, introductions and greetings between me and the old lady were completed. But the old lady continued her head-shaking as before. The woman offered no explanation.

Although gaunt, the erectly seated old lady possessed a singular elegance: Her neatly combed white hair was done up in a chignon, and over her traditional silk jacket with its crisp white collar was draped a soft wool sweater. It was, indeed, an extremely unreal elegance. Compared with what I had seen at first, her head-shaking had abated considerably, now looking more like she was swaying in a gentle breeze. I thought perhaps she might stop after a while, but no matter how long I waited she didn't stop. As my body thawed, I became drowsy. Honeyed sleep was overwhelming me—even if someone proposed to kill me I would have had to sleep on it.

"I'm pretty well thawed out now. I think I'll have a nap in that room we were just in. Oh, yes, how many minutes between buses back to the hot springs?"

"Minutes? In the winter we have only two in the morning and two in the afternoon. Since the one you came on was the last morning bus, the next one will be about four-thirty. Well, now, how about lunch? I'll be preparing some anyway, so why don't you have something to eat before you go?"

All I could think of was sleep—food was the furthest thing from my mind, but I told her to go ahead. The woman thanked me over and over again. I felt pity, believing that she was fussing so much over the little bit she would make by selling one meal. When I arrived at my room, I stretched out on the nice hot floor, pulled the taffeta quilt over me, and fell into a deep sleep.

The head-shaking old lady was the first thing that came to my mind as I woke up. While it was still unclear to me whether I had seen her in a dream or in reality, the picture of the withered old lady shaking her head floated vividly before me. The curiosity I had deferred because of my sleepiness slowly reasserted itself. I looked at my watch—it wasn't even two o'clock.

"Are you still asleep, ma'am? I should expect you're hungry."

I heard the woman's quiet voice outside the paper door. I stirred a bit and slid open the door. The woman, an apron wrapped around her waist, welcomed me out of sleep with the very same show of pleasure as when she had greeted my arrival at her house. She was so pleased to see me up that I even wondered if perhaps she hadn't mistaken me for one of those guests who take some sort of medicine and dispatch themselves to eternal sleep.

The lunch tray soon arrived. Her rather well made preserves, such as the marinated sesame leaves, unripened hot peppers, and wild carrots and the other foods—the kimchi, the spicy radish chunks, the steamy radish soup—were not the least bit like what is served in commercial places. They were gratifyingly similar to what you might receive if you dropped in on country relatives. But my mouth was parched and my appetite did not respond. When she saw me gulp down only the bowl of soup, the woman brought me another hot bowl of radish soup. Urging her to join me in the meal, I drew the woman down to sit beside me.

"Oh, my, that's not at all necessary! I ate earlier with Mother."

Since the woman was first to bring up the subject of her mother, I was able to ask naturally about the old lady's head-shaking.

"Your mother doesn't appear to be much pleased with me. Though she didn't say anything, she was shaking her head all the while I was in the room."

"She's been doing that for some twenty-five years now."

"Twenty-five years!" I was too startled to close my mouth.

"Yes. Twenty-five years, day in and day out, except for when she sleeps . . ."

I thought I saw the woman's eyes grow moist, but her manner of speaking was composed and tranquil.

To shake her head day in and day out, except when asleep, for twenty-five years was, she explained, her mother-in-law's task in life. When she was healthy and in a good mood, the shaking would be serene, barely visible, as if her head were waving in a gentle breeze; when she was in poor health, the movement would become more pronounced and laborious; and when she was agitated or upset by the household, the movement would grow even stronger and more determined until she would be chaotically shaking her head for dear life as if ranting, "I don't know! I don't know, I tell you!" They had scraped together whatever money they could lay hands on and tried all kinds of Chinese herbal medicines and even the most highly rated acupuncture, but all to no avail. The first one exhausted by this ordeal was the woman; but her mother-in-law, on the other hand, though it was distressing, rigorously devoted herself to doing this thing as if it were some fated task she could not set aside until her dying day.

This was a condition that had developed suddenly during the war. Her young husband, who had been a township administrator when the war broke out, was unable to flee in time and had to go into hiding. At first he hid inside their house, but when the ardor of the new circle that came to power began to turn bloodthirsty, hiding at home became so dangerous that it was out of the question.

Late one night, under cover of darkness, the woman hid her husband at her family's home village at the foot of Kwangdŏk Mountain, some five miles from their house. They did their job so well that only she and her mother-in-law knew of it. Conditions only continued to worsen. Informing became rampant as neighbor turned against neighbor, kin against kin, accusing one another of being "reactionaries"— the business had so spread that not a day passed without some bloody and ugly incident in one village or another. These were ugly days. Things had reached the point where the woman began to feel she couldn't rely on her own mother-in-law. She was concerned with what would happen if this unsophisticated old lady, honest to a fault and quite incapable of doubting others, were to fall for someone's deception and disclose her husband's whereabouts. It was not a world meant for people like her mother-in-law.

The woman relentlessly drilled her mother-in-law to say "I don't know," as if she were teaching multiplication tables to a thickheaded child.

"In any case, Mother, simply say you don't know. Even if the most remarkable person in the world asks, you simply must say you don't know where Daddy is. You must insist that he left the house the day the war broke out and you don't know what's become of him since. Lives are lost these days because of a little loose talk. Even if Daddy's brothers ask, you simply must say you don't know. Even neighbors like Ippŭni's grandmother or Kaettongi's grandmother, even if they ask, you simply must say you don't know. You can't trust anyone. There, do you understand, Mother?"

The woman energetically helped her mother-in-law, even with head-shaking, and they practiced the "I don't know" over and over again. Day after day, alone or not, a frightened and lonely expression on her face, the older woman earnestly practiced saying "I don't know, I don't know," also shaking her head at the same time.

Simple villagers, hearing only that war had broken out, were killing and being killed by one another as if possessed by the spirit of the legendary Chinese pillager Tao Zhi. And, in this village that had never once heard the sound of a cannon, suddenly planes had come to strafe and bomb without pause, and for days on end gunfire crackled in the surrounding hills like roasting beans. Then came silence, deep as death. One or two of the villagers, who had been cringing in their houses, still as dead rats, cautiously craned their necks but then quickly shrank back in again. They still hesitated to talk among themselves. There was no evidence that the Reds had left, yet nothing to indicate that they remained. There was no sign of the gangsters who had joined up with them and taken power, but their flag still fluttered from the pole in the yard of the village headman's house, which had been used by the People's Committee.

At this precarious and uncertain time, the woman's impetuous husband had stolen back to their house in the dead of night. Seoul had already been recovered, it seemed. The Reds had held out here, but how many more days could they last?

It was after the kimchi cabbage had already been planted in the kitchen garden and into the season of Cool Winds when young pumpkins, grown waxy, ripen so well. Mother-in-law, who had pushed through the morning dew out into the backyard to pick young pumpkins, suddenly gave out a rending cry.

"I don't know, I don't know! I really don't know, I tell you!"

It was a ghastly shriek, one that raised gooseflesh and made the blood run cold. The woman ran out and, in a moment of bewilderment, her husband joined her. For a moment, they had lost all discretion. Just around the corner of the outhouse, three or four tired and ragged People's Army soldiers, probably stragglers, had the barrels of their rifles leveled at mother-in-law. They, too, looked startled. It may well be that they never intended to cause anyone harm but, rather, that they met up with mother-in-law by accident or that, having met her, they were going to ask for food or clothing. But, before they could say a word, mother-in-law—nailed motionless to the spot—had shook her head madly and repeated in a high, shrill scream like someone deranged, "I don't know! I don't know!" In the moment it would take to catch the bloodthirsty glint in one of the stragglers' eyes, his rifle swung toward the woman's husband and sprayed bullets. The woman's husband toppled over, a wretched sight, and they took flight. This event had taken place in only an instant.

Thereafter the mother-in-law had seemed nearly deranged. After long and devoted care, she recovered somewhat, but the head-shaking, in which she engaged so strenuously upon her son's death by the corner of the outhouse, had diminished in intensity since that time but continued as a chronic condition that she couldn't halt. And so she became known to the neighborhood as Grandmother No-no, a local character.

The woman told this story with distance and detachment, not the least bit garrulous.

"And now, rather than thinking I should find a cure, my only thought is that I must help her."

"Help her? In what way?"

"As something she is not doing of her own free will, this must be very tiring. I do my best to see that she has three meals a day, that she is physically comfortable, and, well, that sort of thing. Can I not do that little bit until the day she completes her great undertaking and departs this world?"

I closed my mouth in failure as I tried to laugh at the woman's joke of referring to the endless days of demented head-shaking as a "great undertaking." Her attitude, after all, was not at all a joking one. Indeed, the woman's face even shone dimly with the pride and sense of duty of one who was actually assisting wholeheartedly in a great undertaking. A shiver passed down my back as I wondered if perhaps this woman was the one accomplishing the great undertaking.

Lunch and the room together came to eight hundred wŏn, she said. Giving her a thousand wŏn, I asked her to keep it all. The woman fussed and bowed and thanked me so much that I felt uncomfortable. She had done the same when I ordered lunch, but, in all, only a tiny profit would be left from the thousand wŏn. For this she was so obsequious? The reason I found her obsequious attitude so distasteful may well have been that I liked and esteemed the woman so much. Furthermore, the woman's obsequiousness seemed unnatural to her and, being awkwardly out of keeping, all the more ugly.

The woman carefully put the thousand wŏn into the pocket of her cardigan sweater and, having made a very relieved and grateful face, said something strange.

"With this as my travel money, I shall go to Seoul. Today."

"Seoul? On such a cold day!"

Having made this remark about the cold weather, I realized with surprise that I had used the very same kind of words that my husband had used to me when I told him I was going on this trip. I suddenly wanted to see my husband, to the point of sadness.

"My son, an only son, attends college in Seoul. The boy was riding on my back that day when he innocently watched his father encounter those circumstances. That boy, he's already so grown up! He did his army service and is now a junior in school. You know, he's really a good, trustworthy child."

"But it should be the middle of winter vacation now."

"Yes. But he's tutoring some children to earn extra money and so he couldn't come back home. I'm quite able to earn all he needs for tuition and such, but, well, that's what he says, anyway. It's lonely like this only during the winter, but from spring to fall business is pretty good here. During the tourist season, especially Sundays, we were running short of rooms and the place was a madhouse. I made enough to cover tuition and lodging for the new semester, which I wrapped up tightly and set aside. We have more than enough food stored away to tide us over the winter. If other businesses do as well, the owners close up and go home for a rest during the winter. We're an inn and this is also our family home, but we always keep one or two guest rooms heated and ready for customers. It's not to make money. We simply enjoy offering a warm room to uninformed visitors who, like yourself, sometimes come looking for the lake. Really. On such occasions we really give no thought to money. But, of course, if they happen to leave a bit so I can get a little meat or something for Mother, that's always nice. But today, that's not the case. Today, I actually waited for a guest, shamelessly calculating the income in advance. Really, if you hadn't come by I don't know what would have happened. Thank you, ma'am."

This time, instead of the servile bowing, she warmly grasped my hand. That left me in a lot better mood than the bowing had. But I was still just as ignorant of the situation as before.

"Well, you see, yesterday this strange letter arrived from Seoul."

"From your son?"

"No. It was from the lady of the house where my son is boarding. She says it's been more than a week since he was last seen there. Ordinarily, in the case of some morally loose student, she wouldn't carry tales over such a matter, she said, but my son was altogether too steady-going. Wondering if maybe something wasn't up, she was letting me know and suggesting that I might want to visit and make some inquiries. And that was the letter. Even though he isn't some loose student, couldn't he easily have stayed over a few days at some friend's, leaving what is not really a home to him but just a boarding house? I suppose as mistress of the house she really shouldn't write letters alarming others, but I guess I'm even worse, thinking every possible ominous thought. I couldn't sleep a wink last night but ransacked my mind from every crazy point of view and finally worked out something kind of, well, superstitious."

"Superstitious, you say?"

"A silly notion, really. I told myself that if a guest came by our inn

things in this world which was not false, I did it with gratitude. To the two rough but warm hands I added my own weak hand, reverently.

"Peace be with you, Grandmother."

The old lady just waved her head gently back and forth, but I could feel what she was saying.

"You have not lived your life in vain. Certainly not! By no means have you lived in vain!"

Translated by Marshall R. Pihl

The Man Who Was Left as Nine Pairs of Shoes

Yun Heunggil

Yun Heunggil was born in 1942 in Chŏngŭp, North Chŏlla Province, and was graduated from Chŏnju Teachers School and Wŏngwang University. Originally a schoolteacher, he has made a living solely from writing since 1976. He made his literary debut in 1968, receiving the *Hanguk ilbo* Newcomers Literary Award. He has since published more than a dozen volumes of fiction and received several other literary awards. Yun is among the best-known Korean authors outside of Korea: many of his works have been translated into Japanese, French, and English.

Yun is one of the exceptionally influential group of young writers who gained prominence in the 1960s and 1970s. Like his contemporaries, he has addressed a variety of social and historical issues, such as the plight of country people transplanted to Seoul and the scars left by the Korean War. But he has maintained a unique voice characterized by gentle humor and an evenhanded treatment of his characters—no mean feat considering the volatile nature of many of his themes. Among his important works are the stories "House of Twilight" (Hwanghon ŭi chip, 1970), "Ganging Up" (Molmae, 1975), "The Wildflower of My Memories" (Kiŏk sok ŭi tŭlkkot, 1979), and "A Very Handsome Umbrella" (Maeu chalsaenggin usan hana, 1987); the novella "Rainy Spell" (Changma, 1973); and the novel *Mother* (Emi, 1982).

"The Man Who Was Left as Nine Pairs of Shoes" (Ahop k'yŏlle ŭi kudu ro namŭn sanae) first appeared in 1977 in *Ch'angjak kwa pip'yŏng* magazine and was the title story of Yun's second volume of fiction.

Right from the start, things hadn't worked out the way we'd expected. We'd gone overboard buying a house in Sŏngnam, and decided to rent out one of the rooms more or less to compensate for our excess. My wife and I were certain we'd be among the best of all landlords in the world, and we concluded that it would be a dream come true for a person becoming a tenant of ours. And so we thought we were justified in demanding that our renters be at least as good as we were. Somehow, though, our expectations had all gone awry, one after another. My own sense of betrayal reached a climax when Yi, a policeman whose rounds included my school, came there in his street clothes to look me up. He started talking about our tenant, Kwŏn, who was listed in the ward register as a resident of our house.

"No need to feel obligated. I'm not asking for a formal daily report. Only when he does something a little out of the ordinary—if he goes away, if someone suspicious comes to see him, if he goes hungry because he's out of rice and coal, or if he suddenly has lots of money. . . ."

It was clear to me that Yi's notion of obligation was off the mark. As far as I could tell, at least, it wasn't something we had a choice about. But to hear Yi talk, you'd think it was something people valued, to the point of fretting in order to obtain it.

"Are you telling me to be your informant?"

"What an embarrassing thing to say!" said Yi, who, unlike most policemen, was a college graduate. He gave a hearty guffaw, then straightaway became serious. "I didn't come here to harp on the duties of a citizen, Mr. O. I'm just asking you to be a good neighbor."

"So all I have to do is squeal to the authorities about Kwŏn's every move, and I can be a good neighbor?"

"Sure," Yi replied, bursting into another guffaw. "But let's drop this talk about 'informants' and 'squealing.' You'll understand by and by, Mr. O. You know, it's not very appropriate the way you express yourself about Kwŏn. Are he and his family getting on your nerves? Or maybe you don't like him?"

"There's nothing about him to dislike at this point. . . ."

"Okay, then, check whether he's out of rice or coal, all right? And see what you can do to help him. I have to keep a low profile, otherwise I'd do it myself. Of course, if he's out of rice or coal we can always blame the people who won't hire him. But then what company would want to hire someone who's being investigated? The bigger problem is Kwŏn himself. He's the kind of person who simply can't put up with a legitimate undercover investigation. The fellow who was responsible for him before me found this out more than once. As soon as Kwŏn senses he's being investigated, he gives up on everything— job, daily routine, even his wife and children—and just lies around in his room. He doesn't eat for days at a time, he tosses down the booze, and sometimes he gets wild like an animal, until he's about to go over the edge. Basically he's a decent, kindhearted man, you know. I think you understand by now what I'm saying. If you can help me to do my duty without Kwŏn knowing about it, you can be a good neighbor—no doubt about it. Frankly, I have a lot of affection for Kwŏn—not as a policeman but as a human being. I'd like to help him as much as I can. I think you'll feel that way too before long, Mr. O. Again, I'm asking from the bottom of my heart—please be a good neighbor."

For me to have a lot of affection for Kwŏn—what an awful thought! I'd much rather pay someone a big fat reward to be nice to him. From the very beginning, our motive for renting out the spare room next to the gate was not human kindness; it was money.

The sight of Kwŏn and his family moving in was no ordinary spectacle but something splendid to behold. It was a Sunday, and I was just getting around to the rare pleasure of a late breakfast when the doorbell rang. My wife went outside and opened the front gate. I could hear her cry of astonishment from where I was sitting in our family room. I went out to see what was going on, and understood right away what the commotion was all about. I was quite surprised myself. There stood a woman dripping with sweat, her chest heaving. On her head was a huge bundle that looked as heavy as she was. A girl who appeared to be about nine standing a short distance from the gate and a much younger boy a couple of steps away from her briefly caught my eye. Their father was far down the steep hill that led to our house, another bundle at his feet. He was just about to have a smoke, but when he saw me, he shoved the cigarette back in his pocket and heaved the bundle to his shoulders. Overpowered by the load, he had all he could do to stagger the rest of the way up the hill. If this was indeed Kwŏn, the man who was to rent one of our rooms, he was carrying out the move on his own, like a sneak attack, without asking our permission, and four days ahead of schedule. As he approached, it appeared he might collapse at any moment, so I snatched the bundle from him. It was much lighter than I thought. This humongous thing was in fact a loosely bundled quilt. His children stared up at me apprehensively. They were holding a bulging plastic bag between them, each with a strap in hand, enduring silently despite the considerable strain evident on their faces. My wife, still looking surprised, was sizing up Kwŏn's wife as if weighing her on a scale. She showed no intention of helping her lower the bundle from her head. I noticed Kwŏn was short. I'm of average height, but I felt like a giant in comparison. Kwŏn remained silent, staring attentively at my sandals, so I felt I had to speak first.

"Is there a truck coming with more?"

"No." He lifted his tired eyes and with his hand drew a long semicircle encompassing his wife's head, the bag the children still held, and the bundle I had just taken from him and placed next to the gate. "That's all." He smiled awkwardly.

Things were sticking out every which way from his wife's bundle—kitchen utensils, I imagined. If Kwŏn wasn't joking, then these few household items—a rice pot, a laundry tub, and some bedding—were, finally, all that they were moving. It was pathetic, even for people who drifted from one rented room to the next. While I was standing there amazed, the fellow quickly wiped the toe of one of his shoes against the bottom of the opposite trouser leg. He then wiped the other toe in the same furtive manner. As he looked down at his shiny shoes cleaned of their dust, his expression brightened like his footwear. His shoes were quite new—a luxury item—and suitably shined. But they didn't match his limp summer shirt with its zigzag pattern, which was old-fashioned and too lightweight for the season. If my guess was right, he'd picked it up at a clearance sale.

"This wasn't part of the agreement," my wife whispered when we were once more by ourselves.

"So what do we do? They had to move today anyway, right? And since we're not using the room, so what if they move in four days early?"

"That's not what I mean."

"Relax. They made a point of promising the rest of the deposit in a few days. They're decent people—I hardly think they'd play innocent and end up paying us only half the money."

"I felt the same way when they signed the rental agreement. But I still think they've got a lot of nerve. They know as well as anybody that two hundred thousand wŏn is quite a bit cheaper than the standard deposit. And yet they barge in early without permission and give us only a hundred thousand. The more I think about it, they're just not to be trusted. If they can't keep their word on something basic like this, how can we expect them to honor any other agreements in the future? Since you're the one who told them it was okay, you get the rest of the money from them."

"Now wait a minute—you're the one who chose these people who won't keep a 'basic' promise."

"How was I to know they'd turn out this way? What am I supposed to do when people put up a front and try to mislead us? And just you wait. They've got something else in store for us."

"And what's that?"

"She's pregnant. Maybe she can fool everyone else, but not me. She must be five or six months along, maybe even seven—who knows? I couldn't tell last time because she was wearing traditional clothing, but today I noticed right away."

"Pretty sharp, aren't you."

Already my wife was trying to act every stitch the landlady, just like the daughter-in-law who finally becomes the mother-in-law. She couldn't have forgotten the days when we had to roam around from one cramped room to another, but she certainly gave that appearance. She had gotten in the habit of talking about that period of our lives as if it were ancient history, and the present as if it were too good to be true. "What we had to go through to get this house!" she would say at the end of practically every sentence, clicking her tongue.

Good point. We *had* gone through a hell of a lot to get this house, and I had every reason to expect my wife to feel a good deal prouder than I about its acquisition.

Before we moved to this house up behind Sŏngnam City Hall, we had lived near Tandaeri Market in a riverside settlement of tightly clustered, oppressive, twenty-*p'yŏng* lots. Our landlord there, Kim by name, called himself a doctor of Chinese medicine. He didn't display a sign, but from the looks of the occasional patient who visited, his specialty seemed to be skin diseases. He sold a homemade ointment of dubious efficacy, but seemed hard put to make ends meet. This self-styled doctor of Chinese medicine spent most of his day taking naps. Then around sunset he started drinking. The liquor launched him on a spree that would usually continue past curfew and stir up the neighborhood till dawn.

Kim was quite drunk the day we moved into his house. This was the first time we had met, and as we shook hands he greeted me in a raspy voice. The next thing I knew, he had put his arm around my shoulders and dragged me into his family room. I felt as if I were being kidnapped. Long into the night he bragged about how he had built this fifteen-*p'yŏng* tile-roofed house in the unbelievably short space of a week. His intimidating voice carried to my wife in the room next to the front gate, where we were to live. At one point, while my wife was doing some chores at the pump in the yard, she had heard Kim shout with glee, "Now that we have a teacher and his wife, there's nothing to worry about!" Finally he had told me, "If anyone in your family is suffering from scabies, pimples, an abcess on the back, cankers, or scrofula, you just let me take care of it." Then he released me to my uneasy wife.

My first meeting with Kim had thus ended without incident. But I wondered why he felt he had nothing to worry about from then on just because he had rented us a room in one of the most jerry-built houses I had ever seen—for three thousand wŏn a month along with a thirty-thousand-wŏn deposit. It took me a while to understand that.

The very next day Kim started announcing throughout the neighborhood that his new tenants were none other than a teacher and his wife. (Think of that—a teacher and his wife!) There were comparatively few teachers in all of Sŏngnam, and one of these teachers was renting from him—that was what he said. On payday every month he would visit us to collect the rent and utility bill. Before leaving he would borrow a small amount, promising as he briskly departed to pay it back. But it wasn't just on my payday: whenever we met on the street or in the house, he would stick out his hand and extort a few coins from me. My wife was in the most difficult situation of all. If Kim borrowed from me, his wife would never fail to come to our room and whine to my wife about it for the better part of the day. We would never get the money back, she would warn her. She would also scold me for lending so readily to her husband—the kind of guy, so she said, who would exchange his wife's underwear for liquor.

It didn't take long for my wife to get fed up with being "the teacher's wife," though she'd found the title rather agreeable at first. Simply because she was the wife of a teacher, the neighbor women and their small fry didn't give her a moment's peace. Thanks to Kim's fervent crowing, we were treated as a species apart in this settlement of twenty-*p'yŏng* lots. The women glued themselves to our kitchen door to learn what kind of supper the teacher ate, and didn't hesitate to peek into our room at any hour to see what kind of makeup the teacher's wife used. An endless swarm of ragamuffins gawked inside to see what snacks the teacher's son preferred. It was the same when my wife did the laundry. When she washed clothes next to the pump, the neighbor women flocked near and marveled at how the detergent foamed up in the water, as if this basic, mundane chemical reaction were some kind of magic.

One day I returned from school a bit late after teaching some supplementary classes. My wife greeted me with a serious expression.

"I think we're going to have to move out of this area."

"What happened this time?"

"Nothing happened, but I'm afraid of the people around here. They're out to cause trouble—I can see it in their eyes."

"Is it the junk dealer's wife?"

"Yes. She followed me to the market again."

This was the neighbor my wife feared the most. She and her husband lived across the alley in a hovel that was half canvas and half mud blocks. Whenever there was a racket in the alley, I would peek through our window and, sure enough, the woman had gotten into a big fight. Her opponent was usually a neighbor, but sometimes it was her husband or their little six-year-old son. No matter who it was, she would call out "Dog!" or "Swine!" over and over and threaten to slice off some part of her opponent with the junk dealer's shears, which were as big as a pair of fodder choppers—though all she really had at her disposal were her teeth and fingernails.

The junk dealer's woman hadn't physically harmed my wife or my son. She had merely shot them piercing looks from a distance on the street, her daughter dangling from her back. That was enough to discourage my wife, though.

One Sunday afternoon, my wife went out for groceries. She was back sooner than I expected. She flung off one of her rubber shoes next to the gate and the other next to the pump, then rushed inside huffing and puffing and made a big fuss of locking the door tight though it was the middle of a peaceful afternoon. Her shopping basket was empty, her face was deathly pale, her chest was heaving.

"The junk dealer's wife followed me the whole way," she panted, her feverish breath flooding my ears.

"And so?" I was taken aback, and couldn't help chuckling.

"Now don't you make fun of me! That woman chased me from here to the market and back again. I was at the butcher's trying to decide whether to buy pork or beef. I had this strange feeling, so I looked back, and would you believe it?—there she was with the girl on her back, staring daggers at me with those sunken eyes of hers. I saw her in the alley when I left for the market, but it gives me the creeps to think she shadowed me all that way before I noticed it."

"Maybe she was thinking about buying some meat too after she saw you with your basket. There's no law that says a junk dealer's family has to eat leftover popcorn."

"Will you listen to me! The way she scowled, I thought she was going to swallow me. My heart started pounding, and I couldn't for the life of me buy meat in front of her. So I left, but then she tracked me down at the fish shop. I was too frightened to buy anything there either, so I decided to go straight home. I looked back along the way, thinking I'd lost her, but she was still there. She kept her distance, but she was dogging me just the same. So, I started running—I couldn't help it. I looked back again, and she was running too. She looked like she was gaining on me, even with the kid on her back. The girl was fussing and crying, but the woman wouldn't give up—she chased me right to the gate."

I quietly rose, opened the window, stuck my head out, and looked past the gate. The woman had planted herself in the middle of the alley, her daughter hanging low on her back. Her eyes met mine squarely. She easily accepted the gaze of an unfamiliar man and seemed determined to engage in a staredown until I retreated. Bewildered, I jerked my head inside and shut the window.

"What on earth is it with her?" my wife pressed me.

"Maybe she wants to be friends with you."

"I wonder what she's thinking."

I couldn't help repeating myself: "Well, I'm not sure, but she probably wants to be friends with the teacher's wife."

" 'The teacher's woman,' 'the teacher's wife,' 'Madam Teacher's Wife'—wherever I go, that's all I hear. I'm sick and tired of it. Why did I have to end up being a teacher's wife!"

Hell! I was caught between a rock and a hard place. After we'd left our hometown, her chronic illness (which was also *my* illness) had settled down for a while, but now she was about to have a relapse. The one reason my wife wasn't so proud of having married a teacher was that most of the husbands of her Edelweiss Club friends from high school earned much more than a teacher did. My wife could never understand how girls with decidedly inferior grades and looks were able to snap up spouses with the "holy trinity" of qualifications—good family, good school, good job. It was as if they had cooked up some plot. And because she couldn't understand it, she couldn't forgive them. Her pride was periodically injured, not because of the discomforts and difficulties resulting from my meager salary, but because the Edelweiss members' eternal friendship with one another, ensured by their biennial meetings, was in her case mixed with pity.

It was the same with me. Meeting classmates who had gotten ahead at an early age, or who at least had high hopes for advancement in the near future, or who had already made their fortune, didn't sit well with me. I couldn't help feeling victimized at the thought of working as a teacher for thirty or forty years in the hope of becoming, at best, a vice-principal, principal, or commissioner of a local board of education. No matter how I looked at it, I felt it was my bad luck in this unjust world to have ended up as a teacher.

On the other hand, there were people who thought the world of teachers and treated them as special. So, my situation could have been worse, but this was no consolation. I had never acted like a big shot in front of the people of Tandaeri who considered me a great figure; nor had I responded in any way to their adulation.

I gave my wife no hint of what Yi, the policeman, had told me about this man Kwŏn Kiyong from Andong. I didn't tell her of Kwŏn's whereabouts during the six years between the births of his two children, Ŭngyŏng and Yŏnggi. Whether I liked or disliked him, I had decided to keep it a secret. Kwŏn's family was already out of favor with my wife, and if she had known that Kwŏn was an ex-convict, she would have fainted on the spot. And if she had known that he had served several years in jail for disturbing the peace and even now was considered dangerous and monitored by the police, she wouldn't have lived with them a day longer under the same roof.

As my wife had said, Kwŏn's family had performed none of their various obligations as tenants. And of course they had violated the rental agreement from the beginning. However, I couldn't evict them then and there for such reasons. I decided to watch them for the time being, until they committed a critical mistake.

Before long my wife's hunch about Kwŏn's wife was confirmed. My wife finally obtained a confession: the woman was six months pregnant. And before I noticed it, my wife had begun counting our coal briquettes, which we stored under the terrace where we kept the soy crocks. She couldn't sleep at night unless she did this every morning and evening. The biggest headache, though, was the children. Why couldn't they consider their parents' situation? Take our little Tongjun, for example. Before, when we were moving from one rented room to the next, he had always ended up hitting the landlady's child, which prevented us from speaking out as tenants. However, now it was he who was getting slapped around by Kwŏn's boy and girl. This not only aggravated us but put Kwŏn and his wife in a tight spot.

One Sunday Tongjun was running about in our yard with a big balloon. Kwŏn's kids were hanging around cajoling him to play with them. When in spite of their best efforts Tongjun didn't respond, they made him cry by hitting him, or scratching him, or some such thing. That really made my wife's stomach churn. Then they went inside, probably to pester their mother. A few moments later Tongjun came in panting and started to badger his mother, asking her out of the blue to buy him, right then, the same kind of balloon Kwŏn's children had. Finally, he led her by the hand out to the yard. My wife came back blushing, and now it was she who grabbed my hand tight and dragged me out to the yard. There I saw Kwŏn's children, happy as could be, with several balloons. I couldn't blame a tenant's children for having fun. The problem was, the balloons had the monstrous shape of huge cucumbers. I recognized them at a glance. Sure enough, they were condoms. I can't tell you how indignant my wife was. She told me that for the sake of our son's upbringing, we couldn't overlook an incident this serious. Fortunately Kwŏn went to work on Sunday, so with a feeling of relief I entrusted this matter of the children's upbringing to my wife. She had kept her eyes peeled for just this opportunity, and she instantly ran to Kwŏn's wife and insisted that she and her husband maintain the dignity one might expect of reasonable adults.

It was after some wretched hardships that we had taken out a bank loan and bought our Western-style house with its slab roof on an honest-to-goodness hundred-*p'yŏng* lot on the hill behind City Hall. Everyone knew this was the most desirable residential area in Sŏngnam. As the lady of such a house, my wife was not that picky in the conditions she presented to prospective tenants. First, tenants must have no more than two children. Second, they must keep their peace. If they could meet these two conditions, my wife would not, for example, begrudge them the use of our appliances or limit the amount of water they could use for washing their blankets, and she would charge them a reasonable amount for the garbage, neighborhood night patrol, and other bills.

Now why must the tenants have no more than two children? Well, my wife had heard this ad nauseam as she followed an elderly real-estate agent around in search of a room. His words had struck home, and my wife believed that a respectable landlady should insist on such a condition as a matter of course. And why did tenants have to keep their peace? My wife set forth this stipulation in order to provide a quiet environment for her "learned" husband (as I would call myself), who had showed the world that material success was simply a matter of education and that education should be a lifelong process. She was saddened that we had to rent out a room even after realizing our dream of buying a house. At the same time, she was clearly quite pleased to exercise a landlady's rights over her tenants. Even clearer to her was the difference between the people who lived in a neighborhood of twenty-*p'yŏng* homes and the people who lived in a neighborhood of hundred-*p'yŏng* homes. In essence, this difference was the gap between a twenty-*p'yŏng* mind and a hundred-*p'yŏng* mind. Whenever she had an opportunity to talk about our new location behind City Hall, she would emphasize that we lived in a house we had bought through the bank.

Early one morning I encountered Kwŏn polishing his shoes on the stoop of the room next to the gate. If he had simply been brushing them like anybody else, I might have taken no note of it. But he was absorbed in brushing and polishing half a dozen pairs of shoes—each a different material, color, and style, all lined up on the stoop.

"Are you having a sale?" I asked, half in greeting and half in jest.

"A sale?"

He immediately stopped what he was doing and looked down at my feet. Or rather he gazed at my shoes. His eyes then crept up my pant legs to the front of my shirt, and when they met mine they had a cool gleam. His face glowed a vivid red, and suddenly a cold smile appeared.

"I gather you don't think very highly of me. . . ."

"I guess that was rude. But I didn't mean anything . . . it's just that all those shoes . . . you have so many of them. . . ."

Kwŏn clamped his mouth shut, clearly intending to deal with me no more, so I was left with nothing to say. On his right he had gently deposited the shoe he had finished polishing, and now he picked up another shoe on his left, put it between his knees, and carefully began removing the mud between the rubber sole and the leather upper with an old toothbrush. In this way he deprived me of any opportunity to apologize. Even so, I dawdled there for some time, having completely forgotten that as duty teacher for the week I was supposed to go to school earlier than usual. So this embarrassing situation gave me my first opportunity to observe Kwŏn up close. Although he had been my tenant for several days now, I hadn't really been able to see him face to face, because we were both gone during the day and didn't have much free time.

Kwŏn was as well equipped as a shoe-shine boy, and he polished shoes as if he had done it all his life. In place of an apron he had spread an old pair of underwear over his lap to protect his only suit. After brushing every speck of mud and dust from the shoe, he smeared polish on a scrap of cloth wound around his fingers and applied it with a circular motion while spitting on the shoe. An even coat of polish followed by light brushing produced a passable shine, and then he polished the shoe to a final luster with a piece of velvet. The result looked terrific to me, but Kwŏn was not satisfied and repeated the process. He sweated as if this were a labor worthy of Hercules. He panted. He spat. And what he spat was not merely saliva but a sticky secretion flowing from a possessed mind—the product of a wild-eyed will to make something more of this shoe, to transform it from something people wore on their feet to a kind of makeup. Kwŏn's hands moved round and round, smartly and ceaselessly, like spindles. Finally the shoe gleamed like gilded metal, and his gaze moved to my feet and then up to my face. He smiled broadly, his eyes as dazzling as the shiny toe of his shoe. Those eyes, in fact, were his best feature. Kwŏn looked prematurely old. His skin was rough and wrinkled, his beard sparse. He had a protruding forehead and high cheekbones, and his bushy eyebrows almost met. His abnormally broad nose was crooked like a journeyman boxer's, and his lips were as thick as those of Mr. Slice (a fellow teacher so nicknamed by the students because a slice of one of his lips would practically have filled a plate). Kwŏn was saved by one feature alone—those large, attractive eyes. Clear and delicate, they showed no trace of viciousness or violence.

Yi the policeman visited me at school again. He said he was just dropping by, but it didn't sound that way from his tone of voice. Right off the bat he started scolding me.

"This won't do. It just won't."

"Well, if I had something to report, I would have called you or something."

"Let's call it cooperation rather than reporting. Anyway, you say there's nothing to cooperate with me about so far?"

"Not a thing!"

"Now look, Mr. O—Kwŏn quit his job five days ago. How does that grab you?"

"He quit? So he's out of work again?"

"That's right. He ditched his job with the publishing company. And this time the circumstances are a bit different. Instead of yielding to the authors and doing what they requested, he kept trying to correct them and kept pointing out their mistakes. So the president of the company called him on the carpet in front of everyone and warned him: 'Who do you think you are? How dare you challenge these distinguished authors!' He hasn't shown up for work since."

"He looked like he was leaving for work as usual this morning . . . yesterday, too. . . ."

"Now you know why I asked you to keep an eye on him?"

"But if you can just sit at your desk and see everything with your X-ray vision, why do I have to go out of my way to cooperate with you?"

Yi gave me a knowing smile. "It's significant that Kwŏn is unemployed again. I think from now on you'll begin to see what your responsibility is. The two of us shouldn't rest easy until he finds a job."

I was tired of insisting that I had no reason to oversee and protect Kwŏn. If I had done something wrong, it was only to rent a room to his

family, and Yi understood that as well as anybody. After talking about
this and that, we returned to the topic of Kwŏn.

"Was Kwŏn one of the people who cooked up that incident back
then?"

"I don't know the details; it happened before I joined the force. But
it's clear he wasn't so much the brains behind it as one of the instiga-
tors. The evidence he left us couldn't have been much clearer. We
have photos of people turning police jeeps upside down and burning
them, photos of people throwing rocks, photos of people commandeer-
ing a bus and speeding down the street, and Kwŏn was right in the
middle of it all."

"That's hard to believe. Are you telling me that someone who can't
even carry a bundled quilt spearheaded a riot!?"

"Well, as soon as he's out of work he skips a meal as often as he
eats. You can believe that, can't you?"

"He can support himself. What's the big deal if he skips a meal?
Maybe he's not hungry."

"My dear teacher, please don't pretend to be so coldhearted. Like I
told you last time, I'm sure you'll end up loving him too."

As if Yi had no idea what a chore it was to love someone, he
laughed confidently and left. He seemed to think that loving your
neighbor was as simple as taking coins from your pocket. For some
time now a somber voice had been echoing in my mind when I was
alone: "Love your neighbor, love the people of Tandaeri, love the
people with the twenty-*p'yŏng* lots. . . ."

It was right after the incident I'm about to describe—an incident
that truly shocked me—that I decided to leave Tandaeri. I was on my
way home from work, and not far from our house I saw a boisterous
group of children playing next to the sewer ditch. Our little Tongjun
was among them. I proudly watched him from a distance, marveling
that he was grown up enough to pal around with the neighborhood
kids. His face looked unusually pale, perhaps because the other faces
were so dark. The junk dealer's boy, in particular, looked like he had
just crawled out of a chimney. Tongjun shouted something to this
sooty-faced boy, who responded by dropping to all fours, as if in
starting blocks, and then hopping like a frog. Tongjun threw something
in front of him, and then I noticed that this little rascal of mine was
holding a box of cookies or some such thing tight against his chest.
The junk dealer's boy picked up the cookie from the ground with his

mouth and crunched into it without attempting to shake off the dirt. When he had finished it he grinned, displaying his white teeth, and resumed his position in the starting blocks. Tongjun again shouted something to him. This time Sootface propped himself off the ground on one arm, took hold of his nose with the other hand, and started turning in circles. But after a few vigorous revolutions he fell on his face. He got up, spun some more, then collapsed again. It looked as though he would fill Tongjun's order, no matter how many trials it took. I couldn't keep track of the number of revolutions, but after the boy was finished he was too dizzy to stand up straight. Next, Tongjun spat on a cookie and threw it on the ground. Then he tried to persuade the other kids to join in. But they merely looked on in a circle with their mouths watering. Perhaps they were dispirited at Tongjun's demands, which had become more and more severe. Tongjun now held up a cookie and threw it as hard as he could toward the stream that ran in the ditch. With no hesitation, the junk dealer's boy slid down a cement pillar to the edge of the stream. I had known about this stream for a long time. Factory wastes and sewage from houses collected there and were carried to a larger stream that fed into the Han River.

This was all I observed. Who knows how long the game had been going on? I went to Tongjun, snatched the box of cookies from him and threw it into the stream, then slapped the little rascal silly. I also wanted to give the junk dealer's son a sound thrashing, but my efforts were directed toward my own little good-for-nothing instead. After I had slapped him several times it occurred to me to look back, and there was the junk dealer's son chasing the box of cookies helter-skelter down the turbid stream.

That night, after shouting at my wife that we should do whatever we could to get out of this awful neighborhood, I couldn't sleep at all. As I tossed and turned, smoking one cigarette after another, I thought about Charles Lamb and Charles Dickens. These two, who had lived in a distant age and in a land that held no special interest for me, took turns keeping me awake.

These two men were known to have had several things in common besides their first name. Both had an unhappy childhood, and sympathy and compassion for slum dwellers seemed to flow from their literary works. But their personalities in real life were as different as night and day, so it was said—as different as their last names. Lamb remained single, looking after his schizophrenic sister, who had killed

their mother. His life was consistent with his writing. Dickens was
self-educated and had worked in a boot-polish factory as a youth. But
in contrast with Lamb, after he had achieved literary fame and a comfortable life, he supposedly used his walking stick to drive away the
slum children who begged him for coppers. If Lamb was right, then
Dickens was wrong, and vice versa. I wanted to be on Lamb's side if at
all possible. But I had to admit that I wasn't blameless enough to be
able to kick Dickens's butt with impunity.

Like my friends, I believed we shouldn't despise the poor. But there
was nothing wrong with looking down on the rich. It was only right
and natural to do so. Calling me a "humanitarian" was by no means the
kind of treatment that might damage a friendship with me. My friends
and I were frustrated that various social benefits bestowed by the government did not reach the bottom rung of society. Whenever we met
people with dead-end lives—on the street, in a coffee shop, or in the
newspaper—we tried to compensate for their pitiable circumstances by
directing vicious insults toward the mercenary plutocrats who were
raking in money any way they could. We considered it our duty and
task as educated people not to ignore the difficulties of those who
could go no further in life.

But this was nothing more than a theory. I had to confess frankly
that I was deluding myself. Generally our outrage was spurred by the
newspaper or a broadcast and then put on display during conversation
at a coffee shop or a drinking place, and that was that. My friends and I
carried one or two packs of gum for emergency use to drive off the
urchins who went around selling gum, and we lumped together all the
young people in school uniforms who sold ball-point pens or newspapers, summarily judging them to be impostors pretending to be
working their way through school. While drinking *soju* we dreamed of
the day we would drink Western liquor. We tossed away tips worth
dozens of packs of gum. While riding the bus we promised each other
we would one day ride in taxis, and while taking a taxi we promised
we would one day drive our own cars. Here was the calculation of
Dickens, which was totally at odds with the humanitarianism of Lamb.
We could do nothing about the tremendous discrepancies between
what we heard and what we saw with our own eyes, or between our
words and our actions. All that night I slept fitfully, kicking Lamb's
butt in my dreams.

The night of Yi's second visit to my school, Kwŏn's son Yŏnggi wouldn't stop fussing. He hadn't behaved like this before. It sounded as if the boy was having trouble getting to sleep, and finally he was scolded for wetting his bed. Then he was left alone until his crying grew quite shrill. When it became loud enough for us to hear it clearly, Kwǒn's threatening voice resounded through the space between the ceiling and the roof. The more Kwǒn shouted, the more little Yǒnggi's crying, so unlike that of a three-year-old, took on a sharp edge, as if it harbored a will for revenge. Finally, we were all half awake. "Listen to that racket, and his mother couldn't care less about calming him down," my wife muttered in a sleepy voice. True enough, Kwǒn's wife didn't say a word. In fact, since the Kwǒns had moved in, I hadn't heard so much as a peep out of her.

"I'm leaving! Is that what you want? You want Daddy to go away?"

Kwǒn's pathetic outburst must have startled the youngster, for his breathless crying suddenly stopped. Or rather it tailed off like a clothesline being stretched out, and finally it became a series of sobs that Yǒnggi seemed to swallow and choke on because of his labored breathing.

The next morning I came upon Kwǒn polishing his shoes again. This time he was more absorbed in his work than usual.

"I'm very sorry about last night."

This polite apology, which was quite unexpected, was directed toward my slippered feet. It was strange: you would have thought he was asking for a reaction to his performance the previous night.

The second day of home-visit week at school found me visiting the parents of my students from Starland Village. On the way there, my homeroom student guide and I came across a school under construction. Workers toting cement bricks on their backs were filing up and down a bouncing wooden footbridge to the scaffolding that towered around the structure's concrete skeleton. Some were stripped to the waist, others had rolled up their pant legs or shirtsleeves; they all looked attractively rugged. But the one fellow who caught my eye reminded me of a soy-sauce bowl among some large earthenware tubs. His trembling legs were barely moving, and I was surprised to see that he was dressed just like an office worker despite such rough work. I walked right under the scaffolding to get a closer look at him.

"Mr. Kwǒn—isn't that you up there?"

The moment I spoke, a brick fell right at me, but I jumped aside and avoided injury. The man hurried down the footbridge to where I stood.

Yes, it was Kwŏn, all right. When I saw his face, white as a sheet and frozen in astonishment, I realized he hadn't been trying to kill me. The man was a sweaty, dusty mess. You wouldn't have believed the stains and wrinkles on the denim jacket he wore over his beige dress shirt. But his shoes were as they always were: the elaborate shine of the chocolate-colored enameled leather was the lonely sentinel of Kwŏn's essence.

"How did you know I was here?" he asked.

"It was just a coincidence. I'm on my way to do some home visits. . . ."

He glared back and forth at my student and me. I could have put the proof right in his hands but it wouldn't have eased his suspicion, so I hurried off.

Kwŏn returned quite late that night. He came directly into our family room, took a seat, and plunked down a small bottle of *soju* as if he meant to plant it in the floor. He was already half loaded.

"I may not look like much, but I'm an Andong Kwŏn!"

His voice sounded rather clear considering he was too exhausted and pickled to budge.

"As I'm sure you know, an Andong Kwŏn gets decent treatment wherever he goes. Your family is originally from Haeju, is it not?"

It was Kwŏn's habit to confirm that I had only one suit and that my shoes were always filthy compared with his, and now he seemed intent on weighing himself against me on the basis of our family origins. I merely smiled, hoping this friendly gesture would penetrate his tipsiness and sink deep inside his agitated mind.

"Mr. Kwŏn, you look pretty drunk. Maybe you ought to get some sleep. We can always talk later."

My wife was standing outside on the veranda, arms folded. Her face was sulky. As I glanced at her I tried to show Kwŏn that my suggestion was purely voluntary and that my subsequent effort to help him up was full of good intentions. But he staved off my good intentions, letting his involuntarily half-raised bottom flop back down. He then snapped off the cap of the *soju* bottle with his teeth.

"So, you don't want to be pals with an ex-con, is that it? Well, I can't let you off that easily. I'm going to have my say, and then I'll leave you alone."

"Ex-con?"

My wife rushed into the room, her eyes gaping as if she had lost her senses. I might have thought she was crying out in unexpected delight at seeing someone, but it soon became clear that she was not in the least delighted.

"Good heavens! Did you say 'ex-con'? Who are you two talking about? Good heavens. Oh, good heavens! . . ."

"Why, you didn't know that, ma'am? Mr. O didn't tell you? It's me we're talking about. Is something wrong? Do I have a funny look in my eyes? Judging from those eloquent phrases of yours, you've never seen an ex-con sitting side by side with a human being before."

My wife jumped back a few steps, as impetuously as she had rushed in. Kwŏn's glare had frozen her into submission, and she appeared ready to do his bidding.

"There's nothing to be scared of. I don't have the energy to harm a fly. Would the two of you kindly relax and listen to me? I won't take long."

Until then I had been keeping an eye out for a chance to mollify Kwŏn and send him back to his room. But I had to change my mind after hearing this confession. If I listened to him, I told myself, maybe I could fathom the mystery of how he could dare to disturb the public peace yet claim he couldn't harm a fly.

"I believe it was Freud who said—" Kwŏn paused to guzzle some *soju* straight from the bottle. "—the saint and the villain are two sides of the same coin. The villain expresses his desires in action; the saint replaces his desires with dreams. That's their only difference."

Kwŏn was about to drink out of the bottle again, so I took it from him, gave it to my wife, and had her prepare a simple serving tray.

"I'm not trying to make the saints look bad in order to whitewash my own situation. But it's true I've taken great consolation from Freud. I feel as if he wrote those words of consolation knowing I'd turn out to be a convict."

The tray arrived. In addition to the liquor there was some pork stew reheated from dinner and a couple of dishes you might see at any of our meals. The first thing Kwŏn and I did was pour each other a shot of *soju*.

"Mr. O, I was at least as good a citizen as you—until the day I got soaked in the rain like the rat who fell into the water jar. And of course, my wife was probably as gentle and sweet as your wife. Sure, we had our complaints and suffered some injustices, but the best we could do was solve them in our dreams; we never knew how to express them through action."

I asked my wife to buy some more *soju*. The more Kwŏn drank, the paler he turned and the more glib he became. The liquor loosened his tongue, that was for sure.

"My whole life has been one big struggle. Probably someone like me shouldn't have been born in the first place. I could have died of typhoid fever, peritonitis, or one of the other diseases I've had, but instead here I am scraping along with a wife and kids. And then that house we had in the Kwangju Housing Development. . . . Somehow, nothing's gone smoothly."

Several years earlier, a most persuasive rumor had spread, especially among the have-nots, that a "Shangri-La" was to be built in the Kwangju area, on the outskirts of Seoul. Kwŏn had taken this with a grain of salt. He had tended to believe that a Shangri-La was nothing special to begin with. But he had been tempted by the prospect of owning a house, and had overvalued the benefit of being within commuting distance of Seoul. He realized now that he had blundered. In the end, he had scared up two hundred thousand wŏn, a hefty sum at the time, and through an elderly, part-time realtor had bought a lot from a displaced family.

"For the first time in my life I owned a twenty-*p'yŏng* lot. I was so happy I paced the boundaries of that lot every morning and every night. I got down on my hands and knees and measured it—I practically caressed it. I knew the land should have belonged to a displaced family—people more unfortunate than me—but that didn't bother me. At that time, the world didn't look any bigger than twenty *p'yŏng* to me."

Kwŏn had barely managed to obtain this land, and now he lacked the wherewithal to lay the foundation and build the frame of a house in order to have shelter. So he let the lot sit, and for the next several months the family made do with an old tent he had rounded up. It was an election year, and the candidates for the National Assembly added various pledges, one after another, to the plans announced for the construction of the "Shangri-La." Magnificent groundbreaking ceremonies were held here and there, and a construction boom followed. In no time the paradise for displaced families, most of them day laborers, was at hand. As the election campaigns heated up, land prices skyrocketed, wages jumped, and real estate speculators buzzed everywhere. None of these developments concerned him in the slightest, Kwon had thought. But then the elections were over, and in the light of the twenty-watt bulb in his tent, he found out how wrong he had been. The realization was like a jolt of lightning.

"The very next day—can you believe it? The elections were held one day, and the next day it all started."

A notice was delivered from the authorities in Seoul: any lot purchased from a displaced family must have a house on it by June 10, or the sale would be nullified. June 10 was fifteen days away. Kwŏn and his wife had to build a house on their lot within that period. Since Kwŏn was not a day laborer and his livelihood was still in Seoul, he had gone his own way in Kwangju, indifferent to the chaotic events concerning the housing development that had surfaced during the campaigns. So now he was off to a late start on the house. He had to run his ass off to catch up. First, he took several days off without notifying the publishing company where he worked, and tried frantically to scrape up some money. As the money materialized he bought cement, cinder blocks, and lumber. With his wife he started building, one row of blocks atop the next. The two of them didn't know the first thing about construction, but they carried out the enormous enterprise undaunted, their instincts telling them that at least the house wouldn't collapse. More than anything else, they felt lucky and grateful that the authorities didn't ask them to build an attractive house worthy of the name "Shangri-La." When they were out of building materials they stopped working and begged friends and relatives for money to buy more. They repeated this process several times, and before they knew it the walls were up and the roof was on. The whole thing took less than the fifteen days. Whatever its quality or outward appearance, the house the Seoul authorities had decreed was finally constructed.

"We felt like we should have thanked the authorities for making us build the house so fast. For almost a month we were on top of the world—we had ourselves a palace. My wife hugged our little Ŭngyŏng, and the tears trickled down her cheeks."

But just as they were about to breathe easy, there was another notice from Seoul. Those people who had bought lots from displaced families would have their ownership officially recognized only if they deposited eight to sixteen thousand wŏn per *p'yŏng* for their twenty-*p'yŏng* lots by the end of July. Otherwise, the sale would be nullified and they would be subject to up to six months in jail and a fine of up to three hundred thousand wŏn.

"They gave us fifteen days this time too. There's something they love about fifteen days."

To make things worse, the Kyŏnggi provincial office sent them a notice to pay a real estate acquisition tax. In this manner, the city of Seoul and Kyŏnggi Province, which supposedly had different jurisdictions, would sometimes whistle a different tune on the same matter, and in this case both the displaced families and those who had purchased lots from them were at their wits' end as a result. A citizens' organization called the Committee for Correcting the Resale Price of Kwangju Housing Development Land was formed (the name set a record for length in those days), and was straightaway renamed the Committee for Opposing and Correcting.... Since Kwŏn was known to be a learned fellow, those who were in the same boat as he drafted him onto the original committee and then its successor.

"I suppose you could call this a position of honor, but to me it was more than I deserved."

Kwŏn was not saying this out of humility. Not only did he feel incapable of performing his duties, but because he regarded himself as a Seoulite through and through rather than identifying with the Kwangju Housing Development, he was reluctant to take on the responsibility. And so he didn't attend any of the nonstop committee meetings. Without a hint of a settlement in sight, the end-of-July deadline for payment of the deposit passed in an atmosphere of taut anxiety. And then on August 10—the day of action decided upon by the committee—things started to happen.

As fate would have it, this high-pressure political atmosphere was greeted with a low-pressure weather system and it began to rain. From early in the morning, leaflets were scattered on the streets and posters appeared on the walls. Yellow ribbons were distributed, to be pinned to the demonstrators' chests at eleven o'clock. Kwŏn remained in his house, not budging, but the sounds of the people moving about outside put his nerves on edge. He sensed that something would surely happen, and that scared him. To Kwŏn, the present situation was better than whatever might happen. The rain fell intermittently. The committee representatives duly presented themselves at eleven o'clock for talks with the authorities, but when the government spokesman did not appear, they decided to wait no longer. Shouts for the citizens to come out into the streets echoed through the alleys of the housing development. "And don't come out barehanded! Grab something—anything!"

Someone knocked so hard on the sliding door to Kwŏn's house that it almost jumped from its track.

"Mr. Kwŏn! Are you there, Mr. Kwŏn?"

Kwŏn's heart sank. He had his wife reply that he had left for work. Only after getting rid of this fellow, whoever he was, did Kwŏn realize it was already Tuesday. Why had he stayed home from work, moping around the house, since the day before? The answer suddenly dawned on him: it was his dependence on others. His was the attitude of an opportunist—one who never jumped into the thick of things, even when they deeply concerned him, but waited for the moment when the efforts of others bore fruit. Kwŏn was shocked. This was an unequivocal awakening, and he was overcome with shame. He sprang up and rushed outside. The streets were choked with people running toward the government branch office shouting slogans and carrying any kind of stick or tool they could use as a weapon. Upon being confronted by them he ducked into a side street like a thief. He might have joined them, given his awakening, but his eyes kept searching for a bus to Seoul. But it was useless: transportation to the outside had been cut off. During this brief search for a bus, he was drenched to the bone by the relentless sheets of wind and water that beat down on the demonstrators. He gave up on the buses and began searching for a quiet alley. He moved aimlessly, thinking these unfamiliar streets he was walking for the first time would eventually lead him to Seoul. And then he came upon a vehicle with the same goal—a taxi that had avoided the club- and rock-wielding mob by zigzagging through the alleys. In desperation Kwŏn jumped into the middle of the alley and blocked the taxi's path—he couldn't have cared less about the fare—and got inside, joining a party of three well-dressed men. The taxi had to pass through the gateway to the housing development, and there it was stopped at a checkpoint. A menacing group of youths armed with two-by-fours, bicycle chains, and other primitive weapons ordered the taxi's occupants out.

One of the youths approached the window where Kwŏn was seated. He bowed, grinned, and spoke congenially.

"Well, well, well, if it isn't our esteemed committee member. Don't you think it's a bit much for you to take on Seoul all by yourself? Would you mind getting out?"

Kwŏn had no idea who this youth was. When he didn't immediately respond, a second youth smashed the windshield of the taxi with a club. The passengers jumped out, and the youths, already hoarse from shouting, raised their voices as loud as they could while threatening the men with their weapons.

"Selfish sons of bitches!"

"We've been on a hunger strike and going all out, and look at you sitting in a taxi like you never had it so good!"

"If we go on a hunger strike, we do it together! We eat, we do it together! We die, we do it together! We live, we do it together! Got it?"

By this time the passengers were frightened half to death.

"Mr. Kwŏn, how about following me over there?" whispered the youth who seemed to know him.

It wasn't the sight of the clubs but rather the kindness of this youth that scared Kwŏn the most. Fettered by the young man's smile, Kwŏn did not resist as he was led to a weed patch beside the road. There the youth delivered a long lecture. "Of course, as you know. . . ." Beginning every sentence with this assumption, he drew a lavish comparison between the leisure class in Seoul—who at that very moment were eating, drinking, dancing, and cavorting in bed—and those living in misery in the housing development. Kwŏn realized that this spiel was designed to rouse his slumbering social consciousness, just as one of the old songs exhorted the children of the "New Korea" to rise and shine. But not a word registered. Instead, Kwŏn asked himself how on earth a person could be cruel enough to treat him so kindly in a situation such as this. The youth decided that his lecture must have sunk in, and led Kwŏn along a steep hillside that provided a shortcut to the center of the housing development.

"It was right over in that area." Kwŏn pointed in the direction of the window.

Regrettably, from where we sat in our family room it was difficult to figure out where he was pointing. Kwŏn realized from our expressionless faces that he wasn't getting through to us, and before I knew it he had sprung to his feet and was out the door. I followed, wanting simply to detain him. At some point Kwŏn's family had gathered at the edge of the veranda near the front door, and they stared up at the two of us as we popped out of the family room one after the other. At the sight of their daddy the little ones burst into tears. Kwŏn's wife, her stomach huge, appeared ready to collapse on the veranda. She gazed in bewilderment at her husband, who had turned as red as a beet.

"You don't have to cry. Daddy's still alive."

I sensed from Kwŏn's low voice that he was well aware of the dignity he enjoyed as family head. He threaded his way between the crying children until he had reached the yard. He spoke clearly, but staggered as he walked, as if his determination to keep his balance could reach no farther than his tongue.

"It was over there," he explained repeatedly. He was much more sure of himself now. A cluster of lights far down the hill flickered beyond the tip of his index finger. They seemed to have poured down from the sky. Although the children must have realized by now that the adults were not quarreling, their torrent of tears did not ebb.

" 'Look at that!' this young fellow shouts. Well, I was already looking. I could see through the rain that the demonstrators had squared off against the police. It was rocks against tear gas. The young fellow was in high spirits—it was almost as if he'd waved a magic wand and created the whole scene. But frankly I wasn't all that impressed by the sight of two groups fighting each other and getting soaked. I was more worried about what my young friend was going to do to me now that he'd brought me this far. But then everything changed right before our eyes. A three-wheeler loaded with a bunch of ripe yellow melons came along and got swallowed up in the crowd. It must have taken a wrong turn. The driver nosed it every which way trying to break out, but it ended up getting turned upside-down. All those melons spilled out and started rolling down the street. Right then and there the demonstrators stopped their rock throwing and swarmed over the melons like bees. The entire load was gone in no time. People were actually picking them out of the mud and chomping in. Eating isn't exactly a pretty sight to begin with, but there was something downright primitive about those people fighting over the melons, and it scared the devil out of me. 'My god, this is human nature at its most naked,' I told myself. I'd never been so moved. I'd always tried to convince myself that I was a different sort from others, but now I wasn't so sure about my reasoning. In fact, I couldn't think about myself in a levelheaded manner anymore."

I had a hunch Kwŏn wasn't going to continue, so for the first time I spoke up.

"Do you mind if I ask what happened next?"

"Why do you need my permission? You've already asked. Three days later a detective showed up at the publishing company and put me in handcuffs. When I saw the photos the police handed me as evidence, I couldn't believe it. There I was sitting on top of a bus; there I was holding a can of kerosene; there I was waving a two-by-four around. It was my face all right, but I'll be damned if I can remember any of that stuff."

I felt I'd heard all there was to hear. Now I could understand why Kwŏn had invited himself in, clutching a bottle of *soju,* and unraveled this tale he had kept to himself. But there was one small matter that still bothered me, and I thought it would be better for both of us if we could resolve it while we had the chance.

"I guess you've known that I've been seeing Yi, the policeman?"

Kwŏn smiled. "More precisely, he's been seeing you, I would think. You know, when one part of the body is paralyzed, another part becomes uncommonly sensitive. In my case, it's a sixth sense."

"I hope you don't think I've been informing on you. Yi calls it 'cooperation,' but. . . ."

Kwŏn smiled again. "There are times when you can do something you wanted absolutely no part of, and not even realize it—remember? Probably you're no exception. Just because you haven't cooperated with him in the past doesn't mean you won't cooperate with him in the future."

"I sure had that Kwŏn figured wrong," my wife whispered to me after we had gone to bed that night. "I thought he was an idiot, but he's something else entirely."

"He had you around his little finger—you were helpless," I replied.

"I know it, and it makes me so mad!"

After I turned off the light, she spoke again in a low voice.

"Her stomach looked bigger than ever today—you saw it. What's the poor thing going to do if it's twins? I know she's only eight months along, but she looks like she's ready right now—goodness. . . ."

"Relax—she's not going to ask you to have the baby for her."

That night I dreamed I was taking turns kicking Dickens's butt and Lamb's butt. And then I was kicking Kwŏn's butt and he was kicking mine.

My wife suddenly began showing an interest in Kwŏn and his family. More specifically, it was an interest in his wife's abdomen, which looked as though it would burst at any moment. From the way my wife talked, I gathered the two of them had contact during the day when Kwŏn and I were out. Kwŏn's wife didn't even know her own due date, my wife giggled. When she had kidded her about this, the other woman had casually replied that it didn't matter. When the time came, she would go into labor and give birth—the result would be the same.

Kwŏn hadn't found a job yet. But even without regular employment, come morning he would put on his work clothes and leave the house. I figured that since he didn't have a trade, he was still doing casual labor at construction sites, though he hardly had the strength for it. His two children still made their way into our family room after a lengthy chorus of "Come on, Tongjun, let's play!" But now they often stood their ground there instead of returning to their mother, even at mealtime. Here was a sign that the situation in the room beside the gate had become serious. Even so, neither Kwŏn nor his wife had ever opened up to us and asked for assistance. If we hadn't made up our minds to help them after witnessing the shape they were in, who knows how far they would have been driven in their wretched circumstances? Just as Yi the policeman had predicted, I began stealing into their kitchen like Santa Claus and leaving them coal, rice, and such. Whenever I did this, my wife would feel too outraged and victimized to finish her supper. When she thought about the expectant mother and her helpless little children, she insisted that this was the least we could do. But when she realized some of this goodwill of hers might extend to an idiotic fellow who couldn't even provide a decent living for his wife and children, she would get so worked up that she had a hard time sleeping. She had already forgotten having whispered to me only a couple of nights before that Kwŏn was "something else entirely," and now she complained to herself over and over about renting the room to him.

Kwŏn's income remained meager, and in no time his wife had reached term. One day I returned from school and my wife whispered to me that the woman had gone into labor sometime after lunch. Then at supper we heard an unfamiliar sound from the room beside the gate. First Kwŏn's wife groaned like someone with the flu, and then, as if a dagger had penetrated deep inside her, she produced a sudden, heart-rending cry that soon trailed off. She did this several times. It was the first time I had heard her voice.

My wife thought it was time to get Kwŏn's wife to the hospital. "Can you talk some sense into him, dear? I tried several times, and he's just impossible! All he did was smirk and tell me not to worry."

"It's not Kwŏn that's refusing—it's their lack of money," I responded.

For some time now my wife had been half critical and half worried about their failure to prepare for the delivery. "A woman with a stomach as big as a mountain having a baby at home in this day and age, and doing it all by herself—the more I think about it, the more I think something bad's going to happen. A fellow who doesn't even have the money for a midwife, and a woman who's nine months pregnant and hasn't bought a single diaper—what a pair!"

I hurried through the rest of my supper and called Kwŏn out to the yard. Just as my wife had said, Kwŏn immediately began smirking and telling me not to worry. You might have thought from his tone that he was the one who was trying to comfort someone in a fix.

"She had the second one by herself, and did a beautiful job."

"It's not your family we're worrying about, but ourselves. I'm not saying something'll go wrong, but if it does, I'll hold you accountable."

Leaving him with these harsh words, I disappeared inside. What a calculating guy, I told myself. I had discreetly offered to lend him the piddling cost of a delivery at the local clinic, but he had turned me down. I had to conclude that he chose to risk two lives rather than going to the trouble, such as it was, of repaying a trivial debt.

But when midnight passed with Kwŏn's wife in the same condition, the situation changed. Women who weren't first-time mothers didn't have labors that long and relentless. This must have scared Kwŏn, because he left carrying his wife on his back and scurried down the steep slope from our house before the end of curfew. It took a load off our minds to see Kwŏn and his wife stealing out of the room beside the gate. The two of them looked like a drum riding on a pair of drumsticks. Before leaving for school the next morning I asked my wife to buy some seaweed for soup for the new mother, and then go to the hospital when word of the delivery arrived.

That afternoon Kwŏn came looking for me at school. A class had just started, but I happened to be free that period and was chatting in the teachers' room, so I was able to meet Kwŏn at the front gate as soon as the custodian called me.

"I'm sorry about this—I know you're busy."

Kwŏn tried to keep a smile on his face, but I had never seen him so self-conscious. I interpreted this in a good light: he had just become a father for the third time. I tried to dismiss the ominous feeling that had come over me the moment the custodian notified me.

"Did everything turn out all right?"

"You know, it's a good thing I listened to you. It would've been a disaster if I'd kept her at home. I don't know whether it's a boy or a girl, but it seems like the kid's giving me a hard time in order to teach me a lesson."

He was still smiling self-consciously. His toe was busy in the dirt drawing some word or picture I couldn't decipher. His shoes were astonishingly shiny considering he had just trudged up a dusty hill to get to the school. No doubt he had been wiping his shoes against his pant legs while waiting for me.

"Could you lend me a hundred thousand wŏn or so?" he blurted right in my face.

His self-consciousness abruptly vanished, and a provocative expression filled his upturned face. He had tried to sound as nonchalant as if he were bumming a cigarette. But then while I was trying to recover my powers of speech, his tone became furious.

"They say she has to have a Caesarean. They X-rayed her, and at first they didn't find any complications. Her cervix is wide open. Her water didn't break early, and the fetus was in the right position. And it's not twins. So everything's like it's supposed to be, except that she's been in labor more than twenty-four hours. The doctor said that in a case like that there's only one possiblity: the baby hasn't dropped because it's turned inside the uterus and got the cord wrapped around its neck. And shit—that's exactly what happened! If the doctor doesn't do something soon, they're both in trouble."

The thing that made me ill at ease was the exclamation "Shit!" This word was so uncharacteristic of Kwŏn, but otherwise his explanation was sincere. Or perhaps it sounded much more sincere because of this vulgarity, which I had never heard him use before.

I couldn't give him a ready answer. His request for "a hundred thousand wŏn or so" was too serious to allow me to convey my sentiments through such tactless, banal expressions as "Oh, that's too bad" or "I really don't know what to say." On the other hand, I still had to pay off more than half of the loan I had taken out from my school to help pay for our house. He wasn't talking about ten or twenty thousand wŏn—the cost of a normal delivery—and to lend him the huge sum of a hundred thousand or so was simply more than I could handle. And I couldn't go ahead with such a big undertaking without my wife's knowledge, because she was the one who controlled the family purse strings.

"If you can lend me the money, I'll do whatever I have to do to pay you back—whatever I have to do," Kwŏn said. He looked as solemn as if he were swearing on a Bible.

It was a good thing he reminded me. Otherwise it might never have occurred to me that getting the money back from him would be more difficult than finding the money to lend him. How was he going to pay me back doing casual labor or some occasional, low-paying translation work for a publisher, when he couldn't even feed his family? So for me the best thing was to avoid lending him the money out of sympathy. And therefore I had to speak harshly to prevent him from raising objections.

"Which hospital is it?"

"The Wŏn Gynecological Clinic."

"It'd be difficult for me to come up with the cash right this minute. Why don't you try the doctor at the clinic again? I'll call him right away and tell him I'll be your guarantor. Doctors are decent people— they wouldn't let someone die. If that's your only way out, give it a try."

Because my response was too slow in coming, Kwŏn seemed to have been expecting this. His aggressive countenance softened, and the self-consciousness returned to those fine eyes of his. He shook his head.

"It's too late—he'd never accept just a promise. From the moment we walked in the door he knew it wouldn't be easy to collect payment from me."

Kwŏn was sweating nervously, but instead of wiping his face he lifted his right foot and wiped the shoe a couple of times against the bottom of his left pant leg. Then he repeated the movement with the other shoe.

"It really was rude of me to bother you when you're busy," he said with difficulty. His "Mr. Slice" lips twitched like those of a baby waking from a shallow sleep.

I thought he would say more, but he quickly turned and began to walk away, his arms swinging. Perhaps I was anticipating the moment he would say in a choking voice from deep inside, "Thank you, Mr. O. Now you go home and have a good meal and live well the rest of your life," or some such thing. I expected the words to fly out of his mouth and stun me. And so I flinched when he abruptly turned back and looked straight up at me.

But this was all he said: "I may not look like much, Mr. O, but I'm a college graduate!" He spoke self-consciously, as a student's parent might do while thrusting a small gratuity in my pocket.

You wouldn't have thought that the arms on that short frame could swing as they did. With every step down the hill he seemed to be cursing the earth and the sky. At the moment he disappeared around a bend in the bare loess hill, I was seized with an urge to run after him and call him back. This too is human nature at its most naked, I felt. It was just like when Kwŏn had seen the people in the housing development suddenly stop throwing rocks and run to the overturned three-wheeler to devour the melons. And then it occurred to me that I was indebted to Kwŏn to a certain extent—that is, if I were to consider his rental deposit as a kind of debt. I don't know why I hadn't thought of that earlier.

At the clinic everything was ready for the operation; all that was missing was the deposit. I had weaseled an advance on my salary from the school and emptied the pockets of my closest friends among the teachers, and barely managed to come up with the one hundred thousand wŏn. As soon as I handed it to the doctor, he ordered the nurse to bring in the anesthesiologist. When the doctor learned I wasn't a close relative of Kwŏn but only his landlord, he clicked his tongue.

"You get all types of people for fathers. I sent him out for the deposit this morning, and haven't seen him since. Can you believe it?"

"Sure, just like there are all kinds of ways to deliver babies, there are all types of people fathering children."

I prayed that the doctor in his gold-rimmed spectacles would get the point, but unfortunately he chose to take it as a joke, and broke into a laugh. So much for my attempt to be serious.

I helped wheel Kwŏn's wife into the operating room. If she wasn't already dead, she certainly looked it.

For an operation that extracted one life and saved the other life that had kept the first one going, it was over all too quickly. I sat in the waiting room and chain-smoked half a dozen cigarettes, as I had the day our little Tongjun was born. Finally I heard the baby crying.

"It's a pepper, a little pepper!" the nurse cried out.

The doctor's wife had assisted with the operation, and as she emerged from the operating room she asked me in a loud voice if I'd guessed from the first cry that it was a boy. Then she congratulated me as if I were the father. I had no choice but to play along and praise her for her efforts. A moment later I looked into the face of Kwŏn Kiyong's new boy, all swaddled. His plump, handsome face betrayed his obliviousness to the Caesarean section his mom had just undergone. His voice was loud and resonant, quite in keeping with my initial impression of the man for whom this medical procedure was named. As I listened to this rugged little fellow cry as though he would lift the whole building, I settled comfortably into the deep emotions of the day our own boy was born.

It was the most peculiar coincidence that we had a burglar that very night. I'd never before had such an experience. As I slept, I felt someone shaking my shoulder. I tried to brush the annoying hand away, but the silent movement continued. Realizing with a start that it was an unfamiliar hand trying to wake me, I opened my eyes, and there in the red glow of the nightlight was a masked man—and the gleaming blade of a kitchen knife pointed right at my neck. The man reeked of liquor. The nightlight tinged the dark shade of the mask with red, and from the eyes and the bit of nose exposed above the cloth mask I could detect the man's considerable drunkenness.

"Get up. Quick, I said get up."

The burglar spoke in a low, measured tone, not wanting to wake anyone. I wanted to get up, but how? The kitchen knife pointed at my throat was dancing up and down. If the burglar happened to stick me in the neck, the wound would be the accidental result of his excessive trembling. This was a burglar without much experience. The moment I saw his eyes, I realized he wasn't a specialist in this area. Despite all his dutch courage, those large, attractive eyes couldn't hide his inherent decency—or his fear of me. If he hadn't become potvaliant and climbed the wall of our house, he would have flunked his course in felonies from the start.

"I'll be happy to get up if you'll just pull that knife back a little."

The burglar did as I asked.

"Give me what you've got—quick," he whispered while waiting for me to sit up.

"Anything you say. But it'll be easier if you do as *I* say too."

The burglar shot me a doubtful look.

"There's not much money in the house," I added. "There's a piggy bank on the bureau, and my wife might have some spending money left—it'd be in the drawer at the bottom of the cabinet. If you can find anything else, help yourself."

The burglar looked even more dubious, and didn't seem to want to act rashly, so I decided to test him by pretending to be irritated.

"Would you prefer to see my wife get up and scream bloody murder? For your own good you'd better trust me and do as I say."

The man drew a deep breath and finally started around our bedding toward the bureau. I noticed that this burglar was polite enough to have removed his shoes. He tottered, and wouldn't you know it, he must have stepped on Tongjun. The boy whimpered, and the burglar flinched, then hunched over and patted him on the shoulder. The man waited until the little fellow was asleep again. Then he rose, glanced at me to make sure I had stayed put, and got down to the job at hand. I noticed his face was sticky with sweat. Suppressing an urge to burst into laughter as I observed the charming movements of the burglar, I slowly sat up and retrieved the knife he had dropped on our bedding while putting Tongjun back to sleep.

"I think I've got an idea of how long you've been in this business," I said, offering him his weapon.

I thought he would faint from the shock. I gave him a friendly smile and gestured for him to take it. After hesitating a moment, he lunged toward me, snatched the knife, and once more pointed it at my throat. Having discovered that our man was not the sort to stab someone on purpose, I had no regrets about returning the knife. Sure enough, he merely stuck it in his belt. His pride had been deeply wounded.

"All this talk of yours, and there's nothing worth stealing here."

"That's why our friendly neighborhood thieves have given up on us."

"You think I wanted to do this? I was driven to it by circumstances —I couldn't help it."

I decided that this was a splendid opportunity to set his mind at ease.

"That's usually the way it is. Someone in your family has a serious illness, or you get in over your head in debt. . . ."

The burglar's eyes immediately filled with suspicion. He retreated to the veranda, trembling in outrage to the point that his teeth clattered. The smell of liquor that he left in his wake was enough to make me sick. It was clear to me that all he embraced in his hurried departure were the shreds of his pride. So, far from calming him, my approach had only frustrated him all the more.

"There's no law that says you have to go it alone when you've got troubles," I called out to his back. "Who knows, maybe you have a good neighbor who's already made things easier for you."

"Don't give me that crap! I don't have any neighbors like that—I found that out myself! I don't believe anybody now!"

He put on the shoes he had left at the front door. I got up to follow him, fighting the impulse to turn on the light in order to see the shoes. He opened the front door and stepped down into the yard. Then he apparently forgot he was supposed to be an armed burglar who had broken into our house, because he turned toward the room beside the front gate. To spare him more embarrassment in the future, I had to point out his mistake.

"The front gate's over there."

He stopped for a moment before the kitchen, then slowly began walking toward the gate. He began staggering. When he reached the gate he looked back at me.

"I may not look like much, but I'm a college graduate!"

Who said you weren't? I asked myself. After this unexpected revelation about his college background, the man opened the gate and was swallowed up in pitch darkness.

I closed the gate but didn't lock it. On my way back in, I peeked in the room beside the gate and confirmed that Kwŏn hadn't returned, and that his boy and girl were curled up in the darkness without their mommy and daddy. My wife was standing outside the front door in her nightgown, arms folded.

"What's going on?"

"Nothing."

Nothing was missing. Everything was in place on the bureau, including the piggy bank. As I had said, nothing had happened. Before I went back to sleep I told my wife I had paid for the operation. She was silent for a time, then turned toward the wall.

"Don't worry about them running out on us—we've got their deposit."

"Are you sure nothing happened?"

She turned back toward me. To the end I never mentioned to her that a poor excuse for a burglar had entered our house.

Kwŏn hadn't returned by the next morning. I dropped by the clinic on my way to school. He hadn't been seen there since his departure in search of the deposit for the operation. Nor did he return home the next day or the day after that. It was clear by now that he had left for parts unknown. It was also clear that my approach had been boneheaded, today, and I used that money to go to Seoul, then I'd find nothing wrong with my son, but, if I broke open that tightly wrapped packet of tuition money and used some to cover the travel expenses, then I would find something wrong with my son. That's all. I can't tell you what a bad time I had of it, so nervous and anxious, waiting for a guest once I had made up my mind. But you came and made it all come out the right way. I really do thank you."

The woman thanked me yet again. My heart nearly burst with pity and compassion for this widowed woman who eased her enormous concern for her son's situation by such curious means. The idea that I had brought her good fortune was not the least unpleasant.

"So, I guess you'll be leaving soon."

"Yes, everything's ready. I asked our neighbor to help with Mother. And now, with the four-thirty bus to the hot springs, I'll be all set."

"So, we're traveling together!"

"Indeed, so we are. You had said you'd take the four-thirty to the hot springs. . . ."

"No, I mean we'll travel together all the way to Seoul."

I decided in an instant that I would also return to Seoul today. An inexpressible peace of mind swept me. I followed the woman into the family room when she went to tell her mother-in-law good-bye. The hands of this mother and daughter, similarly old, held each other tightly.

"Mother, I'm off to Seoul. I have a few things to buy, and I want to see T'aeshik, who's on vacation but says he has to stay there and study. Samsuni from next door is going to keep an eye on you, Mother. Please don't worry about anything and be sure to eat well."

Whether she did understand or didn't understand, the old lady gently waved her head back and forth as always. To me the waving was not "I don't know, I don't know." Rather, it seemed more like "Daughter, there's nothing wrong with T'aeshik, really nothing at all. What sin of ours could be so great that even that boy would have to suffer for it?"

I suddenly wanted to add my hand on top of the still clasped hands of this mother and daughter. There was something flowing freely between these two hands—the intimate hands of strangers, the hands of partners in a great undertaking—something that I wished to measure, to feel, and to have long in my memory. As if this were my first and last opportunity to come into contact with the one thing among all

Land of Exile

Cho Chŏngnae

Cho Chŏngnae (b. 1943) is a prolific writer who made his debut with "Calumny" (Numyŏng) in *Hyŏndae munhak* magazine in 1970. He received the twenty-seventh Modern Literature Award in 1981 for "Land of Exile" (Yuhyŏng ŭi ttang, first published in *Hyŏndae munhak* the some year) and the Republic of Korea Literature Award for "Door to Humanity" (Ingan ŭi mun) in 1982.

As a writer, Cho expresses a belief in the value and dignity of human life and strives to relate the life of the individual to the flow of history. He is particularly concerned with the twin impacts of war and division on the Korean spirit and with the connection between such events and Korea's social history. Like the main character Mansŏk in "Land of Exile," Cho Chŏngnae's people are frequently the unfortunate victims of Korea's history, both ancient and recent.

From 1983 to 1989 Cho devoted himself to a ten-volume, 1.25-million-word roman fleuve, *The T'aebaek Mountains* (T'aebaek sanmaek), named after the three-hundred-mile chain that runs from Kangwŏn Province in central Korea south to the city of Pusan, forming the backbone of the peninsula. Critics have hailed the work as "the masterpiece of the 1980s."

Cho states that the work "deals with the tragedy of Korea's division with a mind to overcoming that division." "Unification is impossible," he adds, "unless we strip away our postwar anticommunism and form a more objective, balanced judgment whereby we criticize the historical blunders and distortions of the right wing and affirm the historical sincerity and meaning of the left."

"Please, mister . . . I'm old and worthless, and my only wish is to close my eyes in peace. I beg you, look on me with pity."

The old man fervently rubbed his palms together. He could scarcely have been more ardent before the Buddha himself. And, as if that were not enough, he knelt on the floor.

"This really isn't necessary, sir," said the director. "I fully understand your difficulty. Here, now, won't you have a seat?" He made an awkward attempt to help the old man up.

"Please, mister, promise you'll take him," the old man pleaded, bending even lower.

"All right. I'll see that he's admitted," the director managed to answer, revealing his contradictory feelings.

"Oh, thank you, mister! I'll never forget your heavenly grace, even when I've passed on to the next world."

Still kneeling, the old man bowed two or three times, palms pressed tight against his chest. His eyes misted over with tears.

"Sir, please take a seat."

Why didn't he just leave the boy at the gate and disappear without all this pleading? I'd have taken him in anyway, thought the director.

The old man reseated himself with some reluctance in the chair, then groped in his pocket, sniffing continuously.

"Here, mister—it's all the money I've got. Take it, will you? It's not much but it's a token of my gratitude."

There in the old man's rough hand were two creased ten-thousand-wŏn notes.

"No, no, no. Keep it, sir, and use it for medicine or something. We'll take care of the boy."

"Take it, I'm begging you. The last expression of the heart of a useless father. If you won't accept it, then how will I be able to turn and leave? Please, mister, take it."

The old man's tear-filled eyes spoke many times more fervently than his words.

"Well, if you insist."

The director accepted the money from the old man's trembling hands.

"And here's some underwear for him."

The old man briefly rubbed his eyes with the back of his hand and then proffered a small bundle.

"Oh, yes."

As the director took the bundle, he heard a groan of paternal emotion.

"I would have bought an extra change of clothes, but after I got him the underwear I didn't have enough money, you see."

The old man spoke as if to assuage his guilt, biting back tears that worked the corners of his mouth.

"There's no cause for concern."

"And please take good care of this."

The old man carefully produced an old scrap of paper. The director read at a glance the six syllables laboriously drawn on the paper: "Father is Ch'ŏn Mansŏk."

"This is my name. 'Mansŏk' means 'ten thousand bushels.' They say my grandfather gave it to me. The life of a poor commoner is nothing but hopes and sorrows, and he wanted me to have this name so I'd become a rich man with ten thousand sacks of rice. But look at me now."

The old man heaved a deep sigh of despair.

"I know I'm a poor excuse for a father, but I thought he should at least know my name."

"Yes, of course. Every son must have a father. It's only natural that he should know."

As he spoke, the director examined the old man anew. Here before him was a man with a pitiful fate, worn out by life and withered like a fallen leaf.

The old man called his son back in from the hallway. Though he had said his son was six, the boy looked thin and scrawny like a wild melon vine in a drought—he was probably malnourished. The child's wretched appearance prompted new pangs of sorrow in the old man.

It'd be a mistake to stay with him to the bitter end, the old man thought suddenly. A father's remorse, rehearsed countlessly before his visit here.

"No matter how hard your life is, you're not helping yourself by neglecting your health like this. You'll have to be more careful. Don't slack off or you'll be in trouble."

The doctor's words had shattered Mansŏk's belief that he would be with his son until the end. That ugly picture showing a jumble of bones—what the doctor called an X-ray—seemed to say that his life was like a candle burning low.

Even before the old man had talked himself into visiting the hospital, he suspected how sick he was. Even before he began bleeding from the mouth, there had been other symptoms. His body would shake strangely if he drank, and as the days passed, he had found it increasingly difficult to exert himself. His co-workers, who worked hard and so ate heartily, were aware of the decline in his health even before the doctor.

He began to fear he might breathe his last on the job or on the street. Either way, it would have amounted to abandoning his son as an orphan. Would he live another year? Another two years? He had no way of knowing. Entrusting the child to an orphanage was the only way, he thought, to maintain the family line.

"Ch'ŏlsu, from now on you'll be living here with the director. I want you to do what the man says. Understand?"

As he spoke, the old man bent down and searched the child's small face.

"And you, daddy?" the child asked briefly, looking into his old father's eyes.

"There you go again. I keep telling you I'll find your mother and bring her back!"

The old man deliberately used a sharp voice.

"When?" countered the child anxiously, all the while staring directly into his father's eyes.

"The moment I find her. . . ."

"What if you don't find her?" the child persisted.

The old man was speechless for a moment. Cold sorrow filled his heart.

"I'll be back. I'll find your mom and bring her back . . . honest," said the old man confidently.

"Daddy, you promise."

The boy stuck out his little finger. But instead of hooking it with his own to seal the promise, the old man stared intently at his son.

Poor little kid. Why did you have to be born to the likes of me and end up this way? I want you to grow up strong and healthy, well fed. . . . Poor little kid.

"Daddy, promise!"

"Okay, okay."

The old man stuck out his finger, suppressing the massive sobs that surged and tore at his throat.

A small, slender finger linked in midair with a thick, rough finger.

"Daddy, you've got to find Mom and bring her back," said the boy, squeezing and shaking his father's finger as he spoke.

"Okay, okay."

"I'm going to pray every night that you find Mom quick."

"Okay, okay."

The old man fought back his tears.

My sweet little boy. How are you going to make it all alone? If I had only known, I wouldn't have let you be born. What a useless fuckup I've been. . . . Poor little kid. . . .

"Ch'ŏlsu, you be sure to mind the director, now. He won't let you go hungry or make you sleep on straw sacks. It's going to be a lot better here than living with Daddy. Now, you mind what the director says. Understand?"

The boy, perhaps anticipating the impending separation, nodded sullenly.

"Now then, Ch'ŏlsu, come along," said the director, signaling that the time had come.

The old man unhooked his finger from his son's and straightened up, then nudged the boy toward the director. The boy's thin back resisted the prodding with a pressure that passed through the old man's hand and spread hotly through his body.

"No cause for concern," said the director, precipitating the farewell.

"I hope . . . you. . . ."

The old man bowed deeply several times, but in the end he couldn't get the words out. He seemed to hesitate over his threadbare satchel, but then hurriedly turned and left the office.

"Daddy!"

The old man didn't look back.

He went down the hallway, and as he shuffled out onto the playground the tears finally gushed forth.

"Daddyyy! You've got to find Mother and bring her back!"

Across the playground, at the main entrance to the orphanage, he could still hear the boy's ringing cries. The old man had intended not to turn around, but that simply was not to be.

He turned. His son, the director's hands on his shoulders, was standing in the vestibule, waving.

"Daddyyy! You'd better come back."

The old man turned away as tears welled up once again.

"That bitch should be drawn and quartered! Abandoning the poor little kid and running off . . . "

The old man trembled and angrily clenched his teeth.

His wife's face, laughing mindlessly, appeared before his tear-blurred eyes.

"Worthless bitch!"

He hurled insults as if somebody were actually there in front of him. Then he wiped his eyes quickly with the back of his hand. The illusion of his wife disappeared without a trace.

Hatred raged again like fire in his heart. He had spent two years searching the countryside, carrying his young boy on his back, determined to spare neither of them once he caught up with the pair.

"What a stupid fool I was!"

The old man released a despondent sigh. He was tormented as much by the undying hatred he felt for his wife as he was by feelings of remorse.

What notion of glory had possessed him, a homeless common laborer, to set his sights on such a blossom? Though he had been a party to the affair, it still made no sense to him at all. The only thing it had brought was regret. It vexed the old man beyond endurance to know that if he had steered clear back then, he would not now be putting his son into a stranger's hands.

"Why do you still live alone, Mr. Ch'ŏn? Aren't you lonely?"

When a woman began to make advances like this he knew he should reject them outright. But he felt agitated, like a cat that had caught the smell of fish.

"Why do you ask such questions when you live alone, yourself? Aren't *you* lonely?"

But even as he parried, his nose began to tingle at the woman's smell, which made him feel so odd.

"Since no one will have me, I live by myself, facing this hard life alone. I was born to be lonely—what can I do about it?" she said, suddenly dispirited.

The old man found he was pitying her, but he could feel his heart hammering at the same time.

How stupid can you get? I've spent half my life on the run or else hiding out. How could I be suckered by the smell of a woman?

He had to steady his throbbing heart. He had to hold out. If he couldn't, he'd have to leave this construction job for another.

This construction project provided plenty of work—unusual for winter. The industrial complex was to begin operating by spring, and before then they had to finish not only the buildings themselves but the workers' apartments, too. So, jobs were abundant and the daily pay was not only generous but always on time.

For over thirty years he had wandered from one construction project to another, but he had never come across one as lucrative as this. And it was winter. If a lucrative job can lead to problems, then this one sure had.

"Life is so short, Mr. Ch'ŏn. What do you do for fun?"

"What sort of crap is this?"

"Is this your idea of a good time, drinking *soju* every night?"

The woman stared directly at him as she poured him a drink.

"Does anyone drink for fun? If I was having fun, I wouldn't be swilling this stuff."

"Then we'll have to find some real fun for you."

"What sort of 'real fun'? I just work and eat, one day at a time."

He tossed down his drink and crunched on some pickled radish.

"Who says you have to 'just work and eat, one day at a time' without the pleasures of a wife and kids? What kind of life have you had, Mr. Ch'ŏn, living this long without a family? Maybe you think you'll live forever, but you'll get old, and what if you suddenly get sick? Think about it. And who's going to bury you when you die? Who'd offer even a bowl of cold water to your memory after you're dead and gone? You drift through this world following construction jobs. In the next world, do you intend to be a wandering ghost?"

"What is this shit? Why the hell are you running off at the mouth like this?" he shouted, suddenly alarmed.

"Oh, dear! I'm scared to death! Come on, don't get angry and just think for a moment. Am I wrong to say this to a man who still lives by himself?"

"Lay off! Tease a leper for being a leper and he gets angry. . . ."

"Then it's not too late—if you'll just give up the leper's life."

"What are you saying?"

As he studied the florid eyes of this laughing woman, he felt something like an electric shock stinging his groin.

Since this woman Sunim worked at a soup-and-rice house, she saw Mansŏk once a day when he came to eat. Vague rumor had it that she had once been married but was driven out, and that the owner of the soup-and-rice house was some distant relative. One thing was clear: she was not one of those barmaids who litter a construction project like rags.

Sunim's words forced Mansŏk to reconsider his circumstances. Sunim had probed, as if with tweezers, at a very painful spot. These ideas had crossed his mind from time to time, but he always tried to forget, to put them out of his mind. On days when these thoughts did come to him, he would get more drunk than ever.

He had experienced countless women while wandering from one construction project to another over the last thirty years. The relationships were not based on feeling but were business transactions. If people looked on manual laborers as the dregs of humanity, then what was to be said of the women who lived off them, spreading their legs to fill their gullets? No matter how long you waited, you'd never hear one of them talk like Sunim just had.

Actually, it had been altogether too long since Mansŏk had heard such words, full of feeling and concern for his future—especially from a woman who was not a barmaid or a prostitute. Mansŏk almost forgot how short of money he was, or that he was forty-nine. Struggling with his surging feelings, he knew he couldn't dismiss these thoughts as easily as in the past.

Why her interest in an old man like him, Mansŏk had asked, when there were so many younger construction workers coming and going at the soup-and-rice house?

"I don't know why. I just felt that way," she answered, her words trailing off and her face flushing.

"If I'm forty-nine and you're thirty-three, how many years do you think separate us?"

"Deep feelings, like the Great Wall, withstand time," answered Sunim, quoting history.

"My aching back . . ."

Mansŏk could say no more.

Hearing Sunim's words, Mansŏk began some personal calculations. He wanted to raise kids to follow after him. If he cut way back on his drinking and saved on eating out, he would probably have enough to support a family. If he tightened his belt and lived frugally, then he might be able to sink some roots and be done with the life of a wanderer. She might be the mate he was meant to have and so live a normal life.

This forty-nine-year-old bag of bones, worn by a life of manual labor, was suddenly revitalized, like a spring tree bursting out in buds. Even his spirits, once always clouded with gloom, now cleared suddenly like the skies in autumn. The booze he used to drink nearly every day barely touched his lips. And he took overtime on the night shift he had once so carefully avoided. Still, he felt no weariness. It was as if he had regained the strength he had known at twenty, when he had worked himself bone-weary in order to bring Chŏmnye home as his bride.

After three months of struggle, he had a tidy sum of money in hand.

"Well, I've saved enough to get us a rented room," Mansŏk said awkwardly to Sunim.

"Already? I guess I had you pegged right all along! Those younger ones could never have managed this. Oh, how I've waited for this day!"

Sunim was much more happy and pleased than he had ever expected.

They didn't need a wedding ceremony. They rented a room and set up housekeeping.

Mansŏk's sudden taking of a bride didn't go unnoticed among the loudmouths at the workplace.

"Better watch out! One whiff of a thirty-year-old woman, and a fifty-year-old man can fall on his face."

"Sure, sure. A woman's clam at twenty may be soft and fleshy, but at thirty it's tight and sticky. You'll come on to her like a stallion at first but she'll turn you to jelly before you're done!"

Mansŏk gave a broad, indecent grin.

"Eat your hearts out, shitheads! I still have what it takes to produce ten sons."

Actually, Mansŏk couldn't have been happier. His much too long life as a wanderer was finally at an end. And now hope began to appear dimly for a future that had once seemed sad and gloomy. He had resigned himself to the idea that one had to fight his way through life with just bare fists. But, to some extent, that was an idea that belonged to an earlier time of frustration. The desire to live one day like a normal person had always lain hidden deep inside his heart.

The evening they moved into their "bridal chamber," Mansŏk's heart was alive with the sorrow and pain of times past.

"I can tell from the way you talk that you're from the Chŏlla region, but is this the first time you've been married?" asked Sunim after they had finished their first round of love to mark the marriage.

"So what if this is the first, or the tenth, or even the twentieth time I've married?" Mansŏk brusquely countered. He was absorbed by other thoughts.

"So what? Well, it's just that I find myself worrying about things, now that we're married."

"Then worry about worms you might have cooked into the food. I don't have a wife and kids somewhere else, if that's what's bugging you. Why don't you think about our future instead?"

"But shouldn't I know where your home is, why you turned into a wanderer, where your parents and brothers and sisters live?"

"Oh, shut up!"

Mansŏk sat bolt upright in bed, his angry eyes bulging with fearsome danger.

"What are you, the town clerk? A policeman? Why are you poking around, digging up useless scraps of the past? You and me, we're just a couple of people whose eyes happened to meet, who rubbed bellies, and now we're trying to live together. What's so important about the past? Why the crazy prying? I had so little to show for my life, so of course I ended up drifting like some cloud. Look, I'm just a plain commoner—no home, no family records. If you need to know that kind of stuff, you'd better pack up and get out—now!"

Mansŏk was agitated—enough to thrash her, perhaps.

"No, no. That's not what I meant at all! I only asked out of concern. . . . I'm sorry. I won't do it again."

The scolded wife, Sunim, rolled over and sank into a deep sleep. Mansŏk, staring intently at her gaunt shoulders, felt sorry. All she had done was ask her new husband a polite question and he had let himself get worked up. But he couldn't help it. Because of his past he had spent nearly thirty years hiding out or being chased like a criminal. You could call it a life, but how did it differ from death? For all that times had changed, he still could not go home again—proof of his continuing guilt. If he were to go back to his home, where the Ch'oe clan lived, they would probably bury him alive, no questions asked. It was a past he'd never told a soul, ever since he had fled his home under cover of the early evening dusk, driven by gunfire of the People's Army, with which he had sided until the day before.

"Dirty slut!"

Mansŏk gave a shudder. Just the thought of it made his body stiffen, sent the blood rushing to his head. And the scenes of that time flashed into his mind unchanged, as if ignoring the passage of time. His memory had never been very sharp, and by the time he was forty he had begun to forget things that had happened only a few days before. But why was that one time implanted so vividly in his mind? Even photographs turn yellow after thirty years, but this memory didn't know how to change. And it wasn't just appearances that hadn't changed. Even the smells of different scenes remained vivid. Why was this?

"They should have cut the head off her dead body!"

Mansŏk closed his eyes tightly and expelled a hot breath.

If that bitch of a wife Chŏmnye hadn't been completely stripped, I probably wouldn't have killed her. If she'd just been naked from the waist down, I could have overlooked it, thinking she was suffering at the hands of that bastard. But that bitch, already pregnant, took off all her clothes and rolled with him.

As vice-chairman of the People's Committee, Mansŏk had to be away from his house for two days to deliver a report to the Municipal People's Committee. The journey had been a great boost to Mansŏk's spirits.

"Comrade Ch'ŏn, your revolutionary struggle has been glorious. Your appointment as chairman, comrade, is only a matter of time. Have a good trip."

The words of the People's Army commander, spoken as Mansŏk set out on the road, rang in his ears. If only he could become chairman. Unseen by the two subordinates walking beside him, Mansŏk curled his hands into fists. The power he had enjoyed as vice-chairman was not enough. It wasn't that he needed reasons to avenge the twenty-five years of hunger he had suffered. But, if only he became chairman, all of Kamgol, Hangnae, and Chukch'on would be his—it was a sure thing.

Actually, there were more than just one or two things wrong with Sugil, the present chairman. He might do rather well for a while, but then there would be times of indecision, when fear or hesitation paralyzed him. Sugil had been made chairman only because he was three years older than Mansŏk.

Even when Elder Ch'oe's oldest grandson Hyŏnggyu, was about to be executed, Sugil had wavered like an idiot. The grandson, who had studied law in Seoul, was rumored to have slipped back into the village. Sugil could have brought the entire Ch'oe household into the matter and ruined them, but he had settled for a secret investigation. For the family had already been devastated by the execution of Elder Ch'oe's son, who had served as town administrator some time before. After four days of hiding, Elder Ch'oe's grandson was apprehended in a bamboo grove dugout at his uncle's house.

He had been dragged out back to a pine tree, his fate clearly determined. Gaunt and tight-lipped, he held his captors in a penetrating stare.

"It was Hyŏnggyu who contributed the pig we sacrificed for my mother's mourning," whispered Sugil in a trembling voice.

"Does that mean we should let him live?" challenged Mansŏk, giving him no leeway.

"Well, I'm not saying we really have to do this. . . ."

"Let us be resolute, Comrade Chairman, for the good of the revolution. . . ." Mansŏk deliberately raised his voice in imitation of the People's Army commander.

Perhaps sensing something strange afoot, the commander came up behind them.

"What are you two doing?"

Sugil's face froze instantly as he gazed, imploringly, at Mansŏk.

"We were saying how we ought to waste no time in dealing with this reactionary," replied Mansŏk quickly, all the while keeping an eye on Sugil, whose head now drooped with apparent relief.

"Good! Then deal with him at once!"

At the commander's word, Mansŏk winked a signal to his subordinates. The three men hoisted their bamboo spears and lunged at Elder Ch'oe's grandson, who was tied to the trunk of the pine. Screams, long screams, spread forth—screams that seemed to tear through the mountains, rend the skies, rip open the very earth. Sugil stood rigid as a post, eyes tightly closed. *You ass, you don't deserve to be chairman,* thought Mansŏk, watching him with a mocking sneer.

Quite unlike Sugil, Mansŏk listened to the drawn-out screams with a pleasure that thrilled every joint in his body. The sense of pleasure was, in fact, one of sweet revenge. All the sorrow and pain and mortification they had all known over generations of slavery, and that he himself had endured for his twenty-five years, was slowly, slowly washed away by that thrilling pleasure. For Mansŏk, this feeling amounted to an exhilaration even more intense and passionate than what he felt on top of his wife, Chŏmnye. That sensation was also maddening in its way, but it was too short-lived, and it was followed by a sudden, precipitous hollowness. But the pleasure he took from the screaming lasted as long as the time it took for the unforgettable memories to float up one after the other and then vanish; and, although he was left with a feeling of loss, there was none of the precipitous hollowness.

Buoyed at the thought of soon becoming council chairman, he arrived at the Municipal People's Council. He accepted the urgent directives handed down there and retraced his twelve-mile route home that same day.

When he got back to the council office the sun was about to set. After walking some twenty-four miles this long summer's day, Mansŏk was about as tired as he could be. There was no one in the office. He sent his two subordinates home. He would have to meet with the commander personally in order to convey the directives. After resting a while, his feet up on the desk, Mansŏk suddenly became aware of something. There was no reason the office should be empty like this—unless there had been some sort of emergency. He couldn't just sit around like this—he had to check things out.

Mansŏk went out back toward the attached living quarters. He sensed somebody was there.

Closer to the quarters, Mansŏk paused instinctively. A kind of human presence that felt strange to him emanated from the place. He strained to listen. It was clearly the sound of a man and woman making love. Mansŏk tensed, a queer sensation writhing within him. Involuntarily, he shot searching glances left and right. What brazen fool, in broad daylight, in the council's quarters . . . ? By now he had pressed himself close to the window.

Mansŏk almost cried out. He couldn't identify the man, whose buried face was turned away. But the one on her back, moaning, eyes tightly closed, mouth half open, was his very own Chŏmnye.

Mansŏk's head spun and everything seemed to turn dark. The next instant, a rush of heat burst from his stomach, fed as if by flames.

He grabbed the biggest rock he could find. Then he kicked open the door and jumped inside.

"You slut! You filthy slut!"

The man, spread out on top, stiffened abruptly and sat up, just as the rock thudded against the back of his head. His naked body vomited up an oddly short scream and tumbled to the floor. At almost the same moment, the naked woman jumped up. Arms crossed over her breasts, blanching with fear, she waddled to a corner of the room. Mansŏk, eyes blazing and teeth clenched, stepped closer to her. Cornered, unable to retreat further, the woman trembled, her nude body shriveling before his eyes. Mansŏk approached her like an animal. He had come to within one step of her.

"Don't—please!"

And then she darted forward, trying to slip away. Mansŏk delivered a hard kick to her stomach. She gave a short cry, like the man had, and rolled onto the floor.

Mansŏk ground his teeth fiercely and turned back to the man. The fellow moved spasmodically, blood streaming from his head. An arm, stretched into empty space, twitched. The man seemed to be clutching for something. Mansŏk grabbed the prostrate man's head and turned it toward him, then stepped back in shock.

"No! You son of a bitch!"

It was the People's Army commander. Mansŏk had thought all along the man was from the army. But who would have dreamed it was the commander, someone Mansŏk had trusted like heaven itself? His rage at being deceived, worse than his anger at the sight of his wife's face through the window, pulsed through him. The commander, his eyes rolled back and his arm still outstretched, was writhing toward a Russian-made submachine gun nearby. Mansŏk grabbed the weapon, aimed at the man's groin, and pulled the trigger. A staccato burst.

Mansŏk turned to his wife. In the moment just passed, she had steadied herself and was crawling on all fours toward the door. His wife's big buttocks loomed before him. The parts exposed between them seemed, like those of a pig, filthy and repulsive. Mansŏk aimed at that spot and again pulled the trigger. Another staccato burst.

When the bullets were exhausted, Mansŏk threw down the gun. The room had become a sea of blood where two sprawled corpses spewed forth their intestines.

Mansŏk had to get away. He ran from the building and lit out toward a path into the mountains.

"The world is a place where we must live according to reason. Who are you? Who do you think you are to beat on people as if they were dogs? It won't do, it won't do at all. You'll face the wrath of Heaven. The wrath of Heaven!"

The sound of his father's voice followed him all the way. He could just glimpse his mother's smudged face, Mansŏk's three-year-old boy was beaming happily as he called, "Daddy! Daddy!"

His new wife, Sunim, never again asked about the past and went on managing the household as it should be done. Mansŏk must have been thriving on this life, for he felt like a new man—embracing a young wife and able to sleep with a deep warmth unknown to him before.

The heat shimmered and danced on the far side of the construction site. The apartment complex was moving toward completion on schedule.

"I've been feeling a little strange lately," said his wife, averting her eyes.

"Maybe it's something you ate," offered Mansŏk, as if to suggest she buy a bottle of digestive.

"That's not it. The flowers haven't bloomed for two months now."

"Flowers?" Mansŏk asked. But then a light turned on inside his head.

"Oh, you mean, you've had news?" asked Mansŏk, excitement in his voice.

"That's what I mean," responded his wife, mimicking Mansŏk's tone and giving him an embarrassed glance.

"Just pop us out a son. I'll work hard and take good care of him," said Mansŏk, grabbing his wife's hand.

"That's disgusting! Children don't 'pop out'—they're born."

His wife laughed bashfully.

"If you had known I'd have to spend my life crushed under the heels of those rich bastards, you probably wouldn't have let me be born in the first place. And then I wouldn't have had this damn luck."

"Listen to this crap—he says anything that pleases him! At your age, what do you know, boy? When you live a few more years you'll understand."

His father had reproached eighteen-year-old Mansŏk no further.

At age twenty-one Mansŏk had taken a wife, though his heart wasn't in it. He cared little for his parents' concerns and, though he regarded wives as an amusement, this one was unusually well turned out. Her face was so pretty as to be wasted on her low class status. So it was that he married as if it were something unavoidable, and having slept with her he became a father. But he still hadn't wakened to the meaning of the word *father*—hadn't even begun to think about it.

But now he was fifty, and his wife was pregnant. And his father's words of thirty-two years before had come back to him, though he didn't know why. Was it because the years had brought understanding with them, as his father had predicted? Mansŏk was dimly aware of something deep and inexpressible in the notion that we live a life only to continue our blood line.

As his wife's stomach gradually swelled, work at the construction site was coming to an end. Sunim was frightened at the thought that they would soon have to take to the road in search of another construction site. So she went out job-hunting for him.

"Don't be foolish. What have I ever learned to do? All I know is farming and day labor—what the hell use is it to go job-hunting?"

Mansŏk tried to dissuade her from the outset, but she wouldn't listen. Several days later, she finally found an opening for a watchman. But just as Mansŏk had suspected, he was underqualified even for a job like that, one requiring only night work. He fell short in several respects. They required at least a middle school education, age thirty-five or younger, financial guarantor, and background investigation. After asking at a few more places, his wife gave up.

"I've been thinking I might as well go back to the soup-and-rice house. We can't live a wandering life."

At the mention of the soup-and-rice house, Mansŏk went through the roof: "We what? Can't what? You rub bellies with me and then decide we're going to live here until we die. Is that it? Now open those ears of yours and listen, before I break off those pretty legs: You just park yourself in a corner and stay put! Whether we eat or go hungry, we'll do as I see fit."

Mansŏk kicked open the door and went out.

But when he thought it over, his wife's feelings made sense. How could he leave her with a baby in her belly, wandering off to who knows where in search of a job? But then, what else could he do? Besides being uneducated and barely able to read, he was an old man of fifty. When he thought of his age, his future seemed black indeed. It was a question of how long he could continue at manual labor. His daily pay at the construction site was already pegged to a rate different from that of the younger laborers.

There was, however, one person he could go to—Mr. Pak, the on-site engineer assigned to the construction of the apartment complex. Even though he was a well-educated young man with an important job, he was quite without arrogance or pride. He was warm and sympathetic even toward the unskilled manual laborers. Mansŏk had gotten to be on quite good terms with him.

After putting it off several times, Mansŏk finally made up his mind and saw Mr. Pak. He spelled out his situation in every detail to the engineer.

"I can see you're up against it. Let me ask around, and then why don't we meet again tomorrow," said Mr. Pak with his usual kindness.

The next day, the engineer had a job ready for him.

"Well, it's not much. You'll have to do odd jobs in the apartment superintendent's office, and the pay isn't very good. I'm not even sure you'd be interested."

"Much obliged, Mr. Pak! If it's really for me, I'll take it—no questions asked. Much obliged."

Mansŏk bowed over and over. Good humor now shone where black clouds had once engulfed his heart.

And so Mansŏk became a handyman. The monthly pay was barely enough to put food on the table. Even so, Mansŏk was as happy as if he had plucked a star from the heavens. He had pleased his wife, and for the first time in his life he found himself drawing a monthly wage. Finding the job less demanding than construction, he applied himself to his new tasks.

His wife bore him a son, and Mansŏk was happy beyond comprehension. But when he thought of his boy growing up and marrying, his face suddenly froze. Even if the boy married at twenty, Mansŏk would then be seventy. Would he live that long? The thought sent a chill into his heart.

The addition of a baby cost more money than another adult would have. His wife began to complain about his pay. But Mansŏk ignored his wife's grumbling and lavished all his attention on the growing baby. When the new year arrived without a pay raise, his wife's complaints intensified. Of course the pay wouldn't increase just because they thought it should. A handyman was only a temporary post.

What is meant by living? For all Mansŏk knew, it was taking time despite my good intentions. Upon seeing those eyes above the mask, I had known immediately that the burglar was none other than Kwŏn. At the time, I'd decided I should treat this masked man as a burglar to the very end so that Kwŏn could save face and be his old self come morning when he was sober. And so I expected him to have been able to visit the clinic as if nothing had happened, to see his wife and third child. I regretted not having caught sight of his shoes at our front door. For some reason I got to thinking that I might have foreseen his fate simply on the basis of how well those shoes had been shined. As long as the toes of his shoes had been polished as bright as a glass bead, his pride would have glowed even more brightly and I could have breathed easy.

My coldhearted reminder as he was about to enter the room beside the gate weighed on my mind. What if he had been thinking that this would be the last time he would see his children? And what then must he have thought of me for blocking his way to the room where his youngsters slept?

My wife decided to visit the clinic. I had the kids tag along with her, and while they were out I scoured the room beside the gate. I hadn't been inside it in broad daylight since renting it out to the Kwŏns. As we had discovered when they moved in, their household possessions consisted entirely of their bedding and a few utensils for cooking and eating. Nothing unusual caught my eye. If there was anything that might afford me a clue, it would have to be his shoes. In the very place where the cabinet or a similar piece of furniture should have been—the place for the most valuable household possession—there were nine pairs of shoes lined up like soldiers awaiting inspection. Six pairs were neatly polished; the remainder were covered with dust. Altogether, then, Kwŏn had owned ten pairs. It seems he would select seven that suited his fancy, shine them all at once, and use them the following week, a different pair each day. While reflecting on the pair missing from the neatly shined group, I was struck by the realization that they would not return soon.

The time came for me to report Kwŏn's disappearance. It would be the first and last time I would notify Yi. I tried to remain as calm as possible while calling the policeman who had assured me time and again that I would one day grow to love my neighbor.

Translated by Bruce and Ju-Chan Fulton

by the spoonful and dying little by little as he drank it. The reckoning of his age, those bundled nodes of time, was truly frightening. Forty-eight was different, as was forty-nine, and fifty showed a face more different still. As tree leaves change the day after a frost, so did his age seem to rush headlong into oldness. Year by year his body was losing its vigor.

The baby, perhaps inherently immune to childhood in a poor family, grew in good health. Mansŏk chose the name Ch'ŏlsu for the baby, hoping his son would grow into a worthy man, the sort who appears in elementary school textbooks. In time, their life became more pinched, and his wife's complaining grew more shrill. But Mansŏk, preoccupied with affection for his baby boy, managed to forget such trials.

Several months before the boy's fourth birthday, Mansŏk had to give up his handyman's job because of an administrative cutback. It was as if he had walked up to the edge of a cliff on a dark road. He had never felt such dark despair for the future. And his agony was made more pressing by his obligation to a wife and child. His livelihood, from the very next day, was in immediate question. Mansŏk collected his wits and went out to the construction site to ask around. But, aside from possible manual labor, there was nothing he could count on. After wandering about for several days, he learned that there might be work at a construction site opening up more than fifty miles away.

"As long as I have life and breath we'll eat. Take good care of Ch'ŏlsu while I'm gone. I'll send money every couple of days."

Mansŏk set out for the construction site immediately.

He saved up his daily wages and sent some home every ten days. The vitality remaining in his fifty-three-year-old body was exhausted beyond what even he had believed possible, but Mansŏk gritted his teeth and bore on. He was driven by the conviction that he could not let his little son go hungry, his son with the bright and shiny eyes. To a manual laborer, liquor is almost like food. But Mansŏk drew the line—no more than half a pint a day. And, for a liquor snack, just kimchi and pickled radish. Finding unique sustenance and joy in saving and sending home his pay, he endured his bone-wearying fatigue day after day for more than two months.

Then one day Mansŏk received a letter. He took one look at the contents, leapt up with a cry, then slumped back down.

He went straight home and found their room coldly vacant and his son, quite unaware, in the care of the soup-and-rice house. His wife had run off with some young guy.

"Just you wait and see, you whore! Until they shovel dirt onto my face, I'll hunt you to the ends of the earth. And, when I've caught you, bitch, I'll tear your crotch into a dozen pieces."

Mansŏk, fiercely grinding his teeth, grabbed the boy into his embrace. Before his raging eyes there came alive a vision of entrails strewn about in a sea of blood and the prostrate, naked corpses of a man and a woman.

"My luck with women was bad from the start. Why should the second time be any better? All I can do now is find her and kill her. Let's just see how far she can run, the stinking bitch!"

A chilly smile formed on Mansŏk's lips and a steely, bloodthirsty glint shone in his eyes.

When he discovered, too late, that she had been careful enough to collect even his modest room deposit, Mansŏk shook with even greater rage. After gathering the few pennies he could from selling off his household effects, Mansŏk hoisted the baby onto his back and set out on a road leading nowhere.

They had probably gone to Seoul, someone said; maybe Pusan, said somebody else—all nothing more than guesswork. He decided to start with Pusan, which was closer, and have a look around. As he and the boy moved from city to city they occasionally went hungry and sometimes even begged. Unlike the days of his youth when he had wandered from one job to another, the world now seemed vast and desolate. At times, on days of endless drizzle or when snow blanketed them, Mansŏk, his little boy gathered in his arms, cried silent and endless tears.

What do people mean by "living a lifetime"? Where am I going? What am I doing here in this strange land where I don't know nobody? They call you a human being, but is this how you end up if you never should've been born? You mean to tell me some people are born noble and some people are born low? Where in hell did they get the idea of nobles and commoners, anyway? We're just the same—same faces, same minds. . . . So, what's the difference? Was it my mistake? Just because you're born low class, do you have to live like you are? Is the passion in me so different from the others? Is that why I did what I did? Maybe this is what I get for slaughtering so many people like dogs for those three or four months. I probably don't deserve to be alive today. But I didn't ask to be low born, like my father. Was I greedy? Can't you be greedy if you're a commoner? I'll drift like this and then I'll die—it won't be long. But then what happens to the kid? How's the little fellow going to turn out? He's all I'll leave behind. As long as I've got the kid in my arms, I can plug on, in spite of it all. Tomorrow's another day, another place I have to go—but where?

Mansŏk was unable to deal with such agony.

After a while, his wandering brought him close to his childhood home. As in times past, Mansŏk's heart throbbed and his legs tensed. He thought he might try slipping into the village under cover of darkness, but the next moment he gave up this idea. He couldn't possibly muster the courage.

Was this what old age did to a man? He was tempted and vexed like never before. Even while strictly avoiding the place all these years, he had twice approached the outskirts of his home village, on both occasions taking advantage of the night. In the end, though, he had forced himself to leave; his crime was still very much alive.

It was after Mansŏk and his son had wandered for a year and a half that he began to spit up blood. His body seemed withered, desiccated. He knew time was short, but still he sought out a hospital, since his young boy's well-being weighed heavily on his mind. The X-ray made it look like he had lived out his term. He headed for Seoul on the last leg of his search for his wife. And so, as his last task on this earth, he wandered Seoul for six months, looking both for his wife and an orphanage. Unable to keep up his strength, he had decided to entrust his son to an orphanage. He was spitting blood more and more frequently. He had come to fear that he would infect and kill his son if he clung to him any longer.

"I was going to raise my kids to be just right. . . . We'd live as bright as bells and I'd make my kids into gentlemen," the old man mumbled to himself as he tottered away, looking as if he were deranged, his back to the orphanage. Tears ran into the sunken hollows of his cheeks.

The images of his two sons' faces, one superimposed on the other, shimmered in the old man's clouded vision. One was his first son, Ch'ilbong, who had died at the hands of the People's Army when he was three; the other, whom he had just left at the orphanage, was Ch'ŏlsu.

The old man knew the time to go home had finally come. This would be his third attempt. Though it might result in his death, he was now determined to set foot on the soil of his home.

It was after the war that he learned that his father, mother, and son, Ch'ilbong, had been slaughtered by the People's Army.

"Who's this? It's not Mansŏk, is it?"

When Mansŏk had appeared one night out of the darkness at a drinking house near the ferry, three years after the fighting ended, Old Hwang was as startled as if he had seen a ghost.

"What are you doing here? What are you up to?"

In spite of the impenetrable darkness, Old Hwang looked all around him as he spoke rapidly.

Mansŏk felt himself propelled into the room. At the same time he stiffened with a chill at the thought that he had actually come where he shouldn't be.

"Just listen—don't make a sound. The very night you ran away those crazy sons of bitches wiped out three members of your family. Who would have thought they'd even go after a three-year-old kid?"

Mansŏk was struck dumb. That was the outcome of three years' unrelenting, anxious fear.

"Since you've come all this way, you might as well spend the night here. You can leave tomorrow morning before dawn."

Old Hwang added, with an agonized expression, that Mansŏk would probably be buried alive were he ever caught.

"I knew I did real bad, and that's why—to clean myself—I volunteered for the army as soon as I ran away. For three years straight I plowed through one battleground after another. I can't count the times I was almost killed. But somehow I've managed to survive so far. . . . "

Mansŏk spoke with a pathetic look, seeming to ask for exculpation.

"Did you really do all that?"

Old Hwang stared into Mansŏk's eyes, apparently surprised.

"Would I lie to you, Mr. Hwang, just to hear a few nice words?"

"Then, you really have done something that counts. But it isn't enough to help the Ch'oe family ease their hatred of you. The people are still mortally bitter. They'll probably never get over it. Go away. Go far away and start another life."

"I'll have to—seeing what I've done. . . . "

Even while saying this, Mansŏk was having trouble dealing with it, overwhelmed by a new surge of sorrow and regret. Cloaked by darkness, he had returned to his native soil, but he could never hope to live here again. He had come to ask about his family. But to hear himself bluntly told to go far away caused a strange sorrow to well up within him, a sorrow he couldn't cope with.

"Our world today is just what it was when you people ran around like maniacs. There's only one difference to speak of—it's under new ownership. This world's as treacherous as a see-saw."

"I must have been out of my mind. Even my mother and father, and they didn't do anything. . . ."

"Think about it and you'll see it wasn't just your fault. Not that I know anything, but I think it's the times that are at fault—the times. If you're guilty of anything, it's for having a temper like a hot pepper. That and your youth."

"We thought our day was coming. . . . We were so angry, so fed up with living like animals. . . . It was all an awful madness."

Mansŏk heaved a long sigh, like a mighty wind that sweeps the hills and valleys before subsiding.

"You know, I still remember. How old were you—about twelve? I mean, when you shoved Elder Ch'oe's grandnephews into the river. Ever since then, your temper's been as prickly as a fruit thorn. Your father had to put up with a lot of hardship because of that."

Old Hwang, with a pained expression, kept clucking his tongue.

"They dragged Father away and kicked the hell out of him. Not me, but Father. And then, they even ran him out of the village. That's when the hate, like a snake's poison, began to fill my heart."

Mansŏk's husky voice had turned hoarse. Though he might forget his birthday from time to time, he was unable to forget those events. All the same, it was also a memory he didn't wish to dwell on.

It was September and a cool wind had been brushing the reeds. Around this time of year the oak leaves were showing signs of changing out of their usual deep green and the hairy crabs were starting to fatten up.

Mansŏk was out catching crabs with two of Elder Ch'oe's grandnephews. The crabs lived in tunnels they dug between rocks on the reed flats. They were such dimwitted creatures that if you carefully stuck a reed-flower stem into the tunnel and worked it around, pausing a few times, they would bite right into it with one of their big claws. A crab that did that was as good as caught. Those things were so stupid that, once they clamped down with a claw they never let go. Even if the claw broke off from the crab, whatever had been grabbed stayed clamped in the claw. Somehow the children got it into their heads that if your finger was bitten you might as well kiss it good-bye. This fear of losing a finger was probably why the children weren't eager to catch crabs—though the animals made a savory treat when roasted and dipped in soy sauce.

Mansŏk was known among the children for his skill at catching crabs. And it was true. He was quick to spot their tunnels, he lured them with impressive skill, and he was adroit at handling a hair-covered crab dangling from a reed-flower stem. The other children were full of admiration at this talent of Mansŏk's.

Mansŏk had come by this accomplishment alone and at a cost in agony quite unknown to the other children. Mansŏk had begun at the age of six to rummage around the reed flats that stretched wide along the river's edge. Unknown to the others, there were lots of tasty things in the reeds to satisfy an appetite. Kingfisher eggs in the spring, their chicks in the summer, crabs in the fall—all filled Mansŏk's empty stomach. His family could not even feed him plain boiled barley and so his empty stomach always growled. Since he would be out to satisfy his hunger, there was nothing scary to Mansŏk about the crab claws. In the beginning, he didn't have a finger that wasn't bitten. Once you're bitten, you have to slam the crab against the ground. When the claw breaks off the crab you grit your teeth and remove the part that's digging into you. But if you try this while the claw is still attached to the crab, you're setting yourself up to get bitten on the other hand by the remaining claw. And if you end up with a finger from each hand caught in each claw, then what?

While he was suffering alone, not a finger without a bite, Mansŏk became rather skillful at handling the crabs. The pain of a crab bite wasn't something you'd soon forget. Sparks would flash inside his eyes and even the tip of his penis would burn. And the finger would hurt as if it were falling off. But he never lost a finger. That much pain was no big deal, Mansŏk thought, if he could rid himself of the hunger that colored his vision yellow and made his knees buckle.

But the pain so scared the other children that they had no heart for catching crabs, and the children of the Ch'oe family, in particular, would back away at the mere sight of a crab flourishing its ten hairy legs. Mansŏk inwardly scorned and dismissed such children: "You kids think just because you're from some rich man's family that I'm not so good. Well, if I was going to take you out, I could do it with one punch!" he would mumble to himself.

On that day, Elder Ch'oe's two grandnephews had offered him three sweet potatoes if he would catch them five crabs. It wasn't a bad piece of business and so Mansŏk set out to provide. Murmuring to himself about well-boiled sweet potatoes, Mansŏk threw himself into the task. He was twitching a reed-flower stem at what was to be the fourth crab when a scream pierced the air. Mansŏk sat bolt upright.

The younger of the two Ch'oe children, a nine-year-old, had been crouching beside a small crock that held the catch. Now he was gasping for breath, jumping up and down, and screaming madly. And there on a finger of the hand on the arm that was flailing the air was attached a crab. The older brother, who was Mansŏk's age, not knowing what else to do, was calling "Mother! Mother!" It was obvious that the younger boy had been playing with the crabs as they crawled around the inner sides of the crock, and had got himself bitten square on the finger.

Mansŏk dashed over, grabbed the boy's waving arm, and swung it downwards with all his might. But still the crab dangled from the finger. He pressed the boy's palm against the ground and drove his heel down on the crab. Its body was crushed and the claw fell off. As usual, the claw still held fast to the finger. The kid was still letting loose his gasping cries, but Mansŏk quickly managed to open the claw and release the finger. It began at that moment.

"You son of a bitch!"

Mansŏk saw stars. The older boy had just punched Mansŏk in the cheek.

"What'd you do that for?"

It was so sudden that Mansŏk was in a daze.

"Don't play dumb."

Again the fist came flying.

Mansŏk had no time to duck, and as he absorbed the blow it began to dawn on him that he was being blamed for something he hadn't done. Perplexed, he retreated several steps.

"I know what you're up to. Lay off the rough stuff," yelled Mansŏk, confronting them and poised for a fight.

He set his teeth and his eyes took on a threatening glint. Surprised by Mansŏk's nerve, the older boy hesitated.

"It's all your fault that my brother got bit, so now I'm telling you to stick your hands down in there."

The bigger boy pointed towards the crock full of crabs while the little one studied his hand and cried mournfully.

"What?"

Mansŏk felt his stomach turning over. Again he was up against the unfairness he had to face because he was a commoner. The prejudice wasn't something expressed in words. Since it was unreasoning, words were unnecessary, completely useless. It all came down to doing as he was told.

But he couldn't stick his hands inside a crock full of crabs. It wasn't a question of being at fault or not. The other kid was his own age, not an adult. He couldn't let that kid order him around. He'd sooner drop dead on the spot.

"Well, are you going to stick them in or not?" the big kid yelled.

"You'd have to kill me first!"

Mansŏk confronted him with a scornful laugh.

"How's that? Someone of your sort defying me? Maybe we'd better take you up on that. Sure, why not? Hey, Tongjin, let's half kill this asshole!" said the big one to his brother and the two raised their clenched fists.

"Hey, boy! Don't make trouble, no matter what you think. Remember your origins. He who endures is the better man."

Every time there was trouble, big or little, his meek and gentle father would repeat these words. Even in the midst of this attack by the two ganged up against him, his father's words popped to mind. But they couldn't ward away this drubbing.

Mansŏk ducked the fists that came flying at him. Though he didn't live or eat very well, he had a body that started hauling firewood before he was ten and, since he turned ten, carried a backrack. And he was skilled enough in fighting to make quick work of the two Ch'oe boys, who had been brought up eating meat.

Mansŏk knew how to win a fight in a single round. The big boy, whose punch had missed, sprang at Mansŏk, panting. Mansŏk took aim at his groin and let his foot fly. The boy, unable even to cry out, fell flat on his back, writhing.

"Get up! Come on, get up!" cried the younger one, shaking his older brother, who lay pale and twisting on the ground.

"Your turn to get punched, asshole!"

Mansŏk pulled the younger one up by his collar and gave him a ruthless thrashing. By now, Mansŏk was not himself. He had a sharp and fiery temper that, once aroused, he could not control. So much so, that his mother would curse him as "tiger bait."

Mansŏk had the fearsome thought that he could kill these two with no one being the wiser. It crossed his mind that he could pummel them some more and then throw them in the river. So he beat them unconscious and dragged them one by one to the edge of the river, and it was then he was discovered by grown-ups from the village.

His father was dragged to the Ch'oe house, beaten half dead, and carried back home. Now barely able to move, he was to be thrown out of the village. His father fell to the ground, crying and pleading for mercy, but the men from the Ch'oe household loaded all the household effects onto a cart and dumped them by the river. His father had to build a dugout for them to live in on a mountain slope across the river. Having lost their tenancy with the Ch'oes, they were reduced to going hungry as often as they ate. But his father neither punished nor rebuked Mansŏk.

"You're just like your grandfather. Your blood's too hot for a commoner!"

His father, bedridden with pain, mumbled half to himself as tears ran down his face.

It was not until four years later that his father was forgiven by the Ch'oes and allowed to move back into the old house.

"Would you know, by any chance, how my parents' graves . . . ?"

He finally let out the words he had so hesitated to say and then dropped his head.

"You should be ashamed. Who do you think would volunteer to bury them in the face of all that bloodthirsty terror? We were all afraid that we'd get into serious trouble, including me."

Old Hwang spoke very directly. Mansŏk, his head lowered, gave no response.

Mansŏk had never hoped that his parents might possibly have a grave. All he wanted was to know their final resting place.

When it came to reactionaries, could any have been more reactionary than him? His mother, father, and three-year-old kid suffered a harsher death than anyone else. Who would have dared to step forward and offer to care for their bodies? In what pit were they buried together?

"Mr. Hwang, thank you. I'll have to leave you now."

Mansŏk rose.

"What are you talking about? Have yourself a nap and leave before cockcrow."

"No, that won't do. If they catch sight of me moving around at dawn, you'll be in a prickly situation, Mr. Hwang. It'd be best to slip away right now."

"Had I known you'd leave like this, I would have made you a rice ball or something."

"Mr. Hwang, as long as I live I'll never forget the time you saved me."

"No, no. Neither you nor I has done anything wrong, except for being born with the wrong blood in our veins. I understand what's going on inside you. When you really look at it, a man like me has nothing to boast of. People like me who seek an easy life, laughing in spite of this and laughing in spite of that, are no better than spineless idiots. Compared with people like me, how much a man you are! You are really what a man is. So, for you to thank me is to insult me. To have kept a secret of your whereabouts was the proper duty of a small man like me who'll never live so boldly as you."

Moisture was forming in Old Hwang's eyes.

"Mr. Hwang, I wish you a long, long life," said Mansŏk in a choking voice, his head lowered in contrition.

"Forget it—every bit of it! Go and live your own full life. That's your way out."

Mansŏk parted from Old Hwang in the darkness.

As soon as Mansŏk's eyes grew accustomed to the dark he could faintly make out the river's course. Looking out at that river, he could no longer move. A ferry across the river could have taken him to his home.

Mansŏk had made his way past the village shrine when gunfire began to sound behind him like beans popping on a skillet. In between the shots he could hear shouts of agitation. Mansŏk was unable to run as fast as his burning heart urged. Today he had already walked twenty-four miles, going and coming, and was thoroughly exhausted. The sound of gunfire came gradually closer. When Mansŏk reached the ferry, Old Hwang was just tying up his boat.

"Mr. Hwang. You've got to help me!"

"What happened?"

"I've just killed the People's Army commander. Please, take me in your boat."

"Are you crazy? If we go out in that boat, we'll get shot dead in the middle of the river. Quick, run to the reeds! To the reeds. The fog's just started to rise and it'll be dark soon. Run quickly! Now!"

Old Hwang stamped his foot and Mansŏk made a dash for the reed flats.

Twilight, the grayish-yellow of a cuckoo, blazed on the river's surface, and the evening fog rose slowly along the shores. Wind, passing through the reeds, raised the sound of a baby's whine, while the stalks themselves undulated in the waves. Mansŏk felt relieved and turned all his strength to crawling through the flats. With this much wind blowing against the reeds, the ripple caused by a single man does not stand out. This he had learned from experience, having been in and out of these reeds since he was a child.

By the time he had made it to the middle of the wide and even stand of reeds, Mansŏk heard three or four gunshots at the riverbank. Mansŏk waited until it grew pitch dark before he leapt into the river. Avoiding the main roads, he went up into the mountains.

At that time his very life had rested in the hands of Old Hwang.

Early July through early September had been like a dream for Mansŏk. For those two months, Mansŏk really believed the world was his.

They said they would liberate the farmer-laborers. They said rich men and landlords would be eliminated and all power would go to the commoners. Mansŏk had no need to think or mull. He was in his element, like a fish in water. He waved a freshly sharpened sickle and a bloodthirsty glint shot from his eyes.

The first thing Mansŏk did was burn down the Ch'oes' ancestral shrine hall.

"Starting now, I'm going to rip the Ch'oe family up by its roots!" he shouted as he stared at the flaming building. "I'll wipe them all out! There'll be nothing left with a cock hanging from it."

Nobody dared get in the way of Mansŏk and the deadly sickle he brandished. Anyone who challenged him would have lost his head to the flying sickle. Some who were fast on their feet managed to escape him, but not the Ch'oe men, who were all caught and dragged in. They were beaten until half dead, and each day one of them died, tied to the pine out back.

Even though the Ch'oe family was in constant mourning, not a single bier was to be seen; they hadn't been able to retrieve the corpses.

Among the entire Ch'oe family there was no food to eat, not in any of their houses. All their cereal and grains had been looted, so thoroughly that they could not even make gruel.

"It's not right. You wouldn't treat animals like that—how can you do it to humans? They have little children there—you've got to at least let them cook gruel. Mansŏk, boy, change your mind and let them at least cook gruel. These things simply aren't done, even if you were avenging your own father's murder."

His father clung to Mansŏk as he pleaded.

"You've got to stop this reactionary talk. You've suffered this all your life and you're still not disgusted? Is that it?"

Mansŏk shook himself loose from his father and shot a look skyward.

"You've got to get rid of this bullheadedness. Whether you like them or not, those people have given us our daily bread."

"Father, is that all you can say? If you don't change your attitude, and soon, do you know what will happen? You'll end up just like those damn Ch'oes."

A cold look had come over Mansŏk's face.

"Unless you change. I think you exaggerate, Father. When have those people ever fed us? We worked our fingers to the bone so the likes of them could get big and fat, and all we eat is chaff and sweepings—it's barely enough to live on."

His daughter-in-law showed with her eyes that she took her husband's side.

Old Mr. Ch'ŏn kept his mouth shut after that. They had all changed so completely, even his daughter-in-law. People who change their minds face death, they said. The two of them were like different people. His son could butcher people without blinking an eye, and overnight his daughter-in-law had cast off her modest manner and turned into a genuine adulteress. His daughter-in-law, as head of the Alliance of Democratic Women, was wielding power just like his son. For this beautiful daughter-in-law, whose eyes had always been demurely lowered, to have changed so much deeply grieved the old man. No, it's that Communist Party that makes people change so. The more he thought about it, the more frightened and fearful he became.

Mansŏk was so intent on being the eagle who, wings full out, soared as he wished that he was totally unaware of the fires that smoldered beneath his feet. He had no inkling that his wife had fallen madly for the pistol-packing People's Army commander, who ran everything so briskly with just a few words. Even when she would turn down Mansŏk's bedtime requests because she was "tired," rather than growing suspicious he would feel sorry for burdening his wife, who had struggled during the day to accomplish revolutionary tasks.

Mansŏk stuck to out-of-the-way villages to avoid being picked up by the People's Volunteer Army. All the while he was tormented by that ugly dream each night—the dream of a man and woman writhing naked, then collapsing, their guts spewn out on the floor in a sea of blood.

If the thought came to him while he was eating, he would become nauseous and unable to eat any more. After about one month on the run, he heard that the People's Army had lost the battle and were, for the most part, withdrawing to the mountains. Mansŏk thought deeply on what would have become of him if none of this had happened and he had remained in his native village. The world would have turned inside out again. Obviously, the Ch'oe people who had managed to escape would have descended on him. He then would have had no course but to run off with the People's Army.

The war had ended. But the mopping up was not yet finished, just as sweeping remains when the threshing's done. There were the Red guerrillas who had escaped into the mountains on the prowl at night, as well as those who had sided with the rebels, still to be ferreted out.

"Needless to say, it's very clear. Don't you think? Some went to the mountains but those who didn't see the handwriting on the wall were overthrown. They were rounded up and faced an ugly fate."

Old Hwang shook his head as if loath to draw his story out any further.

Mansŏk released a sigh, long as the river's course. And he slowly stepped through the darkness. Just as Mr. Hwang had said, he had no choice but to go and live somewhere far away. And now he had nothing—nothing gained, nothing saved, nothing whatsoever. Just emptiness and absurdity.

He really had wanted to go to school. But they told him learning wasn't for just anyone. They told him that commoners had their own tasks that were different—gathering wood, packing a backrack, and grazing cattle. While the Ch'oe kids sat in the shade of a tree eating watermelons until their stomachs burst, he had to be out leaping around the sun-baked paddy paths, shouting himself hoarse to shoo the birds away. In winter, of course, he had to gather up the children's book bags and carry them to school. While dressed in clothing padded several times thicker than his and wearing mittens as well, those children complained they couldn't carry book bags because their hands were cold.

To get two rice cakes to eat, he had to show them his cock and peel back the foreskin, in spite of the pain it caused. To have a single persimmon, he spent half a day as their horse in a horse-riding game. He was willing to do most anything if it meant putting something in a stomach that knew only constant hunger. But that was only until he was thirteen or fourteen. After he turned fifteen, he began to grit his teeth until the roots ached.

"Mansŏk, Mansŏk! You've got to let me go! I'll give you all my fields and paddies if you'll just let me go."

Some of the Ch'oes were rubbing their palms in supplication hard enough to start a fire when they breathed their last.

"Mansŏk. I mean, Vice-Chairman, sir. Your esteemed father and I were friends for thirty years. Won't you spare me? Please . . . "

Some gushed tears as they writhed on the floor of the porch.

"Comrade Vice-Chairman . . . Comrade . . . Vice-Chairman . . . "

Some, lips trembling, couldn't manage to speak.

Some shit their undigested food, some pissed themselves sloppy, some trembled from head to foot but then went stiff as boards.

Not one of them still trumpeted the grandeur, the arrogance, the self-importance, or the authority that they had shown a few days earlier. "You ill-bred trash! You could learn manners from a dog! How dare you act like this before your betters?" Had even one among them responded in such a way, he might well have been allowed to live.

As if guarded by their departed souls, this land was not something he could return to, thought Mansŏk as he turned his back to the river and began to step quickly into the darkness.

Old Mansŏk, constantly wiping away his tears, took three or four hours to walk from the suburban orphanage to the downtown business district. Without a single coin to his name, he had no choice but to walk.

He found the pedestrian overpass that had earlier caught his eye. The old man barely managed the strength to grasp the handrail and climb the steps. He took off one of his black rubber shoes and squatted down at the near end of the bridge where the two flights of steps from the sidewalk met. The single black shoe rested in front of him.

He had to get a meal each day and he had to get the bus fare home.

He could no longer do manual labor. At whatever job site he inquired, they had no work to give him. His wrinkled and desiccated face was still a face, but his drooping shoulders revealed at a glance that this was no longer the body of a laboring man. Even if a sympathetic or even inexperienced foreman were to assign him some task, he didn't have the strength to carry it out. Not only had his body grown loose and slack but he was apt to spit up blood if he taxed himself.

The old man's eyes were closed, his head hung low. In his shabby appearance he was every bit the beggar.

The old man was not at all interested in how many coins had collected in the rubber shoe, for his heart was already home. With the day of his death drawing near, the old man was more inclined this way. At some point, his heart had started to focus increasingly on that place.

Home was a land where nothing whatsoever was left for him, a land with not a single face to welcome him. If there were something there it would be just an ugly past. For what reason could his heart, in spite of it all, be drawn to that place at the very risk of life? For all the thought he gave to it, he couldn't understand his own feelings.

He had wandered some two years with the boy in tow, following the construction sites, as he searched for his wife Sunim. One reclamation project where he worked for a while was no more than twenty-five miles from his birthplace. At first, thinking he might run into some familiar face, he thought about finding some other place to work. But the conditions there were too good to turn his back on easily. Reclamation projects were always long-term, and since they were mostly government operations, they had the advantage of regular pay. He wavered a bit but then settled in with an attitude of resignation.

Two months passed, then three, without his encountering even one familiar face. During that time a hankering stole into his heart. He was taken with a wish to see Mr. Hwang, if only once. Once he got that idea into his head, he began to find himself often disconcerted. Countless people worked at the site. Many shared the same life, each day exerting themselves and putting away three meals. But they didn't have the humanness suggested by a well-baked sweet potato or a warm, snug room on a snowy night. They worked together easily like a team when they were on the job, but when the work was done they would go their separate ways and quite forget their working life. The life of the wanderer has always been like this.

And they were not without women. But, compared with the men, these women were even more like vacant shadows. Selling their bodies for a few coins, they would turn into inert lumps of flesh just as soon as their task was over. Doing it with them, no matter how many times he tried, always left Mansŏk feeling like he had just bathed in a tub filled only to his ankles with tepid water. How he longed to be immersed up to his neck in a steaming hot tub of water! Suddenly the thought of his wife's body came to mind. How he longed to be drenched with sweat and get that faint and listless feeling, like all his body's strength had been drained away! But then came the memory that flooded in and instantly destroyed his longing. In broad daylight, in the council's quarters, writhing . . .

Perhaps it was this rootlessness that made him want to see Old Hwang again.

The men had one day off a week. That day was boring and frustrating for him. He wasn't particularly drawn to drinking or gambling. But his heart did brim with thoughts of buying something like a bottle of rice wine and going to visit Old Hwang.

Mansŏk held out as long as he could and then, sometime after lunch, he ended up on a bus.

He got off the bus at the town of P, about ten miles before his home village. It wasn't long before the sun was about to set. At a roadside shop, Mansŏk bought two bottles of rice wine. Then he found a place to eat. He ordered a double portion of soup and rice and a glass of *soju*. With ten miles to walk in the dark, he had to stoke up well.

"You mean they're still not done with the burying?"

"That's what I said."

"No kidding! How long has it been since the war ended? You mean they've been burying their people for two years now?"

"Hey look. You can't see anything but your rose-colored view of things. Are you telling me you don't know how many of them were killed?"

"I know. If the People's Army had kicked them around for another six months back then, the Ch'oe clan would have been wiped out."

Mansŏk, his glass of *soju* moving to his lips, froze in place. A shock, at which his body seemed to stiffen, hit the back of his head.

With a flick of his eyes Mansŏk examined the faces of the two men. There was nothing familiar about them. Mansŏk unconsciously heaved a great sigh.

"So true. It's a good thing for the Ch'oe family that the national army won when they did."

"Yeah, but were they able to get their dead reburied properly then?"

"What? With so many people just buried like dried fish on a string in this pit or that, how could they tell whose bones were whose?"

"What a godawful mess! With no way of telling, what must the children have thought as they tried to rebury what they hoped were the bones of their parents?"

"God knows! I say devotion like that ought to be rewarded."

"Well, while the Ch'oes care for their departed like that, what about the people who took up the rebel cause or the scattered souls of their families?"

"That's not your worry. At this point the Ch'oe family is blind with rage. What would they care about the souls of dead traitors?"

Mansŏk, emptying one glass of *soju* after another, was growing coldly tensed. Unlike his heart, which told him to clear out of the place, his body, growing heavier, was sinking down into his seat.

"No, that's not what I'm saying. As long as revengeful spirits of the dead, for whatever reason, are out and moving around, that village will never settle down in peace, I mean."

"So, will the Ch'oe clan therefore bury the commoners who they see as their enemies?"

"It's a crazy business. When you think how they buried that silly Chŏmbagu alive—and he was nobody—then you know these Ch'oes aren't normal people."

Chŏmbagu, that dimwit with the coin-sized mole on the left of his forehead. He would dance for joy, grab a spear, and, as if his day had come, carry out whatever was asked of him. And, when he had run a spear through someone's chest, he would show his yellow teeth and make a gaping laugh. That face was not a laughing face; rather, it was very much the look of an angry, growling dog. It was an expression that came of fear, and people called it his "dog laugh." That is the Chŏmbagu who was buried alive. Somewhat deficient mentally, he clearly was unable to sense that the situation around him had worsened. Would Chŏmbagu have been laughing his dog laugh even while being buried alive?

Mansŏk's arm trembled with anger as he raised the glass of *soju*.

"Anyhow, the Reds aren't coming down from the hills these days, so we can get on with life. Even up to last year we were not able to stretch out and sleep easily."

"By now they seem pretty well rounded up. After Sugil, the chairman, was killed last October, not one has come down, even to his village."

"So, then, the one who died with Sugil—his face bashed beyond recognition—wasn't that surely the Mansŏk who had been vice-chairman, like they say?

"Could be. Having died, he would drop out of sight. If only Sugil had died and Mansŏk had lived to run away, then wouldn't the Ch'oe family have suffered some more grim times? That Mansŏk was not your common baggage, I think. He was as venomous as ten poison snakes in one."

"Oh, yeah. That roughneck was roasting snakes to eat before he was ten."

"You bet!"

"But, Mansŏk kills a People's Army commander and his own wife and then runs away. And this nearly two weeks before the People's Army pulled out. Wouldn't Mansŏk have been a candidate for the People's Army firing squad? So why would he have joined up with them again?"

"Oh, you really try my patience! Whatever else may have been involved, who did wrong? The guy who fucked somebody's wife or the husband who killed the guy? And since they'd have their own baggage, too, wouldn't old wounds—long forgotten—get opened up again? And, when the People's Army was running in retreat, where were they to get anyone's support? The help of one fierce specimen like Mansŏk would've been the same as the help of ten ordinary people."

"That's true. That's sure true."

Mansŏk, his face ashen, quickly got up and left. He set out in the direction opposite to where Old Hwang lived. There should be buses headed toward the construction site, he was thinking.

Back at the construction site, Mansŏk drank up the two bottles of rice wine he had bought to give Old Hwang. And for four days he was sick in bed, unable to budge.

He had never gone catching and roasting snakes to eat before he was ten. True, he had often thought about what it would be like to eat roasted snake. People eat cows, pigs, dogs, and chickens. They eat grasshoppers and frogs. Yet there seems to be something about snakes that keeps people from eating them. Come summer, snakes were common in riverside reed patches and thickets in the foothills. Children, when they caught sight of a snake, would turn tail and run away. But then, all it took was for somebody to catch one, then they would all grab stones and go on the attack. They would always make sure that the snake died in a welter of wounds. But, even then, the children would not retreat. If they didn't chop it into pieces, the snake would drink the dew overnight, come back to life at dawn, and surely return for revenge. The revived snake would go around to the house of each boy who had tried to kill it and kill him by biting off his penis. So the children were satisfied only if they could stone a snake to death and chop it into pieces, even at the risk of their lives. A child would grab hold of his crotch with one hand while throwing rocks with all his might. But Mansŏk didn't throw any rocks. He was hungry and weak and had no need to exert himself to kill the snake; he was most concerned with what he might do to roast and eat its flesh. The eels caught in the river were incredibly tasty. Since snakes and eels looked much the same, he would be lost in thoughts of how sweet and nutlike was the taste of river eel when he put it hot and sizzling into his mouth.

It looked like Sugil had turned partisan, attacked the village, and then gotten himself killed. He was, indeed, a miserable wretch. It had seemed to Mansŏk that Sugil, living with a widowed mother, somehow scraped along even closer to starvation than he did.

"With luck like this, what's the point of living? I'm just living for my mother. Once she's dead and gone I'm going to give up this shit-hole world."

He would talk like this, Sugil who had more spirit than muscle.

Becoming chairman of the People's Committee, though, seemed to make him more energetic. Still, he had been somewhat troubled by all the random killing. In the end, he had died on his home turf.

It seemed that Mansŏk had already been taken for dead by the people of his home village, particularly those in the Ch'oe clan. In that case, only Old Hwang and his wife knew of his existence. There was no way that word of his existence would slip out of the tight-lipped Old Hwang. His life had already ended. Now no trace of him whatever remained in his native place.

Mansŏk, sick in bed for four days, thought seriously about his lot in life. It was true emptiness, meaninglessness. If anything had changed, it was just that he went from tenant farmer to migrant laborer.

Mansŏk made up his mind never to go near the land of his home again. He had stuck to that decision for nearly thirty years now. No matter how good the job site, he always avoided it if it was close to home.

An evening fog was spreading thickly along the riverbank, like the aftermath of some sadness. The old man had been standing a long time, shoulders drooped as if weighted and staring vacantly at the swirling of the fog as it spread into a stand of reeds.

Would there still be, even now, so many hairy crabs in those reeds? He had roasted them to eat when he was young and, after he grew, they made the best of snacks to go with liquor. After knocking back a glass of *soju* the taste you could get chewing on a crab leg soaked in mellow soy sauce . . .

The old man swallowed and wiped his mouth with the palm of his hand. The rough surface of his palm on the skin around his mouth felt deeply incised, like the scar of some wound. The old man looked down at the palm of his hand with a wasted feeling: A palm that had callused all it could, and then heaved up many little cracks. Perhaps it was the hardened excesses, but he could feel no pain even when stabbed by something sizable.

The old man gave a long, thin sigh. In the eyes that looked down into the palm there rose a melancholy the color of the fog.

Long years. Years that have flown by so fast. Empty, meaningless years . . .

The old man set his teeth so firmly that the corners of his mouth began to droop as he turned his gaze once more toward the riverbank. The fog, like some living thing, was devouring both the rambling patches of reeds and the wide body of the river itself.

If it weren't for those reeds . . .

The old man's body trembled. Now that he finally stood face to face with the river, the memory of that day approached, tearing at the intervening years, so that it seemed to have happened yesterday.

The fog stopped spreading. Thin darkness was being laid out, one furrow after another. The old man felt a chill run down his back as he looked around. It was dark enough now to blur the outline of the mountain ridge. The old man felt the pang of hunger and a heavy fatigue that made him want to lie down. Now he just wanted to get to some tavern.

The old man turned heavy feet toward the tavern on his left, which stood unchanged from the old days, except that the roof had turned to slate. What worse could happen, he wondered in his miserable state, but still he waited until it was a bit darker. He was invaded to the marrow of his bones by a helpless sense of guilt.

Could Old Hwang still be alive? If so, he would be over seventy. He had left the running of the tavern to his wife while he operated the ferry by himself. This Old Hwang would launch his ferry for even one person, whether late at night or early dawn, winter or summer. This man who always had a smile didn't seem to hate or be hated by anyone in the world. Everyone in any of the surrounding villages—Kamgol, Hangnae, Chukch'on—all felt warmly protective of Old Hwang and his wife. It was Old Hwang who had glanced up at him for the first time and bellowed,

"Why are you doing this? Are you crazy? The world may change and the times can be unpredictable but if you can't rely on a man, he's useless!"

"Be careful what you say Mr. Hwang! Please. As someone who should take the lead, how can you talk like that?"

"Well, now, listen to what I say. Haven't you thought about what happened to the pro-Japanese collaborators after Liberation?"

"What are you talking about? Oh, do you think things today are just like they were back then? Well, I have just one last thing to tell you and I want you to open your ears wide and listen carefully. Since it was you who said it, Mr. Hwang, I'll make like I didn't hear it. But if you ever talk like that again, I'll report you on the spot—no questions asked! Don't forget that!"

Old Hwang, mouth agape, could make no answer.

He doubted whether his father and Old Hwang clearly understood what it was like to live in the world at that time or where the purpose of living a life lay. They both said one had to live by reason. Though he may once have known what reason was all about, he didn't know now.

Old Hwang was probably so old now that even if they collided on some street corner they probably wouldn't recognize each other. The times had rounded a long bend and flowed on.

The old man began to step into the twilight with a bit of a groping gait, as if he were making his way across stepping stones. He had a dilapidated bag strapped to his bent shoulders. After a few steps toward the tavern the old man stopped and began to cough. He covered his mouth with one hand and clutched with the other at the clothing covering his chest. Without any sound at all the coughing only spun and hacked inside his throat. The old man was unable to stop the coughing, and his body shriveled up smaller and smaller.

The old man's body was nearly in a squat when the coughing stopped. When a fit of coughing racked him like this, his chest seethed with a nearly unendurable fever and seemed to flutter like shredded rice-paper. And there came the sweat that drenched his entire body as it was being swept by a chill.

No good. It's all over.

The old man shook his head as he had that thought again. Each time the coughing racked his chest, the old man felt death come another step closer.

His legs shaking, the old man placed his palms on his knees and slowly rose. A stinking dizziness invaded him dimly like the fog spreading across the riverbank.

The old man paused in front of the tavern gate. Should I say something to make myself known? But nothing came to mind and only the amiable face of a young Mr. Hwang flickered before him.

"Hello, anyone home?"

The old man shouted with what strength he had. But his voice, though he could hear it, was very weak and trembling.

"Who's there?"

A man emerged from a shed and looked around.

The old man strained to see. Although the gloom of evening had already settled in, he could sense that the man in the distance was not an old one.

Mr. Hwang's son? the old man thought suddenly. That powerful youth, though a poor substitute for his father, had taken over the oars of the ferry.

"A big help to me. But that kid came into the world three years too early, I think. Ended up getting yanked around—first by this side then by that side. How it troubled me when that happened . . . "

He could hear Mr. Hwang's voice vividly.

"Who is it?" a sturdy man in his forties was asking quietly.

"I, uh . . . are you still running a tavern here?" the old man began, pushing aside a tangle of questions.

"How? When the bridge went in and the ferry was wiped out the tavern naturally dried up, too."

Answering slowly and deliberately, he took in the old man's shabby appearance with a look of dissatisfaction.

"They put a bridge over this river?" asked the old man, unable to hide his surprise.

"That was done some time back. You haven't been around here for a while, have you."

He slowly studied the old man with a different look in his eyes. The old man instinctively assumed a defensive posture. It was a dark refraction of the feelings experienced over the thirty years since that day. But, as a matter of habit, the old man did not in the least reveal the hard mass of those feelings when he opened his mouth to speak.

"I took up peddling as a young man when I got sick of farming."

"Really? Well, were you able to make some money?" the younger man asked with a sarcastic tone. The old man's shabbiness seemed very far removed from money.

"Could Old Hwang still live here?" the old man asked casually, suppressing his unquiet heart.

"Who is Old Hwang?"

The man shook his head, even his neck, showing that he knew nothing at all. Instantly, the old man felt abandoned. This man, clearly the owner of the tavern, didn't know of Old Hwang. Had Mr. Hwang died? Had he moved away?

"You know, Hwang Sundol . . . ran the ferry . . . "

"Ah, the former owner here! He died more than ten years ago. His son sold us the place and moved off to the city."

Nothing registered in the old man's ears. He hadn't come here to see his native turf. He had come to find Mr. Hwang. His heart was drawn to his birthplace while he wandered rootlessly, not just out of heartache for the troubled spirits of his dead parents but also because Mr. Hwang was there. But Mr. Hwang had already died some ten years before. It was money he had barely scraped together as a beggar, but even that bottle of rice wine he had bought and put in his bag—that was for Mr. Hwang.

"So, where are you headed now, mister?"

At the tavern owner's question, the old man came out of his reverie.

"You wouldn't happen to know, would you, where Mr. Hwang's grave is?" The old man asked as he narrowly opened his watery eyes.

"Well, I really don't," the owner answered bluntly.

The old man kept nodding his head slightly.

"Go have a look around."

With that the tavern owner turned away.

"I'm hungry . . . could I get a little something to eat?" the old man asked feebly to the tavern owner's back.

"Well . . . "

"Don't worry, I'm not asking for a free meal."

"No, that's not it. It's just that we don't have much to go with the rice. Let's go in first," said the tavern owner, again turning to go.

The darkness had closed in all around them. The old man looked down toward the riverbank. In the thick gray darkness he could not make out signs of the fog that had risen up in solid billows like a living thing. If only Mr. Hwang had been there. . . . A desolate sorrow spread through the old man's heart like the fog that covered the riverbank.

"What are you doing, mister? Let's go on in," the tavern owner called. "I've got to urinate."

The old man, noncommittal, went in the brushwood gate.

Since it was around dinnertime, the rice was brought right out.

"Could I have a glass of *soju*?"

Even before he gave thought to lifting a spoon, the old man first wanted liquor. As he spoke, he thought of the bottle of rice wine he had kept so carefully in his bag. He had meant to drink it, sitting together with Mr. Hwang. He had bought wine to soothe away, cup by cup, the weakness and weariness that had overwhelmed his flesh and his feelings. This was only the third bottle of expensive rice wine that he had bought in all his life. He hadn't been able to offer the first two bottles to Mr. Hwang and now, once more, it was the same thing.

The old man poured a glass of *soju* to overflowing and drank it in a gulp. "Ahh . . . " He closed his eyes softly as he felt the prickling force of the liquor ride down his throat. Throughout the wasted years he'd spent floating aimlessly about—pushed by the wind, clouds for a roof—what stood by him, unchanged, was just the taste of *soju*.

"Here, won't you have a glass?"

He offered his glass to the owner.

"Oh, no. If I want to drink, I'll serve myself. How can I take a drink from a customer?" said the owner, declining with a wave of his hand.

"Come, now. Don't be so coldhearted, cutting the good feelings that come from sharing a glass. You can tell from the sight of me that I'm not the type who can often buy a second round. Please have one!"

The old man looked forlorn but spoke emphatically.

"If that's the case . . . "

The owner took the glass.

The hand with which the old man poured the liquor trembled slightly but it righted the bottle neatly, just when the glass filled up.

"If you were looking for the ferry, mister, were you on your way to the Chukch'on area?" the owner asked as he returned the glass.

The old man just nodded his head, his eyes narrowed as if collecting many thoughts.

"I learned when I came here that everything from Chukch'on on belongs to the Ch'oe family."

As before, the old man only nodded.

"I'm told the Ch'oe family came forward to build the bridge. And it seems they're going to put up a middle school and high school, too, after a while."

The old man nodded as he pulled out a cigarette.

"Actually, with one of them a national assemblyman, can't they do anything they want? There may be other families around, but they're all like beggars living off the Ch'oes."

"Well . . . "

The old man was about to say something but then made as if to empty his glass.

"You were going to say . . . ?"

The owner gazed vacantly at the old man.

"Well . . . I was wondering what people have control over the Ch'oe household?"

"As far as I know, it's the ones about my age. Not that there aren't any old men but they all seem to stay in the background. All the same, I've heard talk. They say the old ones aren't well received."

"How come?"

"Not so smart, I hear. The really clever ones were all killed off in the war, they say."

The old man fixed his eyes on the wall, his face tightly drawn.

"I understand that the Ch'oes dropped like flies during the war. Except for the Harvest Festival and New Year's, they say the largest observance in the Ch'oe household is their joint memorial service in late July. A spectacle worth watching."

The old man, eyes tightly closed, took one deep drag after another on his cigarette.

"Those Ch'oes had wielded such power, but once the war broke out and they fell into the hands of rabble, their lives weren't worth shit. How could they ever be avenged? Though it seems there wasn't a place those rabble didn't go wild. The Ch'oes got the worst of it here, they say. Did you see such grisly sights then, mister?"

"Oh no, no . . . "

The old man stubbed out his cigarette and shook his head vehemently.

"Where were you living back then?" the owner asked, seeming to look gently into the old man's face.

"I left here a little before the war began. So I don't know a thing about what went on here during the fighting," the old man asserted.

"They say it was one spectacle to behold. You sure missed quite a scene, mister."

The owner seemed to be quietly anticipating some reaction to his story of those days, but when his expectation was frustrated a look of failure showed in his eyes.

"A real good spectacle? What could have been good about it? People killing and getting killed. Have the poor luck to see something like that and you feel sick for life!"

"How could such a scene be commonplace? What an event that must have been, the rabble going wild. Sure must have been worth seeing."

The old man did not wish to reply further. It grated badly on his nerves to hear the man talk of "the rabble this" and "the rabble that" but he told himself not to find fault. What could this man have known? If he's now about forty, then it happened when he was around ten; and if he's thirty-five now, he was five then. The man takes the horrific killing and being killed of that time as simply another entertaining tale of long, long ago. That's what thirty years adds up to.

"I've enjoyed the meal but I'd better be on my way."

The old man struggled to his feet.

"It's pitch black out there. Will you be all right?"

"I know these roads . . . "

Maybe it was the liquor, maybe fatigue, but the old man was staggering as he cut across the courtyard.

"It's dark. Please take care!"

The owner shouted in the direction of the staggering old man as he receded into the darkness, his battered bag clutched tightly to his side.

The old man's corpse was discovered beneath the bridge the following morning, the battered bag still clutched to his side. No one recognized his drawn face. In order to establish his identity, the police went through his personal effects. But all that came out of his bag were a few coins and a bottle of rice wine. About half the wine was left in the bottle.

Unable to dispose of the corpse right away, the police left it beside the road all day long. They made it visible to anyone passing by. But no one turned up who recognized the old man.

Quite a few people were attracted by talk that a man had fallen into the river and drowned. Among them was the owner of the tavern. It gave him a terrible fright, but the next moment he had cooled down. He figured there was no need for him to pretend for no reason that he knew the man and then suffer the annoyance of getting called to the police station.

"If we assume that he drowned himself last night, he probably threw himself in upstream near the old ferry crossing. So, during the night, he would have floated down here. Make out the incident report that way."

A man in civilian clothing was giving the orders.

"I understand, sir."

The uniformed policeman saluted him. With that, they unrolled a straw mat and began to cover the corpse from the head down.

Translated by Marshall R. Pihl

The Bronze Mirror

O Chŏnghŭi

O Chŏnghŭi was born in Seoul in 1947 and graduated from the Sŏrabŏl College of Fine Arts with a degree in creative writing. She made her literary debut in 1968 with a tale of tortured adolescence, "The Toyshop Woman" (Wangujŏm yŏin), a story she had begun as a teenager. She has since won two of Korea's most prestigious literary prizes—the Yi Sang Award in 1979 for "Evening Game" (Chŏnyŏk ŭi keim) and the Tongin Award in 1982 for the story that follows.

In both technique and subject matter, O is one of the most challenging of contemporary Korean writers. She uses flashbacks, stream-of-consciousness, and a variety of narrative viewpoints to good effect. Her vocabulary is rich, her word choice deliberate and evocative. Her best stories are powerful, sensitive, carefully crafted portrayals of family relationships strained by unspoken emotions and unseen external forces. In these works, O probes beneath the surface of seemingly quotidian lives to expose nightmarish family configurations warped by divorce, desertion, insanity, and death. Darkness is a physical presence in many of O's stories, representing among other things these rents in the fabric of the family.

"The Bronze Mirror" (Tonggyŏng, first published in *Hyŏndae munhak* magazine in 1982) examines a couple on the threshold of old age, the husband facing debility and the wife tormented by memories of their dead son, a casualty of the April 1960 student revolution. The anxieties of the couple are personified in the audacious kindergarten girl who lives next door. The impact of the story is enhanced by the stark third-person narrative, which takes the husband's point of view, and by the assignment of a name to only one character—the dead son.

After watching his wife pour flour into a large wooden basin the man left for his midday stroll. He had just started out when he saw the girl next door coasting down the sloping alley on a bicycle. Her face drew tense as she gave herself up to the speed, gripping the brake lever but not applying it. Her calves stood taut below her tight cotton shorts.

He was walking straight toward her, but he couldn't tell if the girl had noticed him as she braced her feet against the oversize pedals, sitting erect instead of trying to cut the headwind. Her wind-blown hair and her forehead, not tanned like the other children's, registered briefly in his mind and then disappeared more quickly than the smile playing on his aging face.

No one else was about, perhaps because of the unseasonable heat, making this unvarying leg of his stroll seem thoroughly unfamiliar. As his eyes pursued the girl's back, the image of her speeding through this alley of linked gray walls and low roofs was sucked into the blur of the bicycle wheels like grass coming together after the wind has cut a swath through it.

It was strangely quiet. Now and then he passed an open gate in the wall, but all he could see were empty yards and limp bamboo blinds that screened the inhabitants from view. It was not yet time for the children to be returning from school.

Twice the girl sounded the bicycle's long, shrill bell, even though the alley was clear. She might suddenly have recognized the dead silence around her, or perhaps she had grown tired of pedaling incessantly down the empty way.

No doubt the girl had sneaked out of kindergarten. She disliked going there, and every morning he heard her crying on the other side of the wall. But in the end she would open the gate in the wall, cross his yard, and set off. On rainy days, wearing a yellow slicker that came down to her ankles, she lingered in his yard, picking out puddles to splash in. On her way home from kindergarten she would rent a bicycle from the bicycle shop or play house in the corner of his yard. His wife didn't like the girl coming and going as she pleased, trampling the grass and picking flowers. Something disappeared whenever she came by, his wife would tell him. And so she would always examine the area where the girl had been playing.

The girl's mother worked at a beauty parlor on the middle floor of a three-story building facing the main street. The building also contained a drugstore, a butcher shop, and a billiard hall. The girl's father, who had been working in the Middle East since shortly after her birth, had supposedly extended his assignment there.

Although the girl's mother rarely came through the side gate to visit, the man saw her frequently. When it was warm enough to open windows, the snip-snip of her shears would carry from the beauty parlor to the road when the sound of the traffic simmered down. Now and then he saw her close the windows with a scowl because of the noise. And late in the evening he would encounter her trotting along with some groceries. Still wearing the plastic apron she used when giving permanents, she reeked of chemicals and hair. On her biweekly day off she would squat in front of the drain in her yard and clear her throat. "You wouldn't believe this hair," he had heard her say some time ago from the other side of the wall; "it gets into everything—even my throat. So I try to keep my mouth shut when I'm working. The customers don't think I'm very sociable, but what can you do?"

The man's slow pace brought him to the playground at the corner of the neighborhood. He saw the girl leaning against her bicycle. Other children, scuttling about like crabs, were playing in a sandbox under the glare of the cloudless sky.

"Hey, has anybody seen my kaleidoscope? Who stole it?" the girl asked.

"I don't know," the other children sniffled.

Although the girl knew it would be in vain, she furiously dug through the piles of sand she had scoured the previous evening and destroyed the caves and sand castles the other children had fashioned. Then she climbed back on her bicycle saying, "Whoever stole it better put it back by the time I come around again. If you don't, I'm going to get you. I know who stole my kaleidoscope."

As the man departed one step at a time, poking about with his cane as if it were a feeler, his stomach came to life. The silence was enough to suffocate him, and the blinding sunlight gave him the shivers. In response to the feeble gnawing in his stomach, his innards, hanging in clusters large and small, began to squirm. Only now did these limp, worn-out organs reluctantly remind themselves of their function and regain some semblance of vitality. When the weather grew hotter he would probably have to abandon this half-hour walk he had prescribed for himself to stimulate his appetite for lunch.

Gradually growing short of breath, he stopped and wiped the sweat from his forehead while gazing attentively at the curtains hanging thick and still in the open windows of the houses next to the alley. His route was always the same, and he would stare at the monotonous path through this neighborhood of low, small houses shaped exactly alike— a scene sufficient to arouse dread—and at everything else that appeared on his retina. But he didn't intend to observe or remember; he was not even conscious of looking.

At any rate, his strolls would have to be suspended when the days grew hotter. His shrunken, hardened internal organs would not endure hot weather, so he would spend the summer sitting in an armchair in the shade recalling scenes he had witnessed but never reflected on.

Though he had walked as slowly as possible for the thirty minutes, the back of his shirt was damp with perspiration as he approached his house. He was satisfied. Exercise that made him sweat profusely was excessive at his age, he believed, and so he made it a rule to exercise only to the point of breaking a sweat.

He considered his efforts to maintain his regimen important and worthwhile. Though it seemed he was force-feeding himself on the passing days, he enjoyed obeying the rules and rhythms that controlled his body and his life, as if he had no idea that one day everything would stop in an instant.

His wife, it turned out, had made enough dough for noodles to feed a dozen people. The expected visitors, however, had sent word that they wouldn't be coming for home worship after all. Instead they were going directly to the mortuary at the general hospital; a church friend had just passed away after a long illness. As his wife told him this, she gave him a brief, blank look, her hands still buried in the white dough filling the broad-mouthed basin.

The dough, much more than the two of them needed, was rising as if it meant to overflow the rim of the basin. A roller, a cutting board lightly floured to make noodle chopping easier, a wicker tray with colored garnishes, and other implements were spread about the veranda.

In preparation for the guests, his wife had begun cleaning the yard and scurrying back and forth between the kitchen and the veranda early that morning. After breakfast he had steeped himself in the vague tranquillity of his wife's busy footsteps, the muted sound of chopping from the kitchen, and the smell of hot cooking oil. Was he anticipating the warmth of living in harmony with such vitality, even though he didn't believe it refreshed him anymore? Or was he simply growing sentimental about everyday life?

Perhaps his wife wasn't nearly as disappointed about the visit as he had suspected. He couldn't believe, now that he thought about it, that her faith had suddenly become that profound.

Was it last month that his wife had taken pity on those two women who were making their way around the neighborhood, knocking on doors and proselytizing everyone? She had asked them in for a short rest, which had turned into a four-hour lecture on church doctrine.

"Death is unconsciousness, not even worth the life of a dog, it is said. Hell is death itself; the word means imprisonment in the earth. . . ." The lecture was clearly audible where he lay in his room.

"I just thought they might want to sit down for a minute. . . ."

Although his wife had spoken apologetically to him after the women left, the following Sunday she went to their meeting place. There they had decided to make their first official visit to her home today.

Life imprisoned in the earth; glimmers of life crying out, imprisoned in the earth.

It must have been twenty years ago that Yŏngno was buried. Twenty years imprisoned in the earth—the same amount of time he had spent among the living.

After his wife left to prepare his lunch, he remained for some time on the veranda looking at the garden, as she liked to do. He tried to see, as if through her eyes, the place where her gaze would come to rest. The roses, hyacinths, dahlias, and other summer flowers were at their peak. Their petals were wide open in the midday sun, exposing the darker, deeper inner parts. Bees and butterflies inflamed with desire inserted their slender tubes deep in the pistils and stamens in search of nectar. Yearning to bloom more and more, the flowers darkened and began a slow trembling that he could scarcely discern. But by then he realized this was not the scene mirrored in his wife's eyes. As he watched the trees in the garden, lowering his head as if pretending to listen to the cries imprisoned in the earth, their luxuriant foliage dropped leaf by leaf, the desiccated branches turned to fibers and burned blue like phosphorus, and presently the places where the branches stretched out so proudly became empty space adrift with callous death.

The bicycle passed the front gate, its bell piercing the empty space. If only he could call out and beckon her, this girl who flew by like an arrow: "Hey, there, come in and cool off—you ride like that all day and you'll get sunstroke." If only he could plant in the girl's mind for the rest of her life the memory, keen as light glinting on a blade, of an old man's trivial kindness.

His wife appeared with the meal tray. She had prepared his usual lunch of homemade noodles and a glass of *soju*.

The noodles, though liberally decorated with the appropriate color of garnish, were completely bland. Without a word he looked across at his wife. Seemingly unaware that the food lacked the slightest touch of salt, she had lowered her head and was skillfully looping her own noodles about her chopsticks.

Was it because of his dentures? But he'd been wearing them for some time now. And besides, these homemade noodles were a regular part of his diet now that he found it burdensome to eat hard food. He couldn't find fault with the way his wife had boiled the noodles. But how could she have forgotten the soy sauce? After all, she made these noodles every day. As she sat there expressionless, eating the noodles, he resented and detested her almost as much as he hated his internal organs for neglecting their role.

"Get me some soy sauce," he said, suppressing his anger.

Sluggishly she got to her feet and returned with a small bowl of the condiment.

Since his teeth had been pulled and he had started wearing the dentures, he had lost most of the pleasure of chewing and savoring but had grown very particular about the flavor of food. This, however, he refused to acknowledge.

Those dentures!

He had spent his working life as a petty official at City Hall. His assignment was almost always the same—drafting clean copies of instructions from superiors or decisions reached by his department. He enjoyed these scribal duties and never copied incorrectly or abbreviated any of the Chinese characters. Although he knew that his drafts were tossed in the wastebasket as soon as they were approved and typed up, he was proud of his clear, precise penmanship. When his department heads saw his finished drafts they always exclaimed, "What a fine hand!"

Then one day his teeth had begun to loosen. When the gums became swollen and blue and the roots could be seen, he realized he'd have to have all his teeth pulled and dentures fitted. He was much more angry than frustrated at this betrayal. From then on, symptoms of debility appeared in all his internal organs, including his stomach. His doctor told him these were common postretirement symptoms. When you stop working all of a sudden you get lethargic, and the body loses its tone and balance. Retirement disease, the doctor had called it.

The doctor had told him it could happen to anyone, but this didn't console him in the least. After all, he'd never had to apologize to his superiors for anything, but now they'd put him out to pasture at retirement age, just like the people who had merely coasted along dawdling away the hours. He had meekly accepted the decades spent in that gloomy, stuffy old office, but he just could not get used to the dentures. He couldn't help resisting those cold, hard, strange objects that irritated his soft gums.

Losing interest in his lunch, he smeared toothpaste on a small cloth and began to polish the silver ornament on the handle of his cane. The simple, gentle movements of his hands seemed designed to soothe the walking stick, and when he saw the silver regain its milky sheen, his anger toward the noodles, his wife, and the dentures gradually subsided. After standing the polished cane next to the shoe cabinet, he sat down on the veranda and stared in boredom at the garden.

He wondered if he had been dozing. He hadn't heard the gate open, but there in the corner of the yard a young man with an iron hook was removing the lid from the concrete housing of the water meter. His wife was squatting with her back toward him, observing the movements of the young man's hands. Above her white hair and bent, bony waist, the noontide stillness, ebbing hardly at all, flowed heavily like quicksilver.

"Hey—will you look at that cricket, ma'am," the young man said, recoiling as the insect sprang into the sunlit open air. "It's not winter anymore, so why don't you roll up this stuff and burn it? That way you won't have any more bugs."

The young man was referring to the chaff and straw spread over the water meter the previous winter to prevent it from freezing. The man himself had seen insects that had hatched in the insulation during winter and then nested and grown along the dark, moist interior of the housing.

His wife nodded in response. Her hair was snowy white. When his had started to grizzle prematurely, hers was already gray. Turning around after seeing Yŏngno into his grave, he had suddenly realized that his wife, still patting down the thin turf on the mound of red soil, had become white-haired.

"My boy was growing just like green bamboo," his wife would say now and then to the peddler women she let into the house, "and when he died, my hair turned completely white." Then she would explain to him that prematurely gray hair ran in her family. "Honey, you look good with your hair dyed," she would tell him, knowing he was particular about the way his hair was barbered and dyed, "just like a young man."

From the time gray first appeared in his hair, he had never been lazy about dyeing it. And now, with the white, shiny dentures complementing his black, well-groomed hair, he looked much younger. Often he would gaze at himself in the mirror as if looking at Yŏngno turned forty.

His wife looked idly at the water meter, then asked the young man as he was about to leave, "How about cooling off before you go?"

"Okay. Could I have some water?"

The young man produced a handkerchief and mopped the sweat from his forehead and neck. He sat down on the edge of the veranda, and before long the woman appeared with a porcelain bowl of sweetened water blended with powdered roasted grain.

The man didn't like the way his wife trotted out from the kitchen, continuously stirring the beverage as if afraid the young man would leave. Clicking his tongue, he muttered to himself, "Don't do that. He's just a common young fellow who does nothing but go around inspecting water meters. You can see his type anywhere."

The young man emptied the bowl in a breath. The man didn't fail to catch his wife's flustered look as her eyes greedily explored the young man's sturdy neck and ripe-red chest revealed by his casually unbuttoned shirt.

"Thank you, ma'am." The young man wiped the moisture trickling from his mouth and licked his lips.

"The way he drinks isn't decent either," the man impotently muttered again. "Haven't I told you, you can learn a lot about people by the way they eat and drink."

Remembering that the water pipe hadn't been covered, the young man crossed the yard and replaced the concrete lid. As a rule, the man recalled, water meter inspectors left without doing this. They merely lifted the lid reluctantly with their hook, as if despising their job, and after reading the numbers on the meter they disappeared. His wife would usually be left with the chore of replacing the cover.

"Say, young fellow, would you do me a favor?" his wife called out as the young man was about to disappear through the front gate. Without waiting for an answer she went into the shed and came out embracing a heavy toolbox, which she set down with a thump.

The young man stared rather impertinently at the woman and the toolbox as if to say, "You cagey old lady, it looks like you'll get your money's worth in return for that drink."

"This clothesline is too high," she droned, ignoring his expression. "Could you lower it a bit? It's so difficult to hang the laundry. Only us old folks live here, and there's no one to help out."

"But if I lower it, the clothes'll drag on the ground—though I suppose you could use it as a jump rope for the kids." The young man stared into the toolbox, arms folded. "Besides, all these nails are rusty. If you've got your heart set on it I can do it, no problem, but I think it's a waste of time. Do you really think it'll do the job if we tie it lower?" Finally he rummaged through the toolbox and picked out a blacksmith's hammer and some of the cleaner nails.

It wasn't surprising that all the nails had rusted. Like the other tools the man had provided himself with—the blacksmith's hammer, a claw hammer, a small saw, a plane, and such—they had been virtually forgotten through long disuse.

"So, can you get a snack now and then while you're making your rounds?" his wife asked the young man.

"Yeah." The answer came indistinctly through the nails the young man held in his mouth. He quickly hammered in two nails, and now the line tightly spanned the yard at the desired lower height.

The line looked too low to the man. Surely his wife would complain of brushing against it and go to the bother of taking it down that very afternoon or the next morning.

"How can I repay you for your trouble?" his wife asked. "If you're not that busy, how about a bite to eat? I can boil up some noodles in a jiffy." She glanced at the dough filling the basin, which she had left in the corner of the veranda. Perhaps because of the warm weather and not just the yeast, the dough looked like a crazy, bloated thing.

"I've got several other houses to go to."

"It must be hard work walking around all day. Don't your legs get sore?"

"I just wish people would tie up their dogs," the young man sullenly blurted. He spat. "My pants are always getting ripped. All I have to do is look at a dog and it starts nipping at my heels."

The man watched his wife grudgingly follow the young man out, but heard no sound of the gate being latched. The house became quiet again. The shadows of the trees in the yard were a little longer, and now the man could sense only the flow of sunlight and time. No more did he hear the scuffing of his wife's shoes. Instead there was the slack, dreary clatter of bicycle wheels. He wondered if the girl, exhausted by the heat, having long forgotten about her kaleidoscope, her face expressing unbearable boredom, was languidly walking her bicycle past the street corner that his wife would be absentmindedly watching, her hand against the gatepost.

He went into his room and sat down at the desk. It had long been his habit to sit there with a blank expression, rubbing faint ink stains, scars hollowed by knives, and scratch marks. He was comfortable in the chair, and much closer to the scenes and sounds beyond the wall, the desk being next to the window.

He had bought the desk when Yŏngno was in middle school. Though he rarely used it for reading and writing, because of its handy drawers the desk had remained there, occupying considerable space in the unheated part of the floor.

He spread out the foil liner from an empty cigarette pack, folded it into a flower shape, and spat into it. Then he opened the drawers, which were filled with water and electric bill receipts in addition to his reading glasses and whatnot. He took out a pair of nail clippers and proceeded to trim his fingernails attentively.

He heard his wife gingerly pacing the veranda. Trimming his fingernails and opening the drawers shouldn't have to be a secret, he told himself, yet he cringed and kept still whenever she passed by the room. She had said she was old enough to have turned into a spirit who could see and hear everything that happened in the house, even if she was sitting quietly in a corner, but how could she know he was brushing away his dandruff, trimming his fingernails, and opening and closing the drawers like children who sit unwillingly at their desks, hating to do homework? And so he strained for any indication of someone out-side the room, thinking that even a trivial hand movement was a terri-ble plot if unknown to her.

Assuring himself that her steps had faded away, he took out the girl's kaleidoscope, which he had stored deep in one of the drawers. It was made of stout pasteboard rolled up and glued into a cylinder, and its surface was alive with crayon colors.

He put the kaleidoscope to his eye and turned it round and round. Tiny pieces of colored paper gathered and dispersed as light was re-fracted by the mirror in the tube, forming various flower shapes. These flowers struck him as neither florid nor original. They were merely imitations whose single and double layers were formed by the conver-gence and diffusion of the bits of paper. Somewhere he'd heard that the people of antiquity had tried to understand the principles and logic of the universe by turning a kaleidoscope.

Was it the day before yesterday? He couldn't be sure. He had left for his usual stroll, and upon emerging from the neighborhood alley onto the main street he found a pattern of light spinning around him wherever he went. He frowned while trying to deflect its rude touch on his shoulders, legs, and chest, terrified that his face would suddenly shrink when the glittering white light came to rest on it. It seemed to dance and jump like someone's soul between the street and the pass-ersby. Closing his eyes to the strong rays, he shouted, "Who's that playing with the mirror?" A bright voice flew to him: "Hello, grandfa-ther." There was the girl, sitting on the steps to the beauty parlor, a sharp piece of mirror in her hand. "Now what are you going to do if you cut yourself?" Unfazed, the girl replied, "They said I could ask somebody in a glass shop to cut this into a circle. Tomorrow we're going to make kaleidoscopes in kindergarten. You know what a kalei-doscope is? It's a magic box where you can see everything." While saying this the girl ran across the street. "Everything?" he responded to her back—not out of genuine curiosity, of course, but merely for the sake of saying something. Then yesterday he saw the kaleidoscope next to her school bag on a bench at the playground. As usual, he knew, she had rushed from kindergarten to the bicycle shop after fling-ing the satchel down, too impatient to go home first. What could she see through this magic box? He picked up the kaleidoscope, craving to see through the girl's eyes all that she had seen. Concealing it inside his shirt, he watched intently all afternoon as the girl vainly dug through the piles of sand to find the lost toy. "Somebody stole my kaleidoscope. Teacher told me to hand it in for an exhibition." In tears the girl looked under the bench where her satchel and kaleidoscope had been, where she had already looked time and again.

"We can see everything," he murmured, mimicking the girl. He turned the kaleidoscope quickly. The faster it turned, the greater the variety of patterns formed by the interaction of the mirror, glass, and bits of paper. What he saw now resembled bacteria dividing and multiplying at an inconceivable speed. Was it because of the vivid sense of color created by the paper? he wondered.

His eyelids grew heavy, his body listless. It was the drink he took with lunch to help his digestion. He could never resist this temptation to sleep, though he knew a nap would make him wake up at night and pace the silent yard as if in a nightmare.

He returned the kaleidoscope to the drawer and started for the bathroom.

His wife was sitting on the edge of the veranda rolling a handful of dough between her palms.

"What are you making?"

"Oh, I'm just playing."

Smiling sheepishly, she crushed the shape she had been forming. A human, a dog, a horse, and other clumsily modeled figures the size of a finger sat beside her.

He entered the bathroom and locked the door in order to remove his dentures.

The dentist had told him to try to wear the dentures until he was unaware of them, but he couldn't fall asleep unless he took them out and soaked them in a glass of clean water, kept within reach. But even then he couldn't get rid of the fear that in the short weightless state just before sleep there were only the dentures hanging heavily by his side, and that one day they alone would wake up and chatter of their own accord until finally his body vanished, leaving those cold, hard, lifeless things glaring cruelly in the void that had once been his life. And when he was talking he would sometimes fall silent, convinced that it wasn't him speaking, but the dentures chattering and rattling.

He took out the dentures and his blackish, flaccid gums appeared in the mirror. Unable to hold their own against the stubborn dentures, the soft gums were squashed and shrunken. Without the dentures his mouth was no more than an empty, smelly, insignificant hollow. After making sure the door was locked, he started carefully brushing the dentures with the same hidden, bitter pleasure and shame he felt when he grasped his withered genitals in search of consolation that was sure to be ephemeral and unavailing. Cleared of the bits of red pepper and the other remnants of his lunch, the dentures shone fresh and clean. Their pink gumlike base looked healthy, like freshly sliced meat. Breathing heavily from his efforts, he looked at the dentures. White with toothpaste foam, they seemed to be laughing. Then he looked in the mirror. His black hair, like that of a young man, contrasted with his collapsed mouth, the shrunken furrow between his upper lip and nose, and his cruelly sunken cheeks, making him appear younger indeed.

He returned to his room and lay down, his head on a box pillow and beside him the dentures soaking in a glass of water. Falling asleep was always like walking down a dim, endless corridor. Haven't I already turned into a spirit, walking along the passage inside a tomb? he wondered.

His wife's outline was clearly visible through the open door. Drifting in and out of sleep, he saw her hands roll dough into the shape of a body with ears and horns and a tail and legs. It was a queer shape he had never seen before. Standing it in line with the other figures at the sunny edge of the veranda, she began muttering to herself: "Grandfather suffered from nightmares till the day he died, and he had these splitting headaches. He himself didn't know whether the headaches came from the nightmares, or the other way around. We asked a shaman to do an exorcism and we had a blind man chant a Buddhist scripture, but those awful headaches just wouldn't go away. . . ." By now he had heard the story of her grandfather, a well-known master carpenter, several times. "He'd wake up screaming from an awful dream—late at night, early in the morning, whenever—and then roam the house like a madman because of a headache. Grandmother used to say he'd built too many houses where graves once were. . . ." Ahead of him, at an indistinct bend in the corridor, he sees a screaming old man with an arched back and a white headband. "That's why Grandfather carved those strange animals with his pocket knife. They looked like elephants or bears; whatever they were, they sure looked strange. Tapirs, I think he called them, and he said they ate nightmares. . . ." His wife continued to form shapes from the dough in the basin. "Grandfather left them at his bedside next to the spittoon. And so he figured that what he had coughed up into the spittoon was actually the nightmares

—the ones the tapirs had eaten all night long and thrown up first thing in the morning. His dying wish was to have the tapirs with him in his coffin. I guess he thought he'd have nightmares even after he died. Do dead people have dreams, too? I was a little girl then, and it was all very strange to me, but now I can understand why Grandfather did that. Back in the old days didn't people make mud figures of their belongings—and their servants, too—and ask to be buried with them? . . . " His wife's grandfather was sleeping comfortably now at the end of the long, faint corridor of time, the tapirs at his side.

As if mesmerized by his wife's slow, low-pitched chanting, he walked on through time, which was part buried in oblivion and part risen dimly before him. It was just like film applied unevenly with sensitizer: part of it clearly defined, almost luminous; part of it obscured, too dark. But he was not all that impatient to remember. Recalling only the things he wants to recall is the insignificant privilege of an old man. But what was this place where he hesitated to stop? An exhibition room in a museum he had once visited?

It was the room where clay figures, bronze mirrors, and other burial artifacts were displayed. When he saw the mirrors, cleansed of tarnish after thousands of years in the earth, he felt he had died long ago. All alone, he couldn't hear even his footsteps on the thick carpet. That was the reason, he told himself, for the mysterious, fleeting sentiment he experienced on his way out the long, dampish corridor.

What he had just buried, he thought as he turned away from Yŏngno's grave, was not a hurriedly decaying corpse that couldn't endure the riotous vigor of spring, but a piece of a mirror.

"Grandmother, what are you making?"

As he heard this voice with its seemingly deliberate lisp, a squat shadow appeared in the front yard. It was the girl next door, and she had changed into a white lace dress. He tried to struggle free from his shallow sleep, and with a desperate effort was able to look more closely at the girl. She was clutching a doll to her chest, and her free hand held a plastic basket with things for playing house. Had she finally grown tired of riding the bicycle?

"Back from kindergarten?" his wife asked as she continued to shape the queer-looking animals. Her voice held no warmth. She always watched the girl with suspicion. His old wife distrusted everything.

"There's no kindergarten today. It's Saturday."

"That's a pretty dress you're wearing."

"My mommy bought it for me." Again the girl made a point of lisping.

He continued to look at the girl, trying hard to think she was pretty. But he failed, as usual. Her pale eyes turning gold as they absorbed the sun's rays and her face sharp as an ax blade were not at all pretty. She always looked a little lonely when she crossed their yard with the basket of her very own playthings, or when she rode the swing in her yard, the doll under her arm. Even when the girl wasn't riding the swing, it sometimes creaked back and forth by itself.

Was it last summer that he had looked over the wall and seen the girl all those times? After stripping naked in the sun-drenched yard she would jump up and down in her large wooden wading tub, splashing water every which way. Almost in agony as he hid next to the rosebushes creeping up the wall, he would hear her sudden, abbreviated laughter and observe her thin, light brown hair trailing down the back of her neck like corn floss, her belly swollen like that of a pregnant woman, her little pink genitals.

"Grandmother, what are you making?" the girl asked again, the lace of her dress fluttering as she swayed back and forth. Denied, rejected, unloved, she had learned early to play the coquette.

With a graceful turn she spread the hem of her dress like the petals of a flower and squatted. "They look strange, grandmother." Still squatting, she moved so close that her forehead was almost touching his wife.

"They're called tapirs. They're animals that eat bad dreams."

"Do you have bad dreams, too? I always have scary dreams." The girl picked a rose moss that had bloomed and crushed it between her fingers.

"Why do you do that?" his wife scolded.

Pretending not to hear, the girl continued in a clinging tone: "I was flying just like a bird, but then I wondered what would happen if I wasn't a bird and I fell. Right away I was falling upside-down. It was so scary."

"It's because you're getting taller. Not going to the bathroom before you go to bed can also make you have bad dreams."

The girl picked a dahlia and trampled it.

"I told you not to do that!" his wife shouted.

The girl stared spitefully at her.

"How many times do I have to tell you? Good boys and girls don't break off flowers."

The words came out one at a time in a much lower and firmer voice as his wife fought to control her anger. But before she could finish, the girl had snapped a hydrangea and an Indian lilac from their stems.

"You just won't listen. Bad girl—it's time you learned a lesson—you understand?" His wife glared at the girl, arm poised to strike. But then she dropped it feebly, for the girl, face ridden with fear, had cuddled up to her as if to be embraced.

"Sometimes my quilt puffs up real thick and covers me all over so I can't even breathe. No matter how much I cry, my mommy can't hear me." The trembling words were like an appeal.

"You weren't dreaming. You were having a nightmare. Here, take one of these and put it right next to you when you go to bed. Then you'll be all right."

"Thank you, grandmother." The girl closed the precious tapir snugly in her palm as if it were a souvenir from a temple or a seedling that would die if the roots were exposed. She looked as if she were crossing stepping stones as she gingerly departed with the doll, basket, and tapir.

"Oh, now your dress is dirty."

The girl looked back and saw a large stain where the hem of her dress had swept against the ground. She burst into tears. "My mommy's gonna spank me if I get my new dress dirty. She told me not to touch it till my birthday party at kindergarten."

"Come here, I'll brush it off. That's why you shouldn't plop yourself down just any old place," said his wife, surprised at the urgency of the terror expressed in these unexpected tears.

But the girl kept her distance. Full of resentment and fear, she flung aside the tapir and picked all the flowers she could grab.

"Damn girl! I'm going to break your arm." His wife sprang up and chased the girl, who continued to wail as she fled. The girl's crying retreated through the side gate, and his wife returned, panting, to her seat at the edge of the veranda. She began kneading the dough more roughly.

He heard a sound like the creaking of the front gate. A visitor? The girl riding her swing? But his wife gave no indication that she'd heard anything. It wasn't unusual for him to hear something she didn't, or for her to see something he couldn't make out at all. Now and then he would hear the swing creaking in the middle of the night. But when he told his wife, she would snort and turn on her side, saying, "Why would a little girl want to ride a swing at night? It's pathetic." Eventually, though, he would go outside as if drawn by the end of a disturbing dream. Hugging the wall, he would gaze with the silliness of the lovesick at the swaying of the empty swing ridden only by the wind.

Untiringly his wife kneaded the dough and formed more tapirs. What bad dream could be disrupting the old woman's sleep? The old don't sleep well, and they have many dreams, he told himself.

Shade was spreading throughout the yard, and the shadows of the trees were quite long now.

Looking at his wife's white hair, the crimson flowers above her head, the trees burning blue in his mind's eye, he heard, as if drugged by another light slumber, a shrill, rending song from the other side of the wall:

Cuckoo, cuckoo, spring is here.
Cuckoo, cuckoo, peach blossoms fall.

"Damn girl, I'm going to have to break your habits the hard way!" his wife gasped, still angry.

Like rays of the sun, the girl's singing clung to his eyelids, made heavy by his brief dozing.

"All she has to do is touch a stem and she breaks it," his wife muttered. Then, as if seeking agreement, she called out to him: "Are you asleep?"

After struggling to open his eyes, he examined his wife.

"You'd better exercise during the day if you want to get to sleep at night," she said. "Instead of a drink with lunch, why don't you go for another walk after you eat?"

She may have been right. The *soju* he'd taken with lunch hadn't stirred his limp stomach.

Without waiting for an answer, his wife continued to speak loudly, her voice full of an incongruous vitality. It wasn't so much a concern to make herself clear; rather, she was struggling to drown out the incessant singing.

"It's so strange. These days I think a lot about the dead. Everything that happened during their lives comes into my mind just as if they were still alive. And yet I honestly can't remember the years *we've* spent together. No matter how I try, they're like a fuzzy dream that I can't remember. Can you remember what it was like in your forties and fifties? I just can't picture how you looked then. I keep thinking maybe I've lived too long. Even the yardwork's getting to be too much. If I skip it for even a day, the weeds come up like hungry ghosts—especially when the weather's like this."

The girl's singing grew more shrill, and his wife paused. Then she continued in a much louder voice: " 'Forget about the weeds.' That's what our boy said back then. What was the point of sorting them out from the flowers? They looked better growing all together, he said."

A smile rose on his face.

"What was it like when you were fifty? How about forty? Thirty? I just can't remember. Tell me."

Her questions were persistent and tantalizing, as if she were hypnotizing him. Afraid of an answer, she quickly continued. Her voice and the girl's singing were like the dissonance of musical instruments competing with each other.

"He was a lovely boy when he was twenty—I was so proud of him. That was the year he went to college. I can remember it just as if it were yesterday. And those itchy feet of his."

He didn't want to listen to his wife anymore. Yŏngno was always telling them his feet were itchy. The boy had never recovered from the frostbite he had suffered while riding atop his father's rucksack on their way south during the war. He said he felt better when he slept with his feet in a sack of cold beans, even in winter.

"Remember the time he lost my shawl at the ballet? I think he was five then. It was made of real silk, something even the Japanese couldn't get all that often. After the performance I put it around his shoulders so I could go to the rest room. It probably fell off and the boy didn't realize it. He could be dumb like that. Everybody said bishop's purple looked marvelous on me. I won't have a second chance at something like that—not in this life, anyway."

How much longer would his wife tell the story of that lost shawl?

Little by little her speech accelerated, as did the hands making the tapirs. As the basin was emptied of dough, the row of tapirs became too tight to admit any more.

"He was just twenty. What do people that young know? He thought he could turn the world around when he should have been squeezing pimples. Can you believe it? The boy's dead, and here we are still living like this."

One spring day Yŏngno, fresh out of high school, had flown out of the house like a nighthawk, his schoolboy crewcut not quite grown out and sticking up indignantly in all directions.

An old man does not reflect on his conduct, he thought; he does not await a new life that would require him to do so.

The girl's shrill singing grew louder and louder:

Cuckoo, cuckoo, spring is here.

Cuckoo, cuckoo, peach blossoms fall.

"She really is a bad girl." Everting her lips, his wife suddenly started crying.

"Kids are all the same." It was a nuisance having to speak with his hollow, dentureless mouth, but he managed to eject the syllables.

"No, the dead ones are special," his wife sobbed, covering her face.

"Grandmother, what are you making?" There was the girl, standing in front of his wife. The signs of her own crying had vanished.

"Go away!" his wife said with a fierce wave of her hand.

"What's the matter, grandmother? Why are you crying?"

"I told you never to come to this house again!"

"Grandmother, I'm going to make a kaleidoscope out of this mirror," the girl said triumphantly. "My mommy gave it to me. Somebody stole the one I made in kindergarten." Without budging, she opened a compact to reveal a round mirror.

"Don't you lie to me. That's brand-new. Don't tell me your mom gave it to you. She's still at the beauty parlor, isn't she? Fool around with your mom's cosmetics and you'll get another spanking from her."

The girl glared fiercely at his wife, then ran to where the sun still shone in the yard. Aiming the mirror this way and that, she found his wife's face.

Blinded, his wife covered her face with one hand and motioned with the other. "Get out of here!"

The girl responded with an amiable smile.

"Put that away! You rotten little girl. I'm going to tell your mother."

"Then tell her! Squeal! Tell her everything!"

Bouncing about the yard, the girl continued to flash the mirror in his wife's face. Frightened, his wife stepped onto the veranda. The light from the mirror coursed by the line of animals drying white and firm and clung agilely to his wife's face, exposing its layers of wrinkles like aluminum foil crumpled and then spread out.

"Child, now child, for heaven's sake go away. Don't do that," his wife pleaded tearfully.

The girl giggled, delighting in his wife's unexpected fright. To escape the mirror, his wife tottered into the room where he was lying.

Now the light glittered constantly on his wife's small, tear-soaked face and on the rims of his eyes and the edges of his broken-down mouth. It seemed somehow a reflection from a mirror buried in the bottomless earth. The girl wouldn't put the mirror away until she found a more interesting game, perhaps not until the rays of the sun had died out, perhaps not until night when her tired mother returned. But what could be more fun for a child than driving the old into a feeble state of terror?

One corner of the yard was already submerged in shade, and the flowers had started to darken and close in the thick gloom spreading up from the ground. How long would it last, that unseen flow of flower-blooming space into the silent abyss?

He wondered what he could say to soothe his wife, who was no longer attempting to conceal her crying. She needed some affectionate words. Feeling boyishly shy and a bit apprehensive, he opened his mouth, but his wife couldn't understand his stammering. Frustrated, she pressed her ear to his mouth and asked over and over: "What was that? What did you say? Did you ask if somebody came?"

He lay there, his hair as black as coal and his broken-down mouth open halfway, incapable of further speech.

The reflection from the mirror flitted from the ceiling to the walls and came to rest on the glass of water in which the soaking dentures glittered bright and lucid. It seemed that they alone were trying to say something in the silence, dark and calm against the light from outside.

Translated by Bruce and Ju-Chan Fulton

A Shared Journey

Im Ch'ŏru

Im Ch'ŏru was born in 1954 on Wando, an island just off the South Chŏlla coast. He studied English literature at Sŏgang University and in 1981 received the Newcomers Literary Award given by the *Sŏul shinmun* newspaper. In 1984 his story collection *Land of My Father* (Abŏji ŭi ttang) was honored with the Creative Literature Award, and in 1988 he was co-recipient of the Yi Sang Award for his story "The Scarlet Room" (Pulgŭn pang). To date he has published half a dozen volumes of fiction. Im presently lives in the city of Kwangju.

Im is one of the most promising contemporary Korean writers of fiction. Stories such as "Land of My Father," "At Sap'yŏng Station" (Sap'yŏng yŏk), and "A Shared Journey" (Tonghaeng) are works of delicacy and sensitivity that reflect a profound interest in recent Korean history. "A Shared Journey" is an autobiographical account of the emotional trauma resulting from the government slaughter of demonstrators in Kwangju in 1980. One of the first such stories, it was written during the regime of Chun Doo Hwan. Consequently, the original Korean text is necessarily obscure and indirect in references to the event. Place-names, appearing only as single capital letters in the original, are, with the author's permission, rendered in full in the translation. "A Shared Journey" was first published in 1984 in *You Know and I Know* (Chialgo naealgo), an anthology of recent fiction.

264

You were nowhere to be seen. We were to meet next to the telephone booth where the road splits about a hundred yards inside the entrance to the apartment complex.

Was I too early? I checked my watch—five to three. I was a bit more restless. Ever since I'd left the house, and all the way here on the bus, I felt as if something had been tugging at the back of my neck. Actually, I suppose I'd started feeling restless the previous night when you called, or, more precisely, that shocking night a week before when you appeared for the first time in a year and a half. You'd come from out of that darkness, stealing over me like a hypnotic drumbeat, and instinctively I had caught the smell of imminent destruction: my repose, the calm and tranquil life I'd guarded until then, would ultimately be stirred up. Worst of all—and this was the dangerous truth of the matter—I might have to put that life behind me once and for all. And so as that hypnotic drumbeat gradually approached, I became more anxious, more restless. For that reason, when the warning light began to flash urgently in my mind, alerting me to the danger, it would have been better had I at least adopted an appropriate defense—or fled.

But I couldn't escape. Because from that same far corner of my consciousness where an alarm was sounding ceaselessly, I was besieged by another voice, one that ordered me with an all-powerful, imperious authority to await this drumbeat and accept it. Finally, I had no choice but to do just that. Overwhelmed by the affection for you that filled my heart, I realized I would eventually have to accept not only you but also the ominous uncertainties you would bring.

Someone was there. Not too fast, I told myself as I turned toward the telephone booth. But then I relaxed. It was a young woman. Through the transparent glass of the booth, I watched her lift the receiver and deposit a coin. She was wearing house clothes, which made me think she might have been cleaning the floor in her apartment.

"Hi, it's me. . . . Yes. . . . Any news? . . . Oh, really? She had the baby? . . . A boy? . . . What! . . . Oh no! After it was born. . . . Oh, my god! The poor thing. . . ."

The woman's face began to contort with tears.

"Another stillbirth. . . . Oh, how awful. . . . That's the second time. . . . Oh, how awful."

The woman hung up. I quickly looked away before she emerged from the booth. Her head drooping, she trudged back toward the apartment buildings, and I saw her heels rising in turn from her sandals. They looked like two mouths opening and closing.

I checked my watch again. It was just past three. Still no sight of you. A mailbox stood next to the telephone booth; its crimson color gave me a feeling of urgency I couldn't explain. Suddenly, the word *contact* came to mind, prompting me in spite of myself to look quickly in both directions. For some reason I was filled with an intense animosity toward this unsavory word, which might seem appropriate in a spy movie or a cops-and-robbers television show. I might have preferred *rendezvous,* a word with more feeling to it. Yes, a rendezvous with a friend—I was waiting for a friend. But the phone booth was the meeting place I had decided on, and I had to admit that anyone might readily use that distasteful word *contact* to describe the act of waiting for you then.

I lit a cigarette to dispel the unpleasant premonition that came over me like goose bumps again and again. Taxis came and went on the road turning into the apartment complex, but there weren't many people about. True, it wasn't rush hour, but it was more likely that the late autumn weather, which had sent the temperature plummeting the previous day, was keeping people indoors. The concrete apartment buildings, looking like so many upside-down apple crates, stretched endlessly in every direction under the oppressive gray sky. They were a uniform composition of neatly arrayed buildings, equidistant from one another and coated with layer on layer of pink paint. Each side wore a number, and the end of each building appeared in sharp relief. The sight of those bold angles provoked an intense disgust in me, and for a time I remained motionless where I was.

It was then that you appeared. I hadn't expected you to come from outside the complex, and I almost didn't recognize you because of your outfit. The cap with the broad visor pressing down over your forehead reminded me of sports day at a rural elementary school. Your navy blue jacket was emblazoned in yellow across the chest with the word *Hyundai.* Dressed like that, you could pass without suspicion. But that cap and uniform, obtained from who knows where, embarrassed me. They were like stage props—they didn't become you. And to my eyes, at least, they were less than convincing as a disguise.

"Well, you made it. Been waiting long?"

"No."

You gave me a pat on the shoulder—an old habit of yours. But you were more restrained than in the old days; the touch on my shoulder was like an afterthought. More evident than anything were the apprehensive looks you kept casting in both directions. On the surface all seemed the same, but in actuality something was completely different. It was obvious that something between us had changed, and that saddened me. I looked up at you.

"Where the hell did you come from? Somewhere around here?"

I felt the same anxiety, the same nervousness, as before.

"You're not supposed to ask—remember? It's better for both of us that way. What you don't know won't hurt you."

"Asshole."

I forced a grin. You responded with an ambiguous smile. The teeth that shone through your beard gleamed exceptionally white. The lush growth of facial hair reminded me of a barley field gone to seed. It was obvious you'd shaved hardly at all. I had asked you about this the day you surfaced. Anything to change the appearance of your face, you had answered.

We set off toward the street, and I explained the train schedule. From downtown, three trains a day left for Mokp'o. But there were more trains from the town of Songjŏng, because the Mokp'o-bound trains from Seoul stopped there. Of course from downtown there was a bus for Mokp'o every ten minutes or so, you had explained to me on the phone the previous day. But any way you looked at it, the train was safer, and that's what you had chosen.

"Good—then we'll go by way of Songjŏng," you finally had decided.

"We're in luck—there's a local train leaving there in about an hour. The problem is, how do we get to Songjŏng?"

I wasn't thrilled about the idea of riding a congested city bus.

"No problem—we'll catch a taxi. I've got some money."

Two men were chatting in the watchman's cubicle at the entrance to the apartment complex. You strode past, with me following. There were several things I was still wondering about, but I decided to keep my peace. As you had said, it would perhaps be better for both of us that way. In any event, you were an enigma. I still didn't know for certain where you had been living. It was always you who had called me—the previous evening, too.

It was just past ten o'clock when you called. You had come straight to the point:

"Can you get me a train schedule for Mokp'o? And I'd like you to go there with me—how about it?"

I had a class the following day, and several courses were supposed to finish then. So it might have been my last college class. But I couldn't have cared less. Instead, I wondered what had prompted you to undertake a potentially dangerous trip to Mokp'o, and why it was me you were asking to accompany you. But these, too, were matters I decided to keep to myself. The answers would emerge in due course during the trip.

We caught a taxi in front of the apartment complex. The driver looked about forty. Since Songjŏng was outside the city limits, we had to pay extra to go there, he informed us. We finally settled on a fare that was five-hundred wŏn less than he had demanded.

The taxi rounded the sports complex and began crawling up an elevated highway. We kept silent for a while. The mountains were visible in the distance. As always, their massive bulk seemed to embrace the city, keeping a silent vigil over all below them. Their sprawling foothills accommodated some of the huddled throngs who had moved to the city. We too had been born and raised there. Before I realized it, the mountains had become a deep indigo—the color of melancholy. They looked gloomy.

As I watched the mountain skyline through the window, I suddenly thought of the year and a half in which we had been separated. And now we were reunited, each of us with an end of the severed thread of time twined about his fingers. Yes. The important thing was, we had met again. But we each realized we were not what we used to be. Like soldiers returning from battle, we were the same people, but then we were no longer what we once were. It had been a year and a half, but in truth it seemed like an eon, like a kind of vacuum. And between us now was an awesome, bottomless canyon, a gaping maw that stretched as far as we could see. There we stood, each on his own dizzying height, gazing at the other in despair and confusion.

I felt awkward sitting shoulder to shoulder with you in the taxi. As I watched you in profile, I tried to locate the source of this feeling. Before long I had found it. It was the melancholy expressed in your thick beard, in your puffy, lifeless cheeks, in the ever worrisome look in your eyes that belied your attempts at indifference. The period of rupture between us was driven home in my mind more than anything else by the comical cap pressed low on your head, and by the navy blue jacket with the unbecoming *Hyundai* written on it. And this was perhaps what pained me so. Why should I have had to witness the pain and melancholy in your face? They seemed trivial signs of weakness in one who had been so imposing, so full of vitality. But there they were, in plain sight, and we had no choice but to accept them. Our psyches, wounded the previous summer, had yet to heal to the point where we could look back dispassionately on what had really caused all these changes.

"How's business?" you asked the driver.

"Don't ask! God only knows when the price of gas is going to drop. And a few days ago they put another two hundred taxis on the streets."

It was discouraging to have so many taxis serving the population, the man continued.

You engaged him in idle conversation, probably to conceal your anxiety. But your tone of voice seemed a bit forced. I noticed that the driver was sneaking looks at us in the rear-view mirror now and then. Perhaps this was nothing more than a habit all drivers had; whatever the case, it seemed to make you quite nervous. It had already been a year and a half since your face had appeared on the wanted posters. Someone like this driver, more concerned with eking out a living, would probably have difficulty matching the face in the poster with the slovenly appearance you had adopted. But of course there were exceptions to this rule. At school the other day I had overheard someone saying you had been seen near Rocky Pass. I was sitting on a bench in front of the literature building. My heart jumping, I looked around to see who had said this, but it was someone I'd never seen before. Probably you didn't know him either. To be identified at any time in a completely unexpected place by people one didn't know—that was perhaps more frightening than anything.

We passed the industrial complex in Kwangch'ŏn-dong and turned onto the road for Songjŏng. The lowering sky became oppressive, making the asphalt stretching before us even more drab. Before long we had sped past the veterans' hospital on our left and crossed a hill. We were now outside the city limits. There were fewer and fewer houses along the road, and fields came into sight. The taxi gathered speed.

That evening a week ago when you had surfaced, I had been watching television with my family when the phone rang. It was Kim, of all people. He had graduated before me, and was studying for the civil service examination.

"Well, this is a rare honor. What's up?"

"Nothing much . . . just something I want to show you. Can you come over?"

"Now?"

I had no idea what this was all about, but suddenly I felt tense. Kim's voice was somehow giddy, and that gave me a hunch. All in a flurry I caught a taxi.

I could barely contain my emotions as I walked down the pitch-black alley to Kim's rented room. I couldn't believe that the prospect of seeing you after a year and a half—not such a long time, really—was capable of stirring me up so. Looking back, I realize that during that period, which had seen the passage of several seasons, the two of us, both almost twenty-seven, had gained more experience in the ways of the world than one might have expected; we had aged too quickly.

My hunch was right. Kim was waiting outside the door to his landlord's house. An hour before, you had shown up out of the blue, he said as he led me into his room.

"Good to see you," you said in a matter-of-fact tone.

We clasped hands and for a moment greedily explored each other's face. And that was it. We could have leaped into each other's arms, as in some grandiloquent drama. Or we could have staged a grand emotional display, complete with tears welling in our eyes after being starved so long for friendship. For, after all, we had assumed you were dead. Amazingly, though, we spoke sparingly. I tried to control my uneven breathing.

"You've put on a lot of weight."

"That's what happens when you spend all your time eating and sleeping. Yes sir, I'm as fat as a hippo."

It was just as you said. You had a large frame to begin with, but you'd never shown signs of becoming as fat as you were now. The extra weight, which reminded me of soft bean curd, and the swollen stomach showing between the buttons of your thin shirt, were completely unexpected. A haggard face and a body of skin and bones were closer to what I had imagined. But I shouldn't have been surprised. Obviously, you hadn't had much exercise; you had passed the time shut up in a room, too anxious to open the window even in midsummer. I soon realized that your health was out of kilter. In a sense, you had swollen rather than just gaining weight.

"Well, you can be thankful for one thing—you must have done a lot of reading. Probably picked up a few smarts along the way, buddy."

"Yeah, more or less. . . . Won't get much use out of books now, though."

I tried the bantering routine, as in the old days, hoping to smooth things out between us, but that didn't work either. Feelings of guilt, awkwardness, wariness, unease—so turbid and tangled they were forming an oppressive, sticky barrier among the three of us. How could it possibly be? There was so much I had wanted to say, but here I was fumbling for words as if I were speaking a language I had learned only superficially. But then, what was the use of talking now about the autumn and winter, the spring and summer we had passed in your absence? How could I describe to you all our gestures of despair, the countless emptied shot glasses, our incessant harping—while all along we tried to ignore those empty seats in our classroom?

"I always thought you'd survive. You must have had a hard time."

"Well, more or less. . . . I didn't have much choice, since I didn't die."

We chuckled at the same time. It hurt me to realize that your laughter was just as superficial as my own, and it was all I could do to stomach it. Nor could I rejoin the severed thread of time. Our awkwardness was much more noticeable now, and we both suffered in silent despair. That awkwardness disconcerted me as much as the disparity between the imagined bag of bones and the real you swollen like a hippopotamus. For an instant I examined the signs of deep exhaustion appearing on your face, and suddenly I shuddered. I had never expected to see such hopeless fatigue emanating from you. Even the eyes of a wanderer wouldn't have been so veiled with fatigue. "I want to rest"—that was what your face seemed to be saying as you sat in front of me.

And so—in this state of exhaustion you had returned to our hometown of Kwangju. But in just a year and a half this city of ours had changed into a neighborhood of strangers incapable of extending you a warm welcome. You were as familiar with the city as always. You knew the alleys and the tiny mom-and-pop stores like the back of your hand, each and every one of them—but the city would no longer remember you as you once were. For that very reason, even now that you were back home, you could only skulk about at night like a bat, under cover of darkness, and it was likewise for that reason that you were compelled to have a third party summon me, your friend.

We crossed a long concrete bridge. Below, the meager braids of the river twisted through flatlands wearing the subdued colors of late autumn. I lit a cigarette and rolled down the window halfway. The air gushed in. The road became a broad straightaway near the airport, and the driver accelerated.

The station plaza wasn't very busy. We crossed this plaza with its directional signs and the banners with their official slogans. There was a police precinct house to the left. We passed a signboard containing information for soldiers on leave, and entered the waiting room.

The timetable was displayed on a board attached to the top of the wall and tilted slightly toward the viewer below. As we had expected, a local was scheduled to leave for Mokp'o in thirty minutes. What could we do until then? You must have been wondering the same thing, because I turned to find you pacing in the corner. Avoiding eye contact beneath the low brim of your cap, you were trying to control your anxiety, but I knew that deep down inside you were agitated. I felt the same way. My nervousness took the form of a foolish notion that we were extraordinarily conspicuous in the fetid waiting room, as if we were a different species of human being. Quite a few people were pacing about this room the size of a classroom. Strangely, there was no seating to speak of. Then I realized that all the seats were outside in the plaza, probably to ease crowding in the waiting room. The cool weather, though, appeared to have driven most of these people inside, here to await their train in boredom.

What were we going to do? We knew there would be tearooms nearby, but you were opposed to waiting there. At the same time, it would have been risky to remain in this crowded, disorderly waiting room. After hesitating briefly, we decided to sit outside.

A dozen long, wooden benches were lined up in two rows. We sat down on the one farthest from the waiting room.

We smoked in silence. Men and women, most of them country people, trooped in and out of the public toilet nearby; the air was ripe with the stink of urine, and their clothes were permeated with the persistent smell of ammonia.

Huddled on the bench across from us was a group of young people. The three fellows looked old enough to be awaiting their draft notices. Their faces had a disagreeable alcoholic flush, and all of them looked like bums through and through. The two girls couldn't stop giggling. I wondered if they were on their way home from a friend's wedding. Peanuts, dried squid, and similar snacks were strewn about them. I couldn't bring myself to dislike them. Instead, I envied their complete indifference to their surroundings as they laughed and ate.

The outside of the station was covered with a dizzying profusion of posters: "Prevent Fires"; "Protect Nature"; a counterespionage poster, "Until Yesterday a Life of Deceit, From Today a Life of Truth." Next to them was a military recruitment poster and then a row of photographs of most-wanted fugitives. "Age—27; Height—5'9"; Physical Description—handsome, tall and willowy build." The description was surely there, and below it the photo of you in your high school uniform. I looked again at the fat man with the thick beard and the ridiculous getup sitting beside me, a man who at first glance you would think to be in his forties. I chuckled at the thought of the youth in the photo, and you turned to me with an uncomprehending look.

"What's so funny?"

"Nothing." I chuckled some more. "Have you seen yourself in that photo?"

"Where?"

Still laughing, I gestured with my chin toward the wanted poster.

You looked briefly in that direction, then shook your head.

"You should thank the fellows who made those posters. They say you're handsome. And—get this—a tall and willowy build!"

I laughed some more.

"Oh yeah?"

Finally you cracked a smile. But before long you gave a soft sigh and looked off into space. I fixed my eyes on the tips of my shoes, full of remorse at what I had just said. I felt prickly all over, as if covered with sand. If only I could have shouted, at the top of my lungs.

During the previous year and a half, we had encountered your face wherever we went—movie theaters, tearooms, restaurants, train stations, drinking places, billiard halls. Anywhere we went, you were right behind us, a nagging presence. The previous spring we had gone to Cheju Island for our senior-class trip, and there in the room of our inn was the photo of you in your high school uniform. You had followed us that far. That night, we drank ourselves silly and put on a disgusting display of behavior. But maybe it was easier to deal with you that way. After all, we could keep you locked up in that thumb-sized photo from the wanted poster, add just the right amount of emotion and a dash of rationalization, and then look at you as if we were leafing through an old photo album from time to time. If you couldn't be with us in the flesh, at least your name lived on in our memories of the past. And as long as you were frozen in those memories, we could at least drink ourselves to sleep. Occasionally an irritating thought would provoke a shower of curses and complaints from us. And having cursed and complained, we actually found it easier to throw ourselves back into the increased tedium and oblivion of our daily lives. We were tired, unbearably tired, and we wanted so much to lose ourselves in sleep. We wanted to sink passively into the misty chaos of a remote hell in which our consciousness was paralyzed, our spirit strangled. Yes. We were sinking. There was no spark in our eyes, and before we knew it we were each sinking little by little into a deep abyss. "Let yourself go . . . into a deep, deep sleep . . . an eternal sleep . . . and never, ever awaken . . . a deep, deep sleep . . . oh, so long. . . ." Such was the whisper that played about our ears like sweet music wherever we went. That whisper. That sweet whisper. As we listened to the blasphemous command, we were sinking. And we were repeating that whisper, one after another. "Forget. . . . Forget everything. . . . The past is over; the memories can't hurt you. . . . Forget the nightmares, every last trace of them. . . . Wipe the slate clean—perfectly clean. . . . Because tomorrow is a new day, a brighter day."

And then you had reappeared. Why now? I had groaned in despair. You had dared to appear, dared to pick from our sleepy brains the distasteful, chilling remnants of our nightmares. You were unmistakable proof that those nightmares were something tangible. Remember . . . remember . . . remember. Somehow, when we were off guard, you had popped out of the square of paper in which we had kept plotting to confine you—whether or not we had realized it at the time—and there you were in the flesh, standing before us. Boldly, recklessly, you had churned and thinned the syrup of our dreamy self-hypnosis. There would be more pain to deal with now.

The wind came up. Pastry wrappers and scraps of wastepaper cartwheeled past our feet. You had been smoking one cigarette after another; I had kept looking at my watch. One of the drunken young fellows who had been laughing and clowning began to retch. We got up.

We went to the gate where the tickets for our train were being punched. We each had our own ticket. You had insisted on this: "Just in case . . ." We passed through the gate without incident, though. We sat down on the corner of a brick-lined flower bed and waited. The salvia planted here and there had withered. The passengers in the train on the far set of tracks cast indifferent looks in our direction. Beyond the train the sky loomed a shade grayer.

"I'm sorry," you blurted. "It's been one errand after another for you. . . ."

"What do you mean, 'Sorry'? Asshole. Why this all of a sudden?"

I smiled in spite of myself, then suddenly wished I could take the words back, chew them up, and swallow them. Nothing was clicking between us, and I had no idea why.

"Innocent people might get hurt on my account, and that keeps me awake nights. Doesn't matter where I move," you muttered as you broke a matchstick in two.

A gust of wind brought with it the smell of rusty metal and the sulfurous odor of coal. Sitting there with your broad back hunched over, you looked like a big kid who had been scolded. People getting hurt. . . . But who was doing the hurting, and who was being hurt? Were you an agent of pain, you who had to keep hidden even after returning home? And was I a victim, I who could strut through life full of composure, without a care? Suddenly I realized we had been making none of our usual attempts at humor. This knowledge filled me with spite. We had never, ever, had such an embarrassing conversation before. Something had made us different from what we had been, and I just couldn't put my finger on it. All I could do was ask myself the same questions as before.

Our train pulled up to the platform, and we boarded the last car. There were more empty seats than we had expected. We sat down facing each other, tucked up against a window. The coach was worn and dingy. The cushioning inside the blue fabric of the seats was almost gone, and wads of gum were stuck here and there.

The train left five minutes late. The sooty station and the low tin roofs of the surrounding houses slowly began to recede. Every last one of those houses looked shabby, dismal. I watched the low, gray sky darken in the distance over the center of the town. I wondered if it would rain. The train gathered speed and open fields quickly unfolded beyond the window. Every now and then I saw a farmer harvesting late-ripening rice with a sickle. We passed a cultivator loaded with sheaves of rice. And then a solitary dwelling with crimson peppers spread about its roof. In the yard, girls with infants swaddled on their backs were playing jump rope with a length of rubber cord.

Finally I began to relax. You had pushed up your cap so that it sat askew, and had cast your gaze outside the window. Suddenly I noticed a shadow of gloom flit across your forehead. It was that same fatigue I had noticed when you surfaced. You hadn't been able to rid yourself of that deep, gloomy fatigue, the exhaustion in your eyes, which made me wonder if you were about to collapse. I felt new pangs of regret.

"I had to move *fourteen* times in Seoul," you had said a few days before. "Sometimes I'd spend just one night and they'd ask me to move on. . . . You really get tired after a while. You get to feel you just can't live like that anymore. Sometimes I think, what the hell, why not just run outside and take what comes."

A man in a uniform emerged through the glass-paneled sliding door at the end of the coach. *Conductor,* read the crimson patch on his shoulder. He briefly stared at us, then passed through the car and out the door at the other end. Our eyes met, almost by reflex, and then we looked away in embarrassment.

"Does Sunim know you're in town?" I asked.

For a time you stared silently out the window. "No. . . ." You shook your head once, still without turning toward me.

"Why not? . . . She's the one who worries the most."

"I wanted to, but . . . I really thought it would be best for both of us if I held off. Another case of what they don't know won't hurt them."

You lit a cigarette.

Perhaps Sunim had received visitors, as you had suspected. "Tell us the truth. We're sure you know. Where is he?" I wondered how she had answered. "I have no idea"—that was what I had said, and perhaps Sunim had answered likewise. "I don't know. You think I'm protecting him? I don't know. I tell you, I don't know." Perhaps she had shaken her head, like Cain did after burying Abel and returning home, concealing his bloody palms. Yes. We didn't know. And perhaps that made things so much more convenient for us. As you had said, what we didn't know wouldn't hurt us. In any event, even though I had to steady my legs and stand straight in front of them, I was somehow able to answer freely that I was ignorant of your whereabouts. This firm denial was the honest truth, and not to be challenged. I had every right to be indignant at having been made the object of unreasonable suspicions. Complete ignorance sometimes makes people brave. And indeed, in this case it did. I was uncharacteristically brave then. In the end they had to send me home without obtaining any information. "We'll give you the benefit of the doubt," one of the men had said as I turned away. "But we'll probably be seeing you again."

"Is she still teaching at that school?" you asked me.

"Who?"

"Sunim."

"Probably. I haven't seen her since I bumped into her last spring, but. . . ."

You turned back toward the window.

Sunim had been looking through some books when I saw her at a bookstore that day. I barely recognized her; she didn't look well, and that bothered me. She said she was teaching language at a middle school in the countryside where you could see the ocean. I asked her how she had been getting along. "So-so." She had smiled forlornly. But she said she enjoyed teaching the children. "I'm living by myself, and when I'm bored, I read poetry. And I've picked up this embarrassing habit of bawling." Then she selected a book of poetry and quickly turned away. She looked so frail as she was swallowed up in the wave of humanity outside. Only then did I realize that we hadn't mentioned you at all.

"Have you been in touch with your mother?" I asked.

"No. But I telephoned my aunt not too long ago, so my mother must know. Of course, I didn't tell her I was back home. All she did was cry. . . ."

You sent cigarette smoke streaming out the window as you talked. Some children were running one after another along a narrow dirt path across a field. Once I had visited your house, to find your mother watering the garden. She had recently begun to attend a Catholic church, and that day she asked if I would consider doing the same. Your room had been left as it was. The books in your bookcase, your clothes hanging on the wall, the English dictionary on the desk—all was the same as before. "He'll survive wherever he goes, the little stinker," she had said as she watered the flowers, which were withering because of a long dry spell. "I'm sure he's alive somewhere. He's not the type to roll over and die."

The train passed a tiny station without stopping. The trains made irregular stops at such places—places that lacked even a station house. I doubted we would arrive at Mokp'o on time. There was a bustle of passengers coming and going every time we stopped. The turbid, murky water of the Yŏngsan River came into sight, coiling among bare fields. The water moved sluggishly, as if it might cease flowing altogether. Reeds half covered with mud stuck out everywhere along the riverbanks.

We kept silent for some time. Now and then we made abortive attempts to break that silence, but there were no words to bring us together. I was always at a loss, because I didn't know what to do with the severed fragments of the words. I talked about the last play we had been involved in. For three months we had spent cold winter evenings in an empty lecture hall rehearsing that play, living on instant noodles. And then the notice had arrived forbidding us to perform it. We had felt like embracing in tears. We had completed the sets and everything else, and two days before the play was to have opened, we had bought some *makkŏlli,* launched into some songs we all knew, and sang ourselves hoarse. Suddenly you had jumped up and gone on a rampage smashing the sets. The rest of us were already feeling the *makkŏlli,* and we just sat and watched. It was just as if the pathos of the drama we were to have performed were being played out in front of us.

And I talked about college—our friends and the few teachers we cared for, our classrooms smelling of chalk and dust, the campus lawns and the wisteria benches, and that sweltering day the previous summer, which was so abnormally dry, when we watched the desperate floundering of the goldfish in the nearly dried up pond in front of the library, and the traces they left in the clumps of mud where they had slithered along on their stomachs.

"There's something different about our hometown—and I don't like it."

I'd been wanting to say that for a long time. It was the truth. I was scared. When I met someone on the street, I could read the shadow on his brow, the shadow of dark, nightmarish memories. And because of that, even the faces of complete strangers would seem altogether familiar. I would see in their faces the same heavy fatigue, something difficult to describe. If our eyes happened to meet, they would conceal their shriveled hearts, as if they were lepers, look through me, and walk by—each and every one of them. And now, almost without my realiz-

ing it, it seemed they all wanted to slip into a deep slumber. Slumber—
that's what it was. I disliked that lethargic slumber of our hometown.
That heavy, oppressive daytime slumber had become frightening. It
felt like a tomb.

"You always did have a way with metaphors," you said after hearing all of this.

You slowly turned to face me, then smiled. You had once remarked
sarcastically that I had a problem—my overindulgent habit of speaking
in metaphors. "I know you like to play it safe . . . but there are times
when too much prudence can be no good," you had said. "Let me put it
this way. Those big eyes of yours see so much, but that little mouth is
afraid to say anything. Come on, open that mouth wide. Or else close
your eyes a little. That way, maybe you'll have less trouble in the
future."

I still remembered those words clearly.

Suddenly everything was dark. And then the overhead lights came
on, glaring fiercely, and for a time the clack of the wheels filled the
coach. We had entered a tunnel. I felt disoriented, as if I were sinking
in fathomless water, suffocating. I felt the urgency of one being pursued by something, and my eyes searched the opposite seat for your
outline, which was growing indistinct.

What are you doing back here? Why are you jumping out at us from
the darkness we wanted to forget? For God's sake, leave us alone. We
want to sleep. We don't ever want to wake from this tranquil sleep, but
only to lie down for a long, long time. We had great affection for
you—you know we did. And we still do—the same amount. And
you'll be remembered by our children, and their children, forever—
like the tailbone has survived to remind humans they once had a tail.
But we've put you to rest, memorial and all—I can't help believing
that. Don't dare show us the pelt of that pure, innocent animal—no, not
even a drop of its blood, a tuft of its fur. For we have removed that
offering from the sacrificial altar. The ceremony is over. We did our
part, and it's only fair that the almighty, benevolent God who returned
Isaac to Abraham should allow us to enjoy nights of repose, tranquillity, even boredom. It's our turn to rest. So, we beg of you, leave us
alone. We are tired. We are ever so tired, and we want to sleep . . .
sleep.

And then it was bright again. The overhead lights immediately went
off. In that instant just before we emerged from the tunnel, I had

hastened to complete my secret betrayal of you in the darkness. For a time afterward, I was afraid to look at you. My feelings were a tangled mess, difficult to distinguish. I felt as if I were swallowing a huge lump of taffy. Perhaps it was guilt and rage toward who knows what, and perhaps self-hatred along with compassion or melancholy toward myself. The darkness disappeared, as if sucked into the tunnel, but even then I couldn't free myself from that chaotic tangle of feelings. The winding river reappeared at a distance through the window. You continued to sit silently opposite me.

The train lost speed, and a mosaic of tiled roofs appeared. Countless television antennas sprouted above them, looking like insect feelers. We were approaching Yŏngsanp'o. From there a good thirty minutes remained to Mokp'o, the end of the line. Passengers began removing their bundles from the overhead racks. An eight-minute stop in Yŏngsanp'o, the conductor announced. The train came to a stop, and we tensed up again, straightening in our seats.

Dusk slowly began to creep over everything. Through the windows we watched the passengers board and leave the train. And then we slowly pulled away, leaving the station behind while the mercury lights over the platform came on one by one. You were resting your head against the seatback, eyes closed, cap pulled low over your forehead. I looked out the window at the gathering darkness. I cracked my knuckles one after another, feeling that a part of me was collapsing, one piece at a time. I felt lonely. It was truly an unbearably lonely evening.

We had reached the outskirts of town. The clouds were darker, as if threatening a shower, and people were scurrying for home. Someone on a bicycle rode by on a path beside the tracks, ignoring the train. Some toddlers waved and shouted at us.

It was an utterly peaceful scene. The roofs clustered like oysters on the hillside began to lose their individual outlines in the dusk and blend into one large mass. I imagined people turning down the paths to their homes, women in the kitchens, their hands busy preparing supper for their families. I counted the lights as they came on in the windows, looking like morning glories beginning to bloom, and I stole several cheerless looks at your face. Suddenly I was choked up with a mysterious sorrow. I jerked my head away and looked outside again.

Fourteen times! It pained me to think about you constantly moving over the past year and a half—a wearisome, tedious journey. And in the end you had returned. You had returned to the city that had nur-

tured you until the age of twenty-seven. But that city—your hometown—had not welcomed you. And because of that, you would have to
wander its outskirts in hiding like some banished heathen.

It finally started to pour. The sparse, heavy drops of rain spattered
against the windows of the coach, forming lines of water. Some of the
windows clicked shut. I stuck my hand outside. The cool raindrops felt
gentle on my palm. Just then it happened. Without warning the emergency brakes were applied. The train lurched violently, and I felt as if
we would be pitched out of our seats. The train slid forward for a few
seconds, then stopped. There was a confused babble.

"We hit somebody!"

"Where! Where!"

Some of the passengers opened the windows and craned their heads
out. Others sprang to their feet and went outside.

"Good lord! Looks like a woman."

"Uh-uh. I think it's a man."

"Is she alive?"

"She couldn't be. You ought to see the blood. My god, it's awful!"

With everyone exclaiming at once, the car was soon in an uproar. I
stuck my head out the window and peered toward the front of the train.
The victim appeared to have been struck at a crossing. Several men in
uniforms—probably the conductors—had gathered at the scene and
were shouting to one another, gesticulating helplessly. A number of
local people had gathered in a semicircle, and their voices added to the
confusion. From my vantage point, I couldn't determine the condition
of the victim. I assumed we were still in the outskirts of Yŏngsanp'o. It
appeared to be a poor neighborhood, with low, wretched roofs abutting
one another. I sat down and ruffled my sodden hair.

"Looks like an accident."

At this needless explanation you merely nodded.

The rain fell in torrents. Eventually the onlookers returned to the
coach, their hems, cuffs, and collars dripping. Before long the locomo-
tive clunked back to life.

"Was she really trying to kill herself?"

"Hell no! There's no stop sign at the crossing, and apparently the
woman was hurrying home and couldn't see in the rain."

"Seems she lived just across the tracks. People were saying she
raised pigs and was awfully hard up."

"God, what a mess! Killed on the spot."

"She must have been toting a bucket of scraps. Bits of rice and other stuff scattered all over. It's a damn shame."

"Is it true the insurance companies don't pay a red cent if you're run over by a train? What a way to go—slaughtered like an animal."

The train heaved into motion. Before we knew it, the city was out of sight and we were passing through fields draped with darkness. For a long while we stared silently at the pitch black of the windowpane.

The raindrops, heavier now, drummed against the window, every staccato attack sounding like a volley of gunfire. I shut my eyes tight. A short time before, when the train had eased its way past the accident site, we had caught a glimpse of the corpse, covered by a straw sack. The instant that cold mass of flesh came into sight, we had examined each other's pale face. Almost immediately we each confirmed in the face of the other the traces of an identical nightmare, and just as quickly we had looked away, as if by agreement. I closed my eyes and tried to erase from my memory that dreadful image, which had come and gone in a flash, like an apparition. The straw sack half covering the body, the inky water collecting on the ground beside it, a lone shoe, the white grains of rice in the light at the crossing, the battered bucket, and the throng of onlookers—the onlookers. . . . The moment we saw these things, the blanket with which we had desperately tried to cover our nightmares was mercilessly snatched away. And finally, beneath that blanket we were exposed in all our humiliating vulnerability. Beneath that blanket were the chilling memories of the rape of our hometown. No, stop it! No! I shook my head violently.

The rain continued its mad drumming against the window.

Suddenly everything was blurry. I stole a glance at your face. Your eyes were closed, your cap still low on your forehead. All in confusion, I wiped away my tears. Some time ago, to my surprise, I'd fallen into this embarrassing habit of weeping. The tears would start dribbling when I was drunk, or after a bad dream deep in the night. They'd quickly gather without reason, whether I was surrounded by inattentive passersby on a familiar street, or tottering down a secluded alley on a dazzling spring day. But you weren't one to cry. In fact, I'd never seen you weep. Perhaps this was the very thing that distinguished you from me. Knowing I was prone to tears, I quickly came to realize the prudence of knowing when to turn my back, and I carried that prudence about with me like a good-luck charm. You stupid idiot—you hardly ever cried, and maybe that was why you were still a man without a name in this country where everyone else was strutting about in broad daylight.

It was completely dark outside. The rain held steady, streaking the windows with water. The bright lights inside the coach glinted on the glass, everywhere illuminating the sleek raindrops. There was only the ceaseless clack of the wheels, producing regular vibrations, to break the deathly silence.

"What a pathetic pair we are—how about a drink?"

You hailed a passing vendor and bought a bottle of *soju* and a dried squid. I stared at you, wondering if we were doing the right thing.

"Don't worry. We're not going to get drunk on one bottle."

You broke out in a broad grin—something I hadn't seen in so long that it almost shocked me. I accepted without protest the plastic cup you offered me. It really had been a long time since we had shared a drink, I realized. A year and a half. We drank to that lost time, and to the odd forlornness that dominated our reunion.

"What you said a little while ago, about being scared of our hometown. . . ." You poured me a drink.

I remained silent, watching your eyes.

"I felt the same way at first. Even the time I spent away, wandering like a leper from one room to the next, didn't feel as painful as living in our hometown. . . . But that isn't the reason I'm leaving this time. I'll be back—it won't be long. I'm sure of it."

"You left the place where you were staying?"

"Um-hmm. You know, I think this is number fifteen, exactly," you chuckled.

At this news I looked at you slack-jawed, my head suddenly empty of thought. An ambiguous smile played about your lips. For some curious reason I couldn't understand, that smile reassured me.

"You know, this is awfully sentimental, but this time I didn't want to leave by myself. I'm not sure why. I guess being alone I'd have felt like I was being exiled. That's why I asked you to come along. I appreciate it."

Again you chuckled.

"But your duties will be over when we get to Mokp'o, so you can relax. Come on, we'll have one more, and that's it."

I stared at the drink you poured me. I couldn't say a word. At every clack and rattle of the train, the liquid came perilously close to slopping over the side of the cup. Something hot was welling up in my throat, and I had to bite my lip.

It was well past eight when we arrived in Mokp'o. We waited for some of the other passengers to get off, watching them exit the platform like water surging toward a sluice gate. Again, I left first, as you had requested. As we set off toward the exit gate, I sneaked a look behind me and saw you following slowly, your large frame lost in a sea of unfamiliar faces. Once again I was painfully aware of the meaning of the short distance between us.

We stopped in the plaza outside the station. The rain fell even thicker now. Traffic sped by, the headlights making me dizzy. We bought a cheap plastic umbrella.

"I guess this is as good a place as any to say good-bye. Thanks. Sorry I dragged you all the way down here for nothing. And I hope you won't miss the last train home."

"Don't worry. There's plenty of time." I grasped the hand you extended. Suddenly I had a premonition that I might never, ever see you again, and in spite of myself I anxiously tightened my grip. "You know . . . I should have figured out by now what to do with my life. But . . . I haven't."

You looked at me intently.

"Well, nobody's going to tell you. That's something only you can decide. But I think everything will turn out well for you. More than anything else, you're perceptive."

Without a word I released your hand. For a moment I continued to feel the warmth of your palm. I told you to take the umbrella, but you stuck it in my hand, stubbornly insisting I keep it.

"I'll be okay. You've got farther to go."

You turned and hurried off through the rain. Soon I couldn't see you anymore. Before I knew it, there was only thick darkness filling the place you had been. Where could you be going? Had you found yet another place to blend into and disappear? Barely sheltering myself with the flimsy excuse for an umbrella you'd forced onto me, I remained where I was, examining the dark, desolate emptiness where you had stood. Only then did I begin to realize that it was now my lot to somehow fill that space you had left me.

I turned and began to stride back toward the station. What you had said was true: I was on my own, and my road home would be a long one.

Translated by Bruce and Ju-Chan Fulton

Marshall R. Pihl attended Harvard University and Seoul National University (Korea), and is a pioneer in Korean studies. He currently holds the position of Associate Professor of Korean Literature at the University of Hawaii and also serves as President of the International Korean Literature Association. Pihl specializes in Korean fiction and teaches all genres from all periods of Korean literature. His work on the traditional Korean oral narrative, *The Korean Singer of Tales,* is being published by Harvard University Press.

Bruce and **Ju-Chan Fulton** are the translators of *Words of Farewell* (Seal Press, 1989), a path-breaking anthology of contemporary Korean women writers. They have translated many of modern Korea's most accomplished writers of fiction, including Hwang Sunwŏn, Yun Heung-gil, and O Chŏnghŭi. The Fultons have received several awards for their translations, which have been carried in numerous journals and anthologies in the United States and abroad.